STILL WIDE OPEN

the Brad Doty Story

By Brad Doty

with Dave Argabright

STILL **WIDE OPEN**
the Brad Doty Story

© 1999
By Dave Argabright and Brad Doty

ISBN 1-891390-03-1

Front Cover photo/Al Steinberg
Back Cover photo/Marty Gordner Racing Photos
Inside flap photo/Yvonne Dolner

Published by:
Witness Productions
Box 34, Church Street
Marshall, Indiana 47859
765-597-2487

Printed in the USA

Acknowledgments

Although just two people are listed as authors of this book, in reality it took the help of many people to make it possible. The authors would like to thank the following:

Rob Sneddon, for his expert editing;
Laurie Doty, for her invaluable archives and records;
Ed Haudenschild, for his keen memory;
and Ed and Susie Watson of Witness Productions, for their leadership and advice.

Also, for their help with research, we thank Richard Day (World of Outlaws); Dennis Gage (Silver Dollar Speedway); and Bob Wilson (Knoxville Raceway).

For their strong support and generous help with production and promotion, we thank Corinne Economaki, *National Speed Sport News*; Doug Auld, *Open Wheel Magazine*; Randy Steenbergen, Print Communications; Tom Schmeh, National Sprint Car Hall of Fame and Museum; and Mark Kuchan, TNN.

And finally, to a whole list of friends, family, and fans who assisted with a name, a date, or a story: You know who you are, and we thank you.

PREFACE

He once had a life that many would envy, then was locked into a world that most would dread. Through it all Brad Doty has proven that he is indeed an extraordinary human being. He was exalted as a champion race driver, hailed as an example of a new generation of racing stars. He was loved by his family, cheered by his adoring fans, and deeply respected by his competitors. He was handsome, well-spoken, polite, and one of the very best sprint car drivers of his time. In short, he had it all.

Then came a grinding, violent crash in Ohio on a hot July night, and it looked as though even life itself was going to be taken from Brad. He survived, only to face the cold, hard reality that a spinal injury had ended his ability to walk. He suffered through terrible depression, but it was during this period that the true spirit of the man was revealed. He rose above his hardship, and has moved forward to enjoy a dynamic and busy lifestyle that few people could keep up with.

He is truly an inspiration, with a story that is both intensely emotional and heartwarming. His attitude is amazing, his smile is infectious, and his spirit is indomitable. He once strived to be the champion of the toughest sprint car group on earth, the World of Outlaws. His injury ended that dream, but at the same time opened up another opportunity that Brad Doty has won with flying colors: Champion of Life.

Dave Argabright

FOREWORD

It was many years ago, and I was spending some free time between races. We were in Florida, and I was spending a few hours surf fishing at the beach. I stood there on the pier, casting and watching the waves roll in. As I enjoyed the sea breeze, two guys came walking up to talk to me. One was George Gillespie of Pro Shocks. The other was a young kid from the East named Brad Doty.

Brad was just getting started with the World of Outlaws. Maybe George felt like I had been racing for a while and knew how to survive, I don't know. But he wanted me to talk to this kid and give him some advice about making it as a sprint car driver. I gave him the usual talk about "To finish first, first you must finish," things like that. I told him to take his time, and be patient.

I didn't realize at the time just how special Brad Doty was, and what an impact he'd have on sprint car racing. We struck up a friendship, and it's one that I'm sure will last the rest of our lifetimes. He always seemed like one of the nicest guys in the sport. When things went wrong, he just said, hey, I'll just keep on going on. He could take things in stride, while a lot of guys in the racing business are so high-strung they just can't deal with adversity very well.

He was a very tough competitor on the race track. He wasn't wild, but he was aggressive. He was on the gas, but he was under control. I'm sure we banged together, but in all the years we raced together I don't remember either of us taking each other out of a race. He was always there, always fast, always aggressive, and he did it without crashing you.

I was probably one of the first guys on the World of Outlaws circuit to get a motor home and take my family out on the road with me, and Brad was probably the second. Our families used to spend a lot of time together – it seemed like we always wound up in the same campground. Each year at Oklahoma City we had a nice get-together at the campground, it was a lot of fun. I have good memories of those times.

Brad was different from most sprint car guys. He always wore clean jeans, a clean shirt, and he always had his shirt tucked in, while Steve Kinser and I would be running around in cut-off jeans and flip-flop shoes. I remember one time we were out on the road, the day after a big thunderstorm. I was out playing golf, while Brad stayed and washed his motor home because he wanted it to look nice. I was lazy, and I never seemed to take the time to do those kinds of things. Brad always kept his things clean and sharp. I admired that.

I wasn't at the track the night Brad got hurt. Looking back, I'm glad I wasn't there. After his accident I remember Norman Martin making a T-shirt for him, and I sold hundreds of those shirts for Brad at Ascot Park. I talked to Brad a year or so later and asked if he was going to do another shirt. He was kind of down, he said, "Aw, I'm not racing anymore, people don't care about that stuff." But I told him people still care about him, and finally talked him into doing another shirt. Since then he's probably begun to realize just how much people love him.

Today, Brad is a role model for anybody who has been hurt in any way. If you've had a setback, and maybe have some kind of hurdle, just look at Brad and realize that he has shown people how you can't let adversity stop you. I call him on the phone and he's out in the garage working under his car, things like that...he just doesn't let his injury get him down. You never hear him feel sorry for himself. He's like a trouper. Really, he's handled things way better than I would have, I'll tell you.

Brad is the clean-cut American boy. I'm glad I got to race against him. More importantly, I'm glad to call him my friend.

Ron Shuman
Tempe, Arizona
Four-time SCRA champion
Four-time CRA champion
1979 Knoxville Nationals champion
Eight-time Turkey Night Grand Prix champion

FOREWORD

The first time I watched Brad Doty race was at Pennsylvania's Lincoln Speedway in 1981. Somebody pointed out to me that he was really good at Lernerville. Well, he's a long way from Lernerville, I thought. Western Pennsylvania drivers hadn't fared very well when they raced in the eastern part of the state. Why should this guy be any different?

But he *was* different. I could see that as soon as I met him a few weeks later at Williams Grove Speedway. Here was this little guy with long hair and a beard trying to look like what an Outlaw racer was supposed to look like back then. But all he had to do was open his mouth to blow his image. He was just so *nice*. He seemed too nice to be racer. I knew immediately that he was a story and I wanted to write about him. Maybe he was the next generation of sprint car racer, I thought. Hell, he even listened to Aerosmith instead of Waylon Jennings.

Then there was the racing part. He *was* pretty good. By September he had won a feature at Williams Grove, beating the likes of Smokey Snellbaker, Lynn Paxton, Steve Smith and Keith Kauffman. That was surely good enough to get him in *Open Wheel Magazine*.

So I wrote the story and he was appreciative. We stayed in touch. We got to be friends. But that part was no big deal, because he was everybody's friend. To this day I don't know anybody who has ever had a bad word to say about Brad Doty.

Meanwhile, his career was taking off. He had good car owners and good mechanics. He was racing against the best in the business every night and he was doing well.

I'd see him when the World of Outlaws came east and we'd catch up on things. I've got a few memories of Brad at Williams Grove. I'll bet Williams Grove holds some memories for him, too, and not all of them would be good. Like the time he got hit with some debris and had to spend the night in a local hospital. They wouldn't let him look in the mirror because that handsome face of his had swelled to twice its normal size.

Then there was the night at the Grove when he thought he had an Outlaw race won going into the third corner of the final lap. But Steve Kinser came out of nowhere and tried what the racers would call a flyer. Steve won the race. Brad's night ended against the fourth turn guardrail.

There were some good times at the Grove, too. I'll never forget the night he showed up driving Gary Stanton's rig. He was all alone. Stanton had gone home for his daughter's graduation and since this was not a sanctioned World of Outlaws event he was not really in favor of having his car race at the Grove. But the race carried a good purse and Brad didn't feel like spending another night all by himself in a nearby motel, so he brought his rig to Williams Grove. He didn't even have anybody to help him roll the car out of the trailer until he bumped into Deuce Turrill, who had just parted company with Sammy Swindell. Doty offered a percentage of his winnings to rent Deuce for the night.

It was a good move, because they won the race. I remember it vividly because I was doing a stint as a pit reporter for the Grove at the time and I watched the feature with Deuce on Stanton's trailer. Brad was obviously excited to win and I still remember the first words out of his mouth that night. "I can't wait to call Gary tomorrow morning," he said. "First I'll tell him I ran Williams Grove. Then I'll tell him I won!"

That was 1984. Four years later he was back with Stanton again. At least for the Kings Royal at Eldora Speedway. I was there that night, too, only this time I arrived late and watched from the press box. I knew the wreck was bad, but I didn't know *how* bad at the time. Although they carted Brad off in the ambulance I wasn't all that concerned. It seemed like he was always getting hurt, but never seriously.

I drove partway back to Pennsylvania that night and was at Susquehanna Speedway the next evening. That's where I first heard some rumors, at least I hoped they were rumors, about Brad's injuries.

Early Monday morning I got a phone call from someone I barely knew who asked me to call Kenny Jacobs. It was a strange request, but I promptly complied knowing full well that Brad's best friend, Kenny Jacobs, was going to tell me something I didn't want to hear.

The news of Brad's injuries really affected me. To this day I haven't been back to Eldora Speedway.

It is gratifying to see what Brad Doty has accomplished with his life since that hot July night in 1988.

He had every reason to be bitter. He had every reason to stay as far away from racing as he could get. Who could blame him if he never wanted to see a sprint car again? But that just wouldn't be Brad Doty.

Instead of shunning sprint car racing, he's become its most prominent ambassador. He took a bad deal and made the best of it. Just like he did so many times when he was driving race cars.

Thanks, Brad, for writing this book. And thank *you* for reading it.

Bruce Ellis
Hazelton, Pennsylvania
Announcer, Williams Grove Speedway
Motorsports Journalist
National Sprint Car Media Member of the Year, 1987

I have a lot of good memories of racing with Brad Doty. We were always good friends, I knew his family pretty well, and we both had young kids growing up about the same time. He ran Gambler cars a lot, and I did too, so we talked a lot about race cars, things like that. I got to know him real well, and I liked him, even when we competed against each other.

Brad was a guy that just loved to race, and he did a super good job of it. He was a guy that you could race close with and never worry about a thing. He would always run you hard, but he'd run you clean.

In all the years we raced against each other, there were only a couple of times that Brad and I had harsh words after a race. When you're out here racing, it's hard for people to understand how competitive it is. Everybody, and I mean everybody, wants to win. So sometimes you have the heat of the moment, and you get in somebody's face a little bit. But Brad and I just never had much of that.

I know there was the one night (at Cedar Rapids, Iowa) when we got together, but I honestly don't remember much about that. Really, I never gave it any more thought. If Brad and I got aggravated at each other a little bit, it was just for a few minutes and then it was forgotten. He was never a guy that you stayed mad at for any length of time, mostly because you seldom got mad at him in the first place.

If Brad had been able to continue driving, there isn't any doubt in my mind that he would have won a World of Outlaws title or two. He had paid his dues, and he was really right at his prime when he was hurt. He really had things going his way; he was a good sprint car driver, one of the best in the business at the time.

When he had his crash and got hurt, I think it affected all of us (drivers) a little bit. Everybody liked the guy, and respected him. It hurts a lot when you see something bad happen to a guy like that. You think about it a lot.

On the night of his crash, I went up to the hospital and spent the night there. It was kind of a helpless feeling, knowing he was hurting but there wasn't anything any of us could do. But I wanted to be there for his family, because I knew they were hurting, too.

I think it's perfect that Brad is working on the television broadcasts. He knows this sport through and through. When he says something on TV, he knows what he's talking about. That surely is good for the sport, because he says things in a way that people can understand, and he's got a lot of credibility.

To have recovered like he has from his crash, you know he's got to be a pretty special person. I mean, you've got to admire somebody who doesn't let his injury get him down. It's unbelievable how people can work through hard times like that, and make a tough situation turn into a good situation. Brad probably inspires others who are in a tough situation.

In 1998 when he got back into his old car for a pace lap at the Kings Royal at Eldora, I thought it was just about the greatest thing I had seen in a long, long time. I loved it when he was out there with us. Just seeing him sitting in that car, running around there, man, it was just great. I had a huge smile on my face inside my helmet, I don't mind telling you.

Brad has always been my friend, and I know I'll always feel that way. He was a tough racer who worked hard for everything he got. You've got to respect a guy like that. I know I do.

Steve Kinser
Bloomington, Indiana
Fifteen-time World of Outlaws champion
Eleven-time Knoxville Nationals Champion
Winner, over 400 World of Outlaws feature events

FOREWORD

When I first heard that Brad Doty and Dave Argabright were collaborating to do this book, I knew there couldn't be a better match to accomplish this endeavor.

Brad's story is one that truly needs to be told. He is a very personable man who is a remarkable picture of determination and class. He has always faced his challenges head-on, both on and off the race track. He overcame obstacles that lesser men would have given up on. He continues to give to the sport that took so much away from him.

Dave Argabright is one of the most likable and respected motorsports journalists in the entire country. And for good reason. Dave's colorful columns in *National Speed Sport News* and other publications have been a favorite of readers for several years. He has an uncanny talent for painting vivid pictures with words and making the reader feel as if he, too, were right there. His burning passion for racing shows through in every word.

With Brad as a canvas and Dave brushing his words, rest assured that all the ingredients are there for a great story. So kick back and enjoy this collaboration from two of sprint car racing's finest.

I can hardly wait.

Paul Wilson
Indianapolis, Indiana
Motorsports journalist
TNN crew member

FOREWORD

I've seen a lot of race drivers over the years, and I've always classified them two different ways: guys who just drive a sprint car, and sprint car drivers. Some guys just drive 'em, and they're just out there. Then you've got guys who do it right. Brad Doty was one of those guys. He did it right.

I've known him all my life, and he's the same guy today that he was when we were little. If all the fame and stardom changed him, I never saw it. I can spend time with him now and tell you in a minute that nothing has changed about Brad: he's still the guy who worries about little stuff, who gets along with everybody, who finds a way to be happy.

His success in racing happened very quickly. He bought his first car from my dad and raced it a year and a half, and the biggest thing was how fast he caught on. We raced for years and did the one- or two-night-a-week thing, but it only took him a couple of years to go from being a rookie to being a very good race driver. He didn't race locally very long, he went to Pennsylvania and it was a quick process from there.

The first race he was going to win, he was leading and I got into the back of him and he spun. He stopped at the flag stand and told them that he got spun out, and he should get his spot back. The officials stopped me and asked me if I spun him, and I said, "Yeah, but it wasn't intentional." So they put me back up front and restarted him on the tail. After the race he couldn't believe how I talked my way out of going to the tail. He wasn't mad, he was ready to have a good time afterwards. He raced hard and he wanted to win, but he wasn't the kind of guy who took it personally.

When he raced, he was always cranked up on adrenaline. He always liked people, and I think he enjoyed being a race driver, and having people look up to him a little bit. It seemed to pump him up. He always worried about what people might think about him – he really wanted to do well.

I saw him at different times in his career where he had a lot of stress and friction with people on his team, and that seemed to bother him a lot. He's a guy that naturally gets along with everybody, and he just doesn't like having hard feelings. I've seen situations where people he's worked with badmouth him, but you'll never hear him say anything negative about that person. That's just not his style.

When he got hurt, the doctors told us all the stages he'd go through. They said there would be a period of "Why me," different things like that. But it wasn't like they said. He never talked much about feeling sorry for himself, and all that stuff.

Only one time did I ever see Brad struggle with that. He and I were talking about something, and I mentioned that it was "a bad deal." He kind of spoke up and said, "Hey, that's nothing. Look at my situation, look at me. Compared to what happened to me, that other stuff is nothing." I argued with him a little bit. I said, "Brad, I know what happened to you was tough, but you can't look at everything in comparison. Sure, you got a tough break. But don't try to tell me that nothing else matters in life, because I'm not going to think like that. You can't think that nothing else matters just because of what happened to you."

He kind of thought about it, and he finally agreed. And that's the last I ever heard him mention it. He is a very strong person, and tough, to get through his injury like he did.

When he started doing TV, I was kind of surprised. I wasn't surprised he had that much knowledge, because I knew he was smart enough. But talking in front of groups, and appearing in front of millions on TV, I didn't picture Brad doing that. But he does a damn good job. I shouldn't be surprised, because he's always seemed really sure of himself. If he decided he could do a job, he was going to do the job. If he sets his mind to something, he's going to be pretty good at it. He's a very determined guy.

I'm proud to have him for a friend. If he would have driven a year and quit, our friendship wouldn't have been any different. He's a guy that I really like to be around. In that respect, he hasn't changed a bit. And I'm glad.

Ed Haudenschild
Fredericksburg, Ohio

FOREWORD

From the moment I met him many years ago, Brad has impressed me as a very strong-willed person. When we met he was already racing, and when I would go and watch him race I was amazed that no matter how much bad luck he had, no matter how tough things became, he wouldn't give up. That's part of what drew me to him. He's always been so strong, so determined.

Watching Brad race was never easy for me. The fear of losing him was very real, and it grew stronger after we had children. After a while I couldn't watch any longer. It was just too difficult.

I feel that Brad had just reached his prime when he had his accident in 1988. It seemed as though everything was beginning to fall into place. Sometimes it's hard not to think about what could have been.

If I were to describe Brad to others, I would say he is devoted, determined, and very courageous. After his accident, the fans' generosity and support both surprised and shocked me. But then I recalled how devoted Brad was to the fans. He always had a smile and time to say hello. He always tried to let them know that they were an important part of racing. Things seemed to have come full circle. The fans left no doubt that Brad was important to them.

Brad really enjoys his work now, but it will never take the place of racing. All of my favorite photos of Brad were taken when he raced. The sheer joy that radiated from his eyes made it obvious that he was really happy doing what he loved.

Sometimes I think about the past 20 years, and I wonder about everything we've been through. Some if it was very hard and painful, but it made us much stronger. We have learned to thank God for all the good He blesses us with, and to have faith that He will help us through the bad. The road has been long, rough and heartbreaking for Brad at times. Most of us would have given up at some point. Brad never did. His determination helped him find happiness again.

I never dreamed he would write a book, but Brad's story could teach us a lot if we allow it. Quitting was not an option for Brad. He had the courage to look for something good in a very bad situation.

I no longer think about why things happened the way they did. I'm just thankful he's still here. He's a wonderful husband, a terrific father, and my best friend. I can't imagine my life without him. Thank you for being the person you are, Brad. You are a special man!

Laurie Doty
Apple Creek, Ohio

STILL WIDE OPEN

the Brad Doty Story

1

In the summer it is green, green like Ireland. For hundreds of years people have found all that they needed here, with the earth providing a living to generation upon generation. Wayne County, Ohio is my home.

I am a product of this land, just like the trees and plants that thrive here. To understand me is not difficult, because you need only look around at these beautiful rolling hills, this rich countryside, and you will see me. A country boy, from start to finish.

In my life I've seen my share of both joy and despair, and whenever the highs got too high, or the lows too low, I would go to the window and look out at the cornfields and woods and hayfields and barns. Somehow that sight always made me feel more secure, more patient, reminding me that with a little courage you can make it through just about anything.

Today, my life for the most part revolves around these seven acres, and my family. I still carry on a 25-year love affair with racing, and it has been very good to me. It took me all over the country and allowed me to see the world, and eventually brought me back home. I am a very lucky man, because I have had a tremendous amount of satisfaction and excitement in my career, and I can thank sprint cars for that.

My place isn't what you call high-dollar real estate. I live near the little town of Apple Creek, Ohio. We don't have cities around here; it's mostly towns, like Fredericksburg, Guerne, Orrville, Holmesville and Millersburg. The biggest town for us is Wooster, which has maybe 20,000 people but is plenty big as far as I'm concerned.

All around me live the Amish. They are a good people, and they generally keep to themselves. When you drive around these country roads, you'll see them riding in their buggies, the horses stepping briskly. Sometimes you'll see a broad, bearded man with a straw hat walking behind a team of strong workhorses, maybe with a plow or some other implement hitched to the horses. The Amish are resourceful and practical, and they have strong beliefs. Depending on their local bishop, they avoid just about all modern technology. I respect them because they follow their beliefs so closely, and because they are so honest and hard-working. Anyone not of their faith is referred to as "English."

The pace here is slow. It is very different than when I was racing. That was a dynamic life. This is more normal, more real.

Around here, most people stay put. They grow up and find a job, get married and raise their kids here. Others pull up their roots and go away to cities like Columbus or Cleveland, coming home every once in a while to visit.

I guess I was different. I wanted to see the world, but I always wanted to eventually come back here. And, for the most part, I've always done that. No matter how tough the racing world was, I could always come home and feel good again.

Maybe the reason I feel that way is that I was born just a few miles from here. Even today, I live in a home that is within sight of the farm where I grew up. That's probably hard for a lot of people to imagine, but for a country boy like me it is pretty normal.

I was born in Millersburg, Ohio on July 27, 1957. My parents, Dale and Doris Doty, already had two daughters at home, Deb and Belin (short for Belinda). Later on, when I was 10, my sister Ami came along. That's a lot of sisters for one guy to have to deal with, but I survived.

My dad is a very outgoing guy, talkative and friendly. Everybody loves him. He's also very hard-headed and stubborn, and you can't win an argument with him. He has always been a Ford fanatic; you would think he's the president of the company. He retired from driving a truck in 1976, then worked on our farm and finally had a one-ton truck with a rollback bed. He used that truck to haul machinery for Amish folks, and others who bought stuff at auction.

My mom is more quiet. I was closer to my mom as a kid, because my dad was gone a lot. Mom kind of raised all of us, especially when we were really young. We had a good family life, not a lot of stress beyond the usual spats every now and then. There were the usual worries about not having enough money, which I'm sure is pretty common, but never any extreme hardships. When I was really small my mom sold Avon, and I would go with her to deliver product to her customers.

I've always had a good relationship with my sisters. Deb and I grew closer during my high school years. Belin and I are only two years apart, so we fought a lot. On the farm you're kind of stuck together a lot of the time, so kids tend to fight some. But today I enjoy a good friendship with my sisters, and I appreciate them.

As long as I can remember, the Haudenschild family was close with our family. My dad and John Haudenschild drove trucks together for years, they knew each other long before I came along. John and his wife Joanne had five kids, including two sons, Ed and Jac. Ed was about a year older than I was, and Jac was just a little younger than me. They lived about a half-mile from us, and between the three of us, we managed to find all the trouble in our area. And then some.

John Haudenschild had a truck garage, where he would rebuild wrecked semi-trucks, things like that. When my dad went to John's garage, I would tag along, and hang out with Ed and Jac. They lived on a hill, and Ed built coaster carts, these little wooden things we would ride down the hill.

Ed was really good at building things. He built one cart that had soapbox-derby wheels; I don't know where he found them. We didn't buy stuff in stores; we just scrounged around and salvaged other people's junk for "recycling." Nobody ever got hurt on those carts, but it wasn't because we didn't try.

When it snowed, we would take our sleds and go sliding on the Haudenschild's hill. There was one place where there was a dropoff of about eight feet or so, and I decided to give it a try. I went down the hill, really flying, and just soared into the air. It was a great feeling, but the elation went away when I found the ground. I hit hard enough to break the sled clean in two. We walked back to the garage, where our dads were working.

I took some nails and tried to fix my sled, and everybody thought that was pretty funny. On the way home my dad realized it was *my* sled I was working on, and he suddenly had a different outlook.

Our gang of three had a lot of freedom. We had ponies, and we would take off and ride all day long, not coming home until dark. We were only eight or nine years old at the time, and it's hard to believe now, kids that age having that much freedom. I can't imagine parents today allowing their kids to roam so far from home, but our world was really very innocent.

We would ride along on those ponies, finding small caves to play in, pretending we were cowboys. Gates and fences meant nothing to us; we'd just open the gate and ride across somebody's property, figuring they wouldn't mind a few kids.

Our ponies didn't seem to enjoy the game very much. We rode them like they were race cars: wide open. They figured us out pretty quickly, because when they saw us coming they would run from us in their pasture. I guess I can't blame 'em. We would spend two hours trying to catch them, holding feed and treats in our hands to lure them. When they got close enough, one of us would grab them and tie them to a gate, then go get another one until all three of us had a ride.

My pony was named "Red Man," and my sister had a pony named "Midget." I loved those ponies, loved them like a kid loves a best friend.

The summer before my fourth grade, my life changed dramatically. My parents bought an 81-acre place near Apple Creek that had formerly been an Amish farm. It was run down and in sorry shape, with trash and junk everywhere. That was highly unusual for an Amish farm, which are typically kept in excellent condition. We moved from town to live in an old farmhouse, and I felt like we had completely left civilization.

It was a sad, painful time in my life. My best friends, Ed and Jac, now lived 20 miles away, but when you're 10 years old that might as well be 2,000 miles. I lost all contact with them. There were a lot of Amish folks living nearby, and since they tend to be pretty private people, I didn't find many kids my age to play with. So I didn't have many friends. I was just stuck on that farm with my sisters.

We all worked hard that first summer to clean up the property. Burning trash, picking up junk – it felt like all we did was work. When you're a farm family, everybody works. I suppose I was too small to do much, but I remember being very sick of working.

My dad hauled steel for CW Transport. He left every Sunday night and came home on Wednesday or Thursday. That was the routine. I became very unhappy during that summer, and when school started it didn't get any better. I guess I was having a hard time fitting in to my new surroundings, dealing with the new culture.

To make things worse, my sister's horse, Midget, stepped into a groundhog hole and broke his leg right before we moved, and had to be put down. Man, I was devastated. I mourned for a long time. In music class we sang the old spiritual hymm, "Swing Low, Sweet Chariot." I would almost cry when we sang it, because it made me think of Midget. Once, I was so unhappy that when our class was going outside for recess, I just sat at my desk, alone, trying to hold back the tears. I remember a little girl trying to comfort me, telling me that it would all get better. I guess she was right. I learned to adjust to farm life, and found ways to be happy.

Our house was like a typical old farm house. At first it was kind of run down, so much so that you could feel the nice country breeze...*inside* the house. My parents always had to pinch their pennies, keeping the furnace turned down to save fuel, and in the winter frost would form on the inside of the windows. It sounds like an exaggeration, but it's not. My sister wore contact lens, and one night the lens solution froze right in the storage bowl on her dresser. If they took one of those infrared pictures that reveal heat loss in a home, our house would look like the sun. But over time my parents fixed up the old house and made it a home for our family. They were very proud of how much they improved the old farm, with good reason. That period was when I began to understand that determination and hard work can accomplish a lot.

My sisters and I were typical farm kids, climbing trees and swimming in our pond. We didn't think anything about jumping in that muddy, murky water, even after watching cows or horses swimming and walking there. Yuck!

I was accident-prone. It seemed like I was always getting hauled to the doctor for stitches or something. But that was small change compared to the time I was nearly killed in the hayfield.

We used a Ford 800-series tractor on our farm to plow and mow and pull wagons, things like that. One day when I was 10 or 11 years old, I was teaching my cousin how to drive the tractor. An empty hay wagon was hitched up to the back, and my sister was riding on the wagon. We were driving around the field, picking up hay bales off the ground and stacking them on the wagon. We had the tractor in gear, with the throttle set, and while we were driving through the field I told my cousin to slide into the seat and drive. When I moved off the seat to let her in, I went to step onto the little steel platform on the side of the tractor.

Somehow, I missed the step, and fell off the right side of the tractor. Before I could even think, the rear wheel of the tractor ran over my midsection, breaking both bones in my left forearm, and rolled across my stomach. I was too stunned to move; my sister and cousin were screaming, not knowing how to stop the tractor, and in a moment the front wheel of the wagon ran over me as well. I remember seeing the rear wheel of the wagon coming at me, and rolling over (on my broken arm, no less) to get out of the way.

My mom had gone into town, and a few minutes later she pulled in the driveway. The girls were screaming for help – it was a very traumatic moment. Mom came and picked me up, put me in the car, and we went roaring toward Wooster. She saw a policeman and flagged him down, and he escorted us to the hospital. I had huge bruises on my stomach, but no internal injuries, and my broken arm eventually healed up all right.

What if the tire had run over my neck? What if the wagon had been loaded? What if we would have had a plow or disk on the back? I've asked myself those questions, knowing that a lot of kids don't get a second chance after an accident like that. But it really didn't change me, in terms of making me more cautious or careful. Life was kind of reckless, like with most other kids.

When I was 11 years old, a boy named Rich Hendrix moved in with us. He was 15, and he helped on the farm in exchange for room and board. He lived with us until he graduated from high school, and when he left I was old enough to take on some of the harder, heavier farm work.

I couldn't let myself be scared of the tractor, because it was a major part of farm life. Later on, I spent many hours standing on that wagon, while my dad drove the tractor, baling hay. I would ride on the wagon and stack the bales, and when you got more than three or four high you could really feel it in your shoulders and arms. It was hot, dirty work. The sun just ate you up, and the dirt and dust would cover every pore of your body. You had to wear long pants and long shirts, or the hay would just wear the skin off of your arms and legs. It was tough, but it helped me grow up.

As a teenager, my world finally started to expand, with my horizons growing a little bit at a time. The Haudenschild's parents divorced, and the kids and their mom moved into Wooster. We reconnected, and I was elated that my buddies and I were back in business.

It seemed like their family was always busy, always had something going on. I envied that. When I visited them in Wooster, we would ride bikes. Riding bikes on paved parking lots, and paved sidewalks, man, that was a luxury. They had a world I longed for: fun, excitement, and paved streets.

Near their house, there was a store in downtown Wooster called Freedlanders. It was a big department store, and out front they had a glass-enclosed display island that had a sidewalk running all around it. We would ride our bikes around that island, racing each other. One time Jac was leaning his bike through the corner, we had these stingray bikes with big sissy bars on the back. The sissy bar slapped the glass of that display case, *wham!* It made a really loud noise. Luckily, the glass was so thick that it didn't break. The cost of that repair would have been huge, at least in terms of our ability to pay.

During the time we were separated, Ed and Jac began riding mini-bikes. Pretty soon, I had to have one, too. The world would never be safe again. We all had "Lil' Indian" brand mini-bikes. It is always more fun to ride in a pack, instead of alone. When you ride as a group, you're always pushing each other, giving each other a challenge.

Jac and Ed showed up one day with the throttle cable broken on one of the mini-bikes. Instead of parking it, they just unhooked the cable, and would reach down to the engine to operate the throttle directly on the carburetor. That meant they had to drive with just one hand, but hey, no problem. They rode that bike for a long, long time, and never did get around to fixing the throttle cable.

At that time a centrifugal clutch cost $12, and we would burn them up pretty quickly. At $12 a pop, it ran us out of money right away. We discovered that we could buy a straight sprocket (dog clutch) for $2, which was really like direct drive. Nothing gentle about these babies. We started out with 3-hp Briggs & Stratton engines, then later bolted on 5-hp engines. Ed figured out how to make them work. We kept breaking the motor plates, breaking the welds on the frames. We were hell on wheels. When we got the mini-bikes, the ponies probably breathed a sigh of relief.

All these years later, I can close my eyes and think about Jac on those mini-bikes, and I laugh out loud. Later on, when he was a famous race driver, he got the nickname "The Wild Child," but people have no idea. They don't know what wild was, compared to those early days. He's mild now compared to then.

They had a cement culvert in front of their house. I can still picture Jac roaring toward that culvert, one hand on the bars and one arm reaching down to the engine, holding the throttle wide open, the little engine just begging for mercy. He would hit the culvert, sail through the air, then hit the ground and go end-over-end, both him and the bike. He'd get right up and brush himself off, nothing hurt.

One day, after a big rain with the grass really wet, Jac and I made a little oval in the side yard on our farm. After just a few laps, we had a very nice, muddy race track. We just tore the grass to pieces, and had a blast bouncing off of each other, sliding all over the place. I got in some trouble for the yard, but not too much. Today, I would probably be much less tolerant with my kids, but I sometimes forget what it's like being a kid, just having harmless fun.

Nobody ever got hurt on the bikes. Not seriously, anyway. Lots of cuts and bruises, though. Once, Jac spilled his bike and the sprocket ground into his skin, and cut him pretty deep. But he healed up. We always healed up.

I envied Jac and Ed because they each had a brother, something I really wanted. They used to fight a lot. It was nasty sometimes, and Ed always got the best of Jac. Ed was bigger, and had more of a temper, while Jac was really mellow and mild. They were really close as brothers, but their personalities were like night and day. Ed was the planner, always thinking things through, while Jac was a "just do it" kid.

During the time of the mini-bikes, when I was 13 or so, I got a steer (that is a male cow, for you city people) of my own to raise. We always kept at least eight or ten cows around, sometimes as many as 50. We fed them grain and hay until they were grown, then sold the beef. We had a tall silo next to our barn, and it was my job to climb into the silo and pitch the silage out onto the ground for the cows to eat. Silage is a nice word for green crops that have been cut up and now stink very badly. I didn't care much for crawling around in that silo, then climbing down to spread the silage on the ground for the cows.

But that steer was really important, because later on I sold it to buy a motorcycle, a Honda SL 125 Enduro. That motorcycle really extended my range, in terms of distance. By that time Ed and Jac had also graduated from the mini-bikes to motorcycles. It was the same game all along; it's just that our toys got more potent as we got older.

Later on, when my Honda was very, very used, Ed went out and got a brand new motorcycle. The first day he got it, we went hill climbing on a neighbor's farm. The hills were very steep and challenging, and it was tough to make it over the top. We would get close to the top and if the bike wheelied back or stalled, we had no choice but to let go and get out of the way as the bike rolled and flipped to the bottom of the hill. After a while we headed back to my house, where we set up a ramp to make jumps over a creek that ran through our farm. We kept making the jump higher and higher and jumping farther and farther. Evel Knievel had nothing on us! By the time we were done, Ed's brand new bike looked as bad as mine: headlight and taillight torn off, paint scratched, and so muddy you couldn't tell what color it was.

I loved to ride wheelies, and I got to where I could do 'em while I stood on the seat. My Amish neighbors would be out in the fields and they would stop and watch and just shake their heads. I can imagine them saying to each other, "That English boy isn't quite right."

There are probably people who lived nearby who still talk about those idiot English kids and their entertaining thrill shows, free of charge to whoever wanted to watch.

A big day for me came when I was 16, and I got my driver's license. Naturally, the first place I drove was Ed and Jac's house. Being able to drive really opened up my world. I had so much I wanted to see and do.

My first street car was a Pinto. I was infamous in that Pinto. As weird as this sounds, I actually *liked* Pintos. I learned to drive on tractors, and even as a kid I would pretend they were race cars. Now, with my Pinto, I would drive on the gravel roads in Wayne or Holmes County, and while rolling along I would grab that back brake handle and lock it up. There were lots of power slides in the 'ol Pinto.

Later on, I realized that the Pinto had taught me how to feel a car with the seat of my pants. Other kids wanted to ride with me because they'd heard stories about my drives in that Pinto. If they wanted a good scare, they'd pile in and hang on. I'm not proud of that now, and looking back I have to admit it was kind of stupid. Driving too fast, taking big chances, sliding through s-curves with the rear brakes locked up. I went through lots of rear tires, and to replace them I'd buy used ones. Living within my means, you know.

The Pinto had been my sister's, and my parents gave it to me as kind of a hand-me-down. When I was done with it, it was pretty much used up. My parents probably looked at the car and shook their heads. I took torch tip cleaners and filed out the jets in the carburetor to "improve the performance." I don't know if it ran better, but it definitely used more gas. That little 4-cylinder wasn't the strongest thing around, but what I lacked in horsepower I made up in wild driving.

I actually was dumb enough at one point to try to outrun the state patrol in that Pinto. One night I was speeding, passing cars on a two-lane road, and I met a state trooper. He did a quick flip and came after me; I saw him in my mirror. I was in an area unfamiliar to me – I didn't know the roads. I killed my lights and turned off on the first side road I saw.

I was going way too fast with no lights, but the moonlight was really bright. But not knowing the road was my undoing. The old Pinto was awesome through gravel roads, and this old road turned from asphalt to gravel. I thought I saw a curve coming, so I set my front wheel off in the ditch to slide the corner. But there was no curve – it was just a rise and a very slight turn. So having the wheel in the ditch took my control, and I slid sideways, facing the ditch. I kind of panicked, and I sat there and waited on the cop.

It seemed like it took him a long, long time to get there. He was pretty calm. He said basically that I had him beat, and asked me what happened. I was really honest. I told him I thought there was a corner and went to slide the corner, and spun. So he had me. He was pretty low-key about it, really, lots more calm than I would have been if I was a cop. He charged me with reckless operation, and I lost my license for 30 days. They didn't charge me with fleeing, which was a much more serious charge. I guess he couldn't prove I was actually running from him, because it took him so long to catch me. The whole thing was just a stupid trick on my part; it all goes back to unjustifiable risk.

Our biggest chase adventure came in Ed's El Camino. As teenagers, we felt like the Millersburg cops had it in for us, or at least a couple of their officers did. It was what you would call a mutually adversarial relationship. Maybe it wasn't just us, but all the young guys. Ed had an El Camino with a worn-out fan belt. Every time he would rev the engine too much, it would twist and throw the belt off. One night in Millersburg he revved the engine at a stop light, and it threw the belt. We pulled off to the side and popped the hood, and Ed worked on getting the belt back on. A cop drove slowly by and looked at us, and we looked at him. A couple of hours later we were riding around town, Ed driving, me in the middle, and Jac in the passenger seat.

We were headed for their dad's house, probably going home for the night. We went through a 35 mph zone doing about 50. The cop was sitting there, and we saw him but it was too late. He whipped out behind us with his pursuit lights on, and Jac and I yelled, "Go! Go!" to Ed, and he hesitated, saying no, no. Then we said, well, maybe we better not, but by then Ed's indecision was over and he mashed the gas, and the chase was on. Ed hustled the old El Camino up to about 120 mph, and the cop could get within a quarter of a mile or so but no closer. We went about seven or eight miles on Route 39, which is hilly and curvy. We were wide open when we topped a hill and there was a bridge out at the bottom of the hill, just like in the movies.

Luckily, they had built a little wooden bridge off to the side. But by then our brakes were hot, and Ed had both feet on the brakes as hard as he could, and the car wouldn't slow down. You could smell the brakes – they were really fried. We had slowed to about 80 when he shot across that narrow, rickety bridge, then slid sideways and bounced over this dirt road that led back to the asphalt. We probably all needed an underwear change right about that time.

When the cop came along behind us, he had to slow so much for the bridge that we lost him. We took back roads to my house. We were scared there would be roadblocks and the whole deal. We all spent the night at my house.

A day or two later we were in town again, and a policeman walked up to Ed and said they had his license number, that they knew it was him. They told him that if he would go and sign a confession they would forget the whole thing. Well, Ed went in and signed the form, and they immediately charged him with all kinds of stuff! Turns out they didn't even have the license number, but once Ed signed the form he was toast.

He went to trial a few weeks later, and we all had to testify. We were scared to death; none of us were 18 yet. The story had a strange ending, though. Ed had begun racing a modified at a local track, and the cops told the judge that it *had* to have been Ed, because he was a race driver. Only a professional could have made the bridge that night, they said. But then the judge pointed out that if he did such a great job driving, then how could the police say he was reckless? They threw the whole thing out. You should have seen the look on the cop's face. Boy, we knew he would have it in for us from there on out, and he did. We really had to be on our toes, because we knew there would be no breaks. I guess it didn't change our behavior, because we still got into just as much stuff. But it did make us pay more attention to where the cops were!

As an adult, I look back at that kind of stuff and I'm embarrassed. It's the kind of stuff that you hope your kid doesn't try. Society is different now, and things like running from the police would be considered far more serious today. I'm really outspoken to kids that you shouldn't do such wild, reckless things. We were lucky, really, because we survived. Just pick up a newspaper today and you'll find stories about kids who took risks like that and paid the supreme price.

Summer nights were awesome for us. We would climb the fence at the Millersburg public swimming pool, long after it had closed for the night. Every so often the cops would come and shine their lights into the pool from outside the fence, so we'd get back against the pool wall toward the fence and be real still, with everything underwater but our lips. We would hold really still until the lights were out. We used to yell at Jac because he'd jump in and out and get the sidewalk all wet; we were afraid if the cops came by they'd see the water and open the fence and take a closer look.

It might sound like we were troublemakers, but I don't think so. None of us ever did anything to intentionally hurt anybody, or damage anything. Most of the stuff was related to cars or driving. But it was kind of a game, probably like kids in every small town who like to give the cops a hard time.

One summer night in Millersburg it was really busy. Even though it was late, there were lots of people riding around and lots of activity. We were hanging out on a street corner near the police station, with the cop car parked nearby, just sitting there. Our eyes kept looking at that car. How tempting, to be so close to an unguarded car...I'm not sure who actually did the deed, but somewhere along the line the hood got popped, and the coil wire disappeared.

In a little while a cop came out of the station and walked past us, giving us a dirty look and a grunt. He got into the car, and we all started to snicker. RRRRR-RRRRRR-RRRRRR. RRRRRR-RRRRRR-RRRRRRR. RRRRRRR-RRRRRRR-RRRRRRR. By now everyone was busting a gut, except the cop, who stepped out of the car and slammed the car door. He walked in front of the car and raised the hood, looked at the engine compartment for a second, then slammed the hood. He walked back by us (not saying a word this time), and went into the station. It seemed like the proper time to go find somewhere else to loiter, and we did so with great haste, you might say.

After my Pinto I got a really nice Camaro, and then an El Camino that I parked in the winter. I had a beat-up Pontiac that I drove in bad weather, and I would go out and slide like crazy on the snowy roads. More driving lessons!

I had never liked school, and during my teenage years it didn't get any better. I went through the hippie stages, I had long hair and patches on my bell-bottom pants. I got sent home from school once because I had too many patches on my jeans. I was a big Neil Young fan; on one of his albums he was wearing these old jeans and I wanted to be like him, I guess.

I took welding during my junior year, then auto mechanics my senior year. My welding teacher, Mr. Harris, was a big stock car racing fan. That was really unusual for that period, a mainstream person talking about NASCAR. Growing up on the farm, we had an AC welder, a little red stick welder that was called a "buzz box." I learned to weld with that little thing, and by high school I did all the welding on the farm. I knew I didn't want to weld for a living, but I figured on being a good enough welder to build a race car. That's what I was thinking. That would probably have broken Mr. Harris' heart, because he encouraged me to make welding a career. But I really didn't have any interest in that. When I was 13 or 14, I built a tow trailer for our farm, before I ever had a class. I wanted to learn MIG welding and TIG welding, they taught me some of that during my junior year, even though I was supposed to wait until I was a senior. My dad knew how to rebuild wrecks, so I had always been around a lot of mechanical work. It was second nature to me.

It's ironic that even though I didn't want to make my living as a welder, later in my life that's probably the skill that's served me best. Even today I weld a lot, building aluminum clothing irons for the Amish.

This might sound odd, but I really don't remember when I became interested in racing. It was like it was always there, just kind of a passing interest. John Haudenschild drove a modified at Lakeville Speedway, near our house, and we would go to watch him. Ed and Jac and I would play with our toy cars up on the dirt bank near the grandstands, oblivious to the real racing. Later on, when I was a teenager, my interest in racing just perked up.

In no small way, I know it was because of Ed Haudenschild. I looked up to him a lot, I really admired him. And when he turned 16, Ed went racing. This farm boy was about to see a big life change.

2

Racing has a way of sneaking up on you. It starts out as a hobby, then becomes a passion, then ultimately is a master, owning all your possessions. If you're lucky, you'll keep your soul, and that's about all.

But I'm not complaining. On the contrary, getting involved in racing was an exciting, wonderful thrill for me, beginning when I was just 15.

John Haudenschild was a big winner in the modifieds at Lakeville Speedway and Hilltop Speedway. Both tracks are quarter-mile dirt tracks, and both were close to home. John won a lot of modified races in his day at those tracks.

My dad raced one time, and said never again. He'll admit that it scared him. He drove a stock car. I can vaguely remember it, kind of like a street stock car. He was helping another guy build the car, and the plan was that the other guy would do the driving. But when the moment of truth came, the guy's wife said "No way!" So dad drove, and during the race another car got into his driver door and shoved him "all the way around the race track," he used to tell us. That was the end of his driving days. He quit on the spot.

When Ed Haudenschild turned 16, he and his dad set him up with a modified. It was a worn-out old car, and Ed and John went through the car, reworked it, breathed new life into it.

Ed, Jac, and John would go right by my house on their way to Wayne County Speedway in Orrville, and they started picking me up and letting me go with them. Jac and I were only 14 or 15 or so, and we couldn't get into the pits. So he and I would sit in the stands, watching Ed race. John had retired from driving by this time, and he stayed in the pits helping Ed.

I remember a funny story from that time, a story that sort of sums up the era we were living in. I was in the hippie stage of my life, with long hair and wide bell-bottom jeans, and John was pretty much a conservative guy. He considered me a hippie, and I thought he was a redneck. It was never ugly between us; mostly a lot of teasing about clothes, music, that kind of thing.

One day John told me that if I was going to go to the races with him, I had to get a haircut. Well, there was no way he was serious, or so I thought. I had no intention of cutting my hair for anybody. So that next week, there I was, standing down by the mailbox on Saturday afternoon, watching for them to come along. Before long I could see them coming, their truck bobbing over the gentle hills on our road.

You could hear the engine slow as they got close, and I could see them all staring at me. They were looking to see if I had cut my hair. When they saw that I hadn't, John just gassed the old truck and they rolled right on by.

I was devastated! But I must have either cut my hair or found another ride, because I didn't miss many races.

I hung out around their garage a lot, really interested in what they were doing. Once, Ed had the car up on jack stands, and it fell off and tipped onto its side. We laughed that he had flipped the thing even before he got to the race track.

Up until the time Ed started driving, I had no idea he was interested in racing. Actually, none of us ever talked about racing before that time. Sure, we went and watched John, but we never dreamed about becoming race drivers. If any of us did, he sure didn't share it with the others.

John's car was always No. 277, and Ed's car was No. 27. I was really impressed with Ed, racing against grown men when he was just 16.

Really, almost everything Ed did impressed me. Being a little bit older, he was truly a role model for me as a kid. He was very influential on my life. Even today, he is somebody I respect immensely.

Not only was he racing at age 16, but he worked at a gas station. There wasn't a more cool job for a teenage boy at that time. Ed had learned to weld at a young age, so naturally I wanted to weld also.

Ed was an innovator. He could fix things, make things. We were riding bicycles once, and the front wheel on my bike messed up. To get it back to my house, Ed rigged up a wooden thing with a soapbox-derby wheel, and rode it home for me. I believed Ed could fix anything, absolutely anything.

Working at the gas station, Ed saved up his money to buy a magneto for his race car, replacing the old distributor. That was my first experience at trick parts for race cars!

I can still remember the night that the idea came into my head to be a race driver. Ed was leading the modified feature at Wayne County Speedway, and the car got away from him and he spun. But he was good enough that he kept the thing going and got back underway without losing a position.

To me, that was really impressive. To see someone have such control over their car, that was just about the neatest thing I had ever seen, really awesome. That night, that very minute, the fluttering in my heart started. I knew I wanted to be a race driver.

The question was, how? My parents didn't have the money to buy a race car, so that avenue was out. I didn't know how to build one. So I kind of thought it over, mulling in my mind how I might get a chance to do this.

At first, it was something I never really thought I would get a chance to try. You know, you sit there in the stands, and wish you could drive one of those cars, but deep down inside you don't really think you will. But the more I thought about it, I became convinced that I could do it. Other guys had managed to do it…why shouldn't I?

I was only 15, so there wasn't a lot of urgency anyway. You couldn't race unless you were 16, so I had time to think it over.

My big break came a month or so before my 16th birthday. Ed decided to move up to a sprint car, which meant there was a modified ride available. Hmmm….

The deal was soon struck. I would sell my motorcycle, using the $450 to buy the old modified from Ed. He needed his 327-

inch engine for his sprint car, so the deal was he would build a new engine for the modified.

Ed put together a stock 283-inch engine, with a 30/30 cam and a four-barrel carburetor. Although the class was called modifieds, the cars weren't like the modifieds they race out east. It was more like today's IMCA modifieds: a really basic, inexpensive open-wheel car with most of the components coming from junkyards.

When Ed raced, he raced in a T-shirt. But I wore some old white cotton coveralls that had been dipped in fire-retardant stuff. I got a premier full-face helmet, and I was ready to go.

When Ed ran the car it was No. 27, so we took tape and changed the 7 to an 8. That's how my No. 28 came about.

I was excited about my race car, and maybe a little intimidated. Ed had been successful in the car, so I was sitting in a proven winner. But for the most part I just wanted to have fun, so I guess my priorities were in the right order.

A week or so before my 16th birthday, the people at Lakeville let me run my first race. I finished either second or third that night, I can't recall exactly. It would have made for a great story if I had won, but it didn't happen.

But I did win on our second night out, so I felt really great. Maybe I could do this after all.

My parents didn't object much, but I remember my grandparents saying I was crazy for racing. Some of my relatives thought I was just playing race car driver. Racing wasn't the most respectable occupation you could choose back then.

When I started, there was no career path, no World of Outlaws or anything like that. I just wanted to have some fun. And that's what we did. We lived Saturday to Saturday. When Saturday was over, we couldn't wait until next Saturday. I look back and realize now that it was great to be a kid.

But man, that old car was hard to steer. It had big old butyl rubber tires, and an old Ross steering box. Our "feature" was actually a 15-lap B-main, and after 15 laps it was all I could do to unhook my seat belts, I was so spent. Coming off the farm, I thought all that shoveling and hay baling had me in pretty good shape, but...whew! That old car just wore me out.

After I won that first race, I started thinking, "I can do this!" The notoriety, even at a local level, was kind of neat. We towed the car on an open trailer, and my name was on the side of the car. So I'd go through town to the car wash, and I knew people were seeing my name.

If I won my heat and the B-main I made $75. At age 16, I thought I was a full-time racer!

All we did was buy gas. Later on I blew the 283, so I dropped in a 350 with a cracked cylinder, and water would get in the oil. Every week I'd pull the drain plug and let the water out. When it started coming out oil I'd put the plug back in. Then I would refill the radiator and go buy 5 gallons of gas, and I was ready to race. I never bought tires. Once I punctured the sidewall of a tire, and rather than replace it we just had it vulcanized. We just didn't spend any money.

There were hardly any adjustments on the car, it was so old. The frame was bowing so badly that we had to weld a skid plate on the oil pan because it was dragging on the race track. I didn't know it then, but the low center of gravity probably helped the race car work.

The front suspension was an old spring setup, and all the bolts were rusted and frozen. I don't know if Ed ever changed them, but I sure didn't, because I *couldn't*. I just checked the oil and water and put gas in it, and that's it.

John Haudenschild had built our trailer. It was an old double-axle trailer with no springs and no brakes (we didn't have 'em hooked up). I don't think we even had taillights. I pulled it with an old Ford Bronco, with a little six-banger engine.

There was a big hill on the road near Lakeville, and I had to drop the Bronco into low-range and hold it wide open to make the hill. I used to pray that the engine wouldn't die, because I knew the Bronco's brakes wouldn't have been enough to hold the thing from rolling backward down the hill.

I was truly a low-buck operation, no doubt about it. The car ran on gasoline, and it had an old bus seat that was mounted almost on top of the gas tank, a steel tank. Incredibly unsafe. The bus seat was too big for me, so I sat on this big feather pillow. The driveline was open, with a little short driveshaft that ran just a few inches from my seat.

One night the driveshaft broke and it caught that pillow, and in a split second yanked it right out from under my butt. Feathers just exploded everywhere! Inside the car, in my mouth, all over the race track. Everyone had a big laugh, saying, "See, I told you Doty was chicken!"

Another humbling moment came that fall. My vocational-school class rode buses out to the track for a field trip, where I was going to hot lap the car and explain everything to them. On just my second lap, a spindle broke and the wheel and suspension bounced far from the track, out into this field. I was totally embarrassed, and I never did find the wheel.

One of my tight buddies at the time was Scott Drown. His brothers were into racing, and I met Scott the summer before I started going to vocational school. He went to a different high school, but we met at Lakeville. My first day at vocational school I walked into class and there he was. At vocational school you meet guys from different high schools, so to start with you're not familiar with many people. But when I walked in and saw a fellow race fan sitting there that first day, we naturally hit if off and that was the start of a good friendship.

At Lakeville they only ran 15 races or so during their season, and the main event was 15 or 20 laps. If the sprint cars had a short field they would put us in there, but we couldn't keep up with those guys. So I didn't race against Ed much.

What a change from today...now, kids just starting out race two and three nights a week, running 30-lap races. They're able to get a lot of good experience.

Although the frame was already sagging when I bought the car, it was progressively getting worse. Finally, my second year in the car, we crashed big-time, and that took care of the sagging problem. In fact, it pretty much killed the old car.

Three weeks before the end of the season, several cars crashed in front of me. I couldn't miss them, and bounced off somebody and spun. I was sitting crossed up on the track when Dick Byerly came along and just t-boned me. He had nowhere to go. It ripped my engine loose, shoved the frame over – it was a big mess.

Dick got out of the car yelling and screaming at me, he was so mad. I was just a kid trying to keep from getting my head knocked off, so I just sat there with my mouth shut. I didn't say anything back.

My car looked like it was destroyed, and my brief career appeared to be over. But my old buddy Ed, like the Lone Ranger, came to save the day.

I had to bale hay the day after the crash, and early that morning Ed came over and said we were going to fix the car. I told him he was crazy, because it was so severely bent. I just couldn't imagine how it could be fixed. I didn't know where the money was going to come from, or the knowledge. But Ed kept saying that we had to at least try.

We got it off the trailer and got it into our shed, then I left to go to the field. By the time I got back later that afternoon, Ed had torched the frame out from under it, and the only thing left was the roll cage and rear suspension, tank, body work on the back. That was the end of the old frame.

When I saw it, I began to think, "Hey, we can fix this thing!" That week was intense. We weren't morning people, being teenagers, so starting bright and early usually meant around noon. But we worked till very early in the morning, so it was definitely a full work day, every day.

To replace the frame, we needed some steel. I didn't know what chrome moly was; I was still pretty green. We figured the strongest pipe we could find was the black steel pipe that lots of oil companies used in this area. Ed knew a place that stored the stuff.

I probably shouldn't be telling this, but late one night when it was good and dark Ed, Jac and I went out and found 3 or 4 pieces of this 20-foot section of inch-and-a-half pipe. Talk about heavy. We were in my mom's '66 Mustang, and I was terrified of scratching the side of the car.

How do you put a 20-foot pipe in a Mustang? One of us sat in the front passenger seat, with another guy sitting right behind him in the back seat. Hanging our arms out the window, we each held on to the sections of pipe.

I'm glad it was dark, and not just because we might have been in trouble; I'm glad nobody saw how stupid we looked! Like a bunch of hillbillies, driving down the back roads, with arms hanging out of the right side of the car. I kept praying we wouldn't dent my mom's car. I could picture those sections of pipe just gouging into the paint and tearing the chrome off the car.

We were going down the back roads, trying to get back to the shop, when we saw a car coming. One of us dropped the pipe and the other didn't, so we just about messed it all up there. But we hung on and finally got the stuff home.

Ed was the designer and fitter – whacking and cutting – and I helped with the welding. I thought we were pretty high-tech; we built new spring perches with adjustable bolts to jack weight (no more frozen bolts, but I still didn't mess with them because I didn't really know how they worked!). We worked all that week – didn't even take the time to sweep the floor or pick up the junk we had cut up. We were wading in this stuff.

Toward the end of week, we were bolting the engine back into the car, and I fell asleep and fell down onto the engine. That's how weary I was.

By that weekend, John was apparently kind of mad that Ed had spent all his time on my car, because he hadn't turned a wrench on his own car. By Saturday morning Ed was still at my house until about noon, when he went home to work on his sprint car. That left it up to me to finish, and I just ran out of time. I still had the belts to put in, the body panels to hang with pop rivets, stuff like that. I didn't feel there was any way, so later that evening I just washed up and headed for the race track to be a spectator.

When I arrived at the track without the car, Ed was pretty upset. He thought I should have had the car finished. I think he was really disappointed in me, that I couldn't get it finished.

A couple of weeks later came the season championship. Roger Rush was a driver in my division that was really good; I always had to race hard to beat him. I beat him that night for the season championship, and it was really a proud moment for me. Without Ed, there is no way I would have even been there. If I didn't say it then, I'll say it now: thanks, old buddy.

3

Have you ever heard a sprint car calling your name? I have. That sharp, loud growl as they paw and scratch at a dirt track for traction, that blast of exhaust as they pitch into the corner. Then they rocket off of the corner down the straightaway, making the hair on my neck stand up.

I had seen sprint cars race locally for years, at places like Wayne County and Lakeville. I thought they were cool, but until I ran my modified for a couple of seasons, I never really thought about driving one. They were out of reach, or at least that was my perception.

When I was 14 years old, Jan Opperman came to Wayne County Speedway to race, along with Bobby Allen and Steve Smith. Opperman made a huge impression on me. Just enormous, so much so that I can't really describe it. His persona, his character, his ability in the car - my gosh, he reached out and touched me all the way to my soul.

I think he is largely responsible for my long hair and freaky clothes during my teenage years. I went home and made a little leather cross, just like his, along with a leather necklace. I even soaked the leather in water, to make it look weathered, like Jan's. His Bogar car had "race winner" stickers all over it; later on when I started winning races I put stickers on my car just like he did. It was a case of hero worship.

After winning the championship at Lakeville, later that fall Ed, Jac and I talked my parents into letting us use my dad's camper truck to go to Williams Grove for the National Open. I'm amazed that they allowed me to go that far from home at just 16 years old. In fact, not one of us was 18. I think we told them the Grove was just across the Pennsylvania line, when in fact it was about six hours from our place.

As usual, our trip turned into quite an adventure. On the way out we picked up a hitchhiker, an older guy who was carrying a guitar, and he went to the races with us! When we got to the Grove, that night they had a big campfire where everyone sat around, and our hitchhiker buddy got drunk and strummed the guitar and sang. As long as they kept supplying him with beer, the guy played, getting more wound up with every round. I remember him doing the Johnny Cash song *Orange Blossom Special*, and everyone making the train whistle sound, *whoooo-whoooo*, really loud. It was a hoot!

To be 16 years old in the midst of all this was just tremendous. I took it all in, and you might say that it was a watershed event for me, because it was another step farther out into the big, wide world.

As far as the racing, I can use three words to describe my thoughts: wow, wow, and wow! Jan Opperman, Kenny Weld, Steve Smith, Lynn Paxton, Bobby Allen, Smokey Snellbaker. Could it get any better than this?

I had my picture taken with Opperman, and got his autograph. In his signature, when he wrote the "O" in his last name, he would make a little smiley face. Later on, when people began wanting my autograph, I put the smiley face in the "D" in Doty. Like I said, I wanted to be just like Jan.

I didn't care about NASCAR, or Daytona, or even Indy. The only thing that meant anything to me was going to Williams Grove to see Jan Opperman and Kenny Weld. That was the top of the world, as far as I was concerned.

Weld won the main event that weekend, and we headed home. On the way back the truck quit running, and we were broke down on the side of the turnpike after dark. As always, Jac and I counted on Ed to figure out how to fix the truck, and naturally he got right on it. It looked like the points in the distributor were bad. So Jac stayed with the truck while Ed and I started hoofing it down the side of the road to find a gas station to buy another set. As we walked along, we thought we heard something in the bushes.

We were convinced that these big Pennsylvania hills and woods just had to be full of bears. We'd hear that noise, and we'd stop and listen. Then we'd walk some more, and stop and listen. It was kind of like Dorothy in the Wizard of Oz, hurrying through the woods thinking about lions and tigers and bears. Finally we panicked and took off running for the gas station, and in our imagination that old bear was just one step behind us. I could almost feel his hot breath on the back of my neck, thinking that he was going to eat us up. We surely looked goofy, two teenagers sprinting down the shoulder of the highway as if the bogeyman was after us. We never saw anything, of course, and it was probably nothing more than a possum nosing around for his dinner.

We found a set of points, but the truck still wouldn't run. We finally figured out that the fuel filter was plugged, and Ed poked a hole in it and we were on our way. He sure was a handy guy to have around.

After that trip, it was pretty hard not to think about driving a sprint car over the next couple of seasons. Ed was doing pretty well in his sprint car, and I was winning races in my modified. I didn't keep any kind of records back then, but when I look at pictures of my old car I can see 14 win stickers on the wing, so I guess I won at least 14 races that season.

All of this racing had made school seem less and less interesting. I went to Waynedale High School for grades 9 and 10, then moved on to Wayne County Joint Vocational School, which we referred to as "The Joint." When I was a freshman, my sister introduced me to another kid from our school who was also interested in racing. His name was Kenny Jacobs.

Kenny had already moved on to "the Joint" by this time. He was a couple of years older than me. My sister Deb knew Kenny from school. The thing I remember most about him was that he had a Chevelle with a 396 big block. I could hear him rumble into the high school every day, with a load of kids in his car. Way, way cool. When Deb introduced us, it was really no big deal at the time. I didn't realize that I would have a life-long friendship with Kenny, just like Ed and Jac Haudenschild.

Kenny didn't like my hippie clothes, I remember that. Once I had this old jacket on, really grungy looking, and he wouldn't even talk to me.

Kenny's dad also drove a truck, and was a well-known race driver in both modifieds and late models. But I hadn't heard of him, mainly because they didn't run Lakeville or Hilltop much. They focused on Orrville, where I went only every once in a while. Kenny, Sr., was a track champ at Orrville, and everybody called him "Jake."

So now we had four wanna-be sprint car drivers, right in the same little circle. Actually, Ed was already a sprint car driver, which sure helped fire me up, because I could see that he was getting it done.

I ran my modified for another season or two, then decided to sell it at the end of the season. My plan was to use the money to buy a sprint car. With the success Ed had, I felt like I was ready to move up as well. By then Jac also had a sprint car, a No. 17 that looked like Ed's No. 27: blue with a white plywood wing. On their second week out at Lakeville, Jac tipped his car over in turn two and it caught on fire. He got out okay, but the car just literally burned up. His car had a carburetor, and when it tipped the fuel leaked out and that was all it took. The car had brand new belts, lots of new stuff, and it was just eaten up. They dragged the car home and went through it, and eventually got it going again.

This was early 1976, and I had no car. I couldn't get anything going. The season wore on, and it began to look more and more bleak for me. I felt like I was in trouble, because I didn't have the money to buy a car on my own, and lacked the experience to get a chance in somebody else's car. I hung around with Ed and Jac, watching them race, and Kenny, too. It galled me. I hated it.

Ed and Kenny were battling every week against guys such as Roger Wiles, Don Davidson, Dick Byerly. They were all pretty good. Roger was especially tough. He had been winning at Lakeville for years and he was in a good, full-up sprint car.

At that time in our area a typical sprint car was a simple car with a spring front end. That was considered pretty good equipment. A lot of guys were still running carburetors. In western

Ohio, places like Findlay and Fremont, those guys ran fuel injection and four-bar suspensions. They were ahead of us technically.

There were some pretty good cars at Lakeville, though. A CAE car was the hot setup (CAE is Culbert Automotive Engineering out of California). CAE built a lot of parts, in-out boxes, rear ends, chassis, they made lots of good stuff. Guys started going to four-bar cars right after I got started, and running quick-change rear ends. Don Davidson had a four-bar car, with Weber carburetors. Dick Byerly's car was a four-bar car too, I think. Ed was competitive right away. He was a natural. Kenny ran a modified with a quick-change rear end, which had been his dad's car at one time. It had a six-cylinder GMC engine. His dad won a lot of races in that car. When Kenny got the car, it still had the Jimmy engine.

Then Kenny got into a sidewinder asphalt sprint car, but ran it on the dirt at Lakeville. He used to pick the left front wheel up on the car coming off the corner, really up high. But I was pretty low, because I had nothing going in terms of finding a ride.

Finally, in the middle of the '77 season, I was allowed to drive a sprint car. It was on the half-mile at Mansfield, and I talked my way into the car. The guys who owned the car agreed to give me a shot. The car had fuel-injection and an open-tube rear end, with a three-inch axle with tapered hubs. The rear end had a key-way cut into the axle, but when they put the car together the guys forgot to put the key back into the key-way. Basically, the rear end was driving only one wheel.

When I got out on the track, every time I pressed the throttle, one rear wheel would bite and the car would turn severely. It was scary and a downright horrible experience. Already I had no confidence, and then this. I was devastated, because if that was what it was supposed to feel like, I couldn't do it. I got out of the car, and they put another, more experienced guy in it, and he didn't do any better than I had.

That week I was feeling very, very low. Then the next weekend those guys apologized and laughed, and explained that they had later discovered the key was missing. It was kind of a relief for me, and it gave me renewed hope, but the bottom line was that I didn't get another chance in the car.

Not too long after that, Wayne Yerian let me drive his Trevis car, a maroon No. 75. A solid, fuel-injected car. I settled in and ran that car for a few weeks, and when I beat Roger Wiles in a heat race I figured I was on my way. I'm not sure why that deal fell apart - I don't remember getting fired or anything - but by the start of the '78 season I got the opportunity to drive the No. 00 car owned by Ken "Speed" Botkins.

This car was from Galion, Ohio, west of Mansfield. Speed was a lot of fun, a real jokester who could always make me laugh. He owned a car repair business over there and he was a really likable guy. We clicked pretty well; I was really enjoying the experience and having a lot of fun. Speed gave me my first real opportunity, my first steady ride.

Early in the season, I got my first sprint car win. It's hard to believe, but today I don't remember much about it. I wish I could remember more. I didn't realize what an important event that is in a person's career. I just felt like, well, neat, let's go on to the next race. You only win your first one once; I should have savored it more.

Even when I won, though, I didn't feel like I had "made it." There was no sigh of relief, no feeling of great satisfaction. Being a race driver is a life of stress and pressure, I would later discover, and no matter how much you win you are only as good as your last race. So you can never be content, never be satisfied, until you quit.

After winning that race, I really only thought about next week. I never thought very far ahead.

But for me and my three buddies, it was a special time. It quickly became obvious that all four of us had some potential in sprint cars. I didn't realize it until much later, but for three or four guys to come from one little place, one little track, and make it to the pro leagues, that's really unusual. It's kind of like four kids in the same high school class all going on to play in the NFL. It's really, really unlikely.

Kenny was running a No. 6x car owned by John Harmon, John Gantz, and Dave Pope. The car was one of the first four-bar cars built by LaVerne Nance. Before Kenny, they had Roger Wiles in the car, so this was a top-notch ride, at least for our area. When Roger was in his prime, they ran a spring-front CAE car.

Roger was from Creston, a little town north of Wooster. There had been two or three sprint car teams up there; somehow along the way they joined forces, combined their efforts. Roger ended up driving their car. He ran a great big wing, like a four-by-eight sheet of plywood standing almost straight up. With the spring-front car he could turn the car sideways and that wing was like an air brake. When they later went to the four-bar, when he tried that it lifted the right side completely off the ground! The style then at Lakeville was to back the car in like a non-wing car. They started trimming the wing down, learning the four-bar suspension, and it was an interesting period technically, a period of a lot of progression.

When Roger retired, the team hired Kenny. After Roger quit I remember him telling me, "Kid, you'll know you've made it when they call you a son of a bitch." That was good advice! He was a great guy, and a very dominant racer in his time. I was still young enough that Roger was a good person to emulate on the race track. He was a guy you could respect.

As my racing interests grew, the day soon came when I graduated from high school. That meant it was time to think about a job, which to me was nothing more than a necessary evil. I wanted to race; who cared about a job, anyway? I wound up getting hired at an auto parts store in Orrville, and man, was I terrible at that job. I was supposed to be hired into the machine shop they had at the store, but to begin with they put me on the counter, looking up parts. They didn't have computers then, and we had to look all the part numbers up in great big books. I was so s-l-o-w. The customers were really steamed. It would take me three times as long to find a part number as other guys who could blitz right to them. So I quit after 2 weeks.

Not long after, my vocational school scheduled a job interview for me at a welding shop. I was driving over for the interview when it occurred to me that I didn't want to spend the rest of my life in a hot old welding shop. So I turned the car around, turned up the radio, and forgot all about that interview. I didn't know what I was going to do, but I knew I didn't want to be a welder.

Finally I got a job at Magna-Fab, a small fabrication company near Wooster on Route 30. I worked there for two years, and in spite of that the company survived! Actually, they were great people, and it was a good experience for me. They built the covers for Genie garage door openers, and other things like that. They had a paint line, with parts on a chain, and the operator had to put parts on the chain as fast as he could. If you screwed up and got behind, they were pretty irritated. That was kind of the entry-level position; I hated that job.

After a couple of months I moved over to operate a press, and I was really efficient at that job. To me, just about everything was competitive, like a race. I figured out how to operate the press faster than the other guy, turning out more parts per day even though he had been there for years. That didn't sit very well with the other guy, but the plant manager, the supervisor, and the foreman were excited! They started watching me to try and figure out how I was able to work so quickly. They were pleased, but they told me to be careful, because that old press could chop off your thumbs in a heartbeat.

Later I started doing some MIG welding, then worked in the shipping department, and also drove a forklift. I used to see how quickly I could get a truck loaded. I was hell on wheels on that forklift. One day I was on the forklift and needed to go outside, and my trick was to slip the forks under the garage door and lift them, and the spring on the door would bring it the rest of the way up. But little did I know that somebody had locked the door, and when I raised the forks it just mangled that garage door. Whooops.

Naturally, I was taking a lot of time off, and after a while they got pretty tired of it. I'd like to blame it on racing, but that wasn't really all of it. I just hated the factory, being cooped up inside, the confinement. The guys that I worked with were really neat people. After I had been racing for a while, I found out that a lot of them became race fans, that made me feel good. They would show up at Eldora with a big sign, "the gang from Magna-Fab".

One day I finally told my foreman, Ben Schaffter, that I was quitting to go racing full-time. He kind of laughed and said I would be back in six months, and that they would have a job for me. Ben is still working there; he's moved up the ladder a lot since the day he told me that. We still chuckle about it.

Although I won a race in the No. 00, they fired me midway through the '78 season, on my birthday, July 27. No hard feelings – they were just ready for a change, I guess. So I was idle again, wondering where I would go from there.

At a time like this, it's good to have friends. Luckily, I had plenty. Late that season, Kenny left the 6x car to drive a 3x car for Harold "Flake" Kemenah. Kenny pitched the guys that owned the 6x car, John Harmon, John Gantz, and Dave Pope, to give me a chance. You know, he didn't have to do that for me, but that's the kind of friends we were. We truly tried to look out of each other, and I would have tried to help him if the roles had been reversed.

The guys with the 6x car were pretty skeptical at first, I know. After all, I was still pretty much of an unknown, and had only won one race. Hardly enough to impress anybody. My first race with them came at Lakeville, where I started on the tail of the main. They told me to watch the gauges, because above all they couldn't afford to hurt the motor, and if it got hot or lost oil pressure to bring it in right away. The car had power steering, which I had never tried before, so I was really worried about being squirrely. I didn't want to get in anybody's way. That's why we started on the tail. Right off the bat I was passing cars, trying to glance at the gauges, and the car worked perfectly. It was awesome. I didn't want to crash or break, because I felt like this was my big chance. I had to prove I was as good as the car. I just rolled around the corners, real easy, just like on asphalt, and hammered it down the straights. When it was over I finished second.

I should have been happy with that, but I wasn't. I thought I could have won, if I would have just driven the car. But then again, maybe if I had hustled the car I would have crashed, which would have cost me the ride and ended my career before it even started. But it says a lot for my mindset at the time: I wasn't at all satisfied with second, when under the circumstances I should have been.

I drove that car until the end of our local season, when they parked it. I learned that Kenny and Ed were going to head west late that year, to run the Western World at Phoenix.

Now the road trips were getting more serious.

4

Things were happening quickly for our fearsome foursome. Jac had a steady ride, and in late 1978 he finished second at the Eldora Nationals in a car that didn't have power steering. Very impressive. Kenny was running a good car, Ed had a good ride, and I was in Kenny's old ride.

Late in the '78 season, Kenny was planning on going out West. Ed and I didn't have rides lined up out there but decided to tag along with Kenny and his guys. The 6x car was parked for the season, and I had quit my Magna-Fab job by then, so I had nothing but time on my hands anyway.

Kenny and "Flake" (his car owner) and their crew were planning on running both the Western World at Phoenix and the Pacific Coast Nationals at Ascot. I talked about trying to find a ride in somebody's car out there, and everybody kind of teased me about that remark. I had only won one race in my life – back at little old Lakeville – and there I was wishing for a ride at two of the biggest sprint car races in the country. Yeah, sure.

We made our way out West and went to a party at Lee James' house in California. Lee was a great sprint car racer from that region. We were sitting around in their shop, and there was this old bolt-on roll cage sitting under the workbench. Kenny started teasing me, saying that was my next ride, maybe I could wheel that thing. He probably didn't mean anything, but it sure lit my fire. Deep inside, I vowed that "I'll show 'em."

During the earlier time when I was out of racing, I felt like I fell behind Ed, Jac, and Kenny. I believed I was as good as any of them, in terms of ability. I knew they were good, but I wanted to prove I was just as good. It was a good, friendly rivalry. It was actually healthy for me, because it kept me fired up and ambitious, always trying to find a way to make it as a race driver.

While we were out West we went to a non-winged race at Chula Vista, California. I saw Sammy Swindell crash Gary Stanton's car there, he went completely out of the place in turn three. Through a fence, out into a field, it was a very violent ride. We found out later that he broke his arm in the crash. I had seen Sammy some time earlier when he came to Wayne County Speedway in Bobby Davis' black No. 71, with "Bobby Davis Electric" on the hood. That was Sammy's big break, I think. Boy, he looked so young. To be at that level, with that equipment, traveling, we were impressed. A little bit after his Wayne County visit we saw him at Eldora Speedway (in Ohio), and I walked up and asked him what chassis he ran. He gave me that dry, distant look, and said in his Tennessee drawl, "I built it." Years later Tom Sanders said *he* built it, so who knows. I laugh about that now.

That night at Chula Vista there was a team owned by a guy named Howard. His son drove the car. They had some kind of falling out, and he needed a driver. Ed managed to talk his way into the car, but he didn't have a helmet or uniform. He borrowed a helmet from Rick Ferkel and a suit from someone else. I was glad for him, but extremely envious. I had one feature win to my credit, and here were Kenny and Ed racing with the big boys of CRA. Ed's car blew a head gasket in hot laps, so he didn't have much luck.

That winter I talked my car owners into going to East Bay for the 1979 Florida Winter Nationals. On that trip I also ran Lake City, Florida, which was my first time in a car without a wing. Lake City was a small, oiled sand track. We put a Firestone double-diamond tire on the right rear, and they pushed me off for hot laps. I had never tried that tire before, either. A double-diamond had a different tread pattern, with two stacks of rubber, so that when you wore the first layer off you got to the second layer, with a new edge. All I know is that on an abrasive racetrack, the Firestone drag tire that we usually ran wasn't durable enough. To

Jac Haudenschild and I at the county fair photo booth, 1969. (Ed Haudenschild collection)

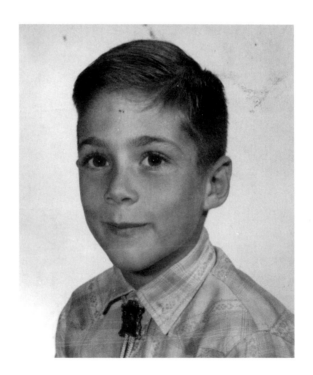

Just a little country boy from Ohio.

Jan Opperman was my idol. I got to meet him at Williams Grove in 1973. What a thrill!

I was just a kid here, making one of our trips to Williams Grove.
(Ed Haudenschild collection)

June 10, 1978, and my first sprint car win at Lakeville Speedway. Kenny Jacobs' sister Mary-Beth is presenting the trophy.

Winning my first race in a modified at Lakeville in 1974.

Running without a wing at Lake City, Florida in 1979.
(Gene Marderness photo)

I don't look very interested after this win at Lakeville in 1979.

The 1979 season championship at Lakeville came down to this race between Ed Haudenschild and me. I won, and Ed was second.

Winning a race at Lernerville Speedway was special because I liked the promoter, Don Martin, so much. Don offers a handshake after a win in 1980.

Top: Shaking hands with Bert Emick after an All Star win in 1981. Sam Bowers is standing next to Bert, and Gary "Deuce" Turrill is on the right.
Bottom: Passing Steve Kinser in hot laps at East Bay in 1981. That was a thrill!

Things weren't always great. I'm burning up the track at Lernerville – literally – in 1980.
(Orren Zook photo)

Tom Sanders (left) and Sam Bowers (right) were a big part of my career in 1981.

Ooops...this little miscalculation came at Lawton, Oklahoma in 1982. I heard later that Sammy Swindell hung this photo in his trailer with a sign that read, "My hero." Sorry, Sammy!
(Jeff Taylor photo)

Top: Jac Haudenschild is in the No. 18, and Kenny Jacobs is in the No. 4J. I like to tell them that I'm about to lap them...

Bottom: On the gas at Eldora in 1982 in Sam Bowers' car.

Finally! My first World of Outlaws win at Oklahoma City in 1983. (D. Bennett photo)

Everybody is talking but me! Good conversation with Ron Shuman, Danny Smith, and Tim Green. (Spekis Bros. photo)

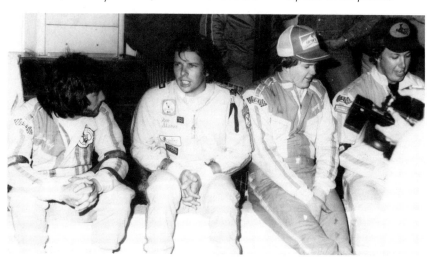

Just sitting around, waiting on the next race. This was 1984, when I was running Gary Stanton's car. Of all the racing photos we have, this is Laurie's favorite.
(Marty Gordner photo)

By the end of the season, our race cars were always pretty beat up. All the wings and bodywork are bent and cracked in this shot, taken in late 1982.
(Steve Koletar photo)

A WoO win at Lernerville in 1984. That's Scott Stanton on the left, with Mike Dutko and Don Martin of Lernerville. Scott was later killed in a very tragic highway accident.

1985, at Lakeville Speedway, my first time back since 1979. I seem to be having a serious discussion with Jac Haudenschild, Ed Haudenschild, and Kenny Jacobs! I won the dash and the feature that night in Ron Pack's No. 4A. (Jim Wilson photo)

I ran this car just once at Buckeye Speedway, when Kenny Jacobs called late one afternoon. I was going on no sleep, but I wanted to race with Kenny. We started side-by-side on the front row, and I beat him to the flag by a foot!
(Cyndi Craft photo)

I spent some of 1983 driving for Gil Suiter in the No. 1az car.
(John Mahoney photo)

This was my one ride in a USAC Silver Crown car. It was
Nazareth in early 1983. I was running third when the clutch
blew with 10 laps to go.
(John Mahoney photo)

Posing for the photographer at Eldora on April 8, 1984.
(John Mahoney photo)

I ran the alphabet soup at Knoxville in Ron Pack's No. 4A in 1985.
(Max Dolder photo)

Running without the wing at Ascot in 1984.
(Dan Mahony photo)

I borrowed Doug Wolfgang's steering box to win the Jerry Weld Memorial at I-70 Speedway in 1985. Thanks, Doug!
(J.R. Photos)

tell the truth, we put the double-diamond on because that's what everybody else was doing. We really didn't know why. We just followed what the more experienced people did.

When you take the wing off, a sprint car feels like it weighs half as much. It's like you took half the car away, the way it sits on top of the racetrack. The back of the car is constantly wiggling around under you. When you enter the corner the car feels like it is going to slide forever, even if the car is right and the track is right. It's like a long, giant four-wheel slide. Even though the car is slower, it feels like things are happening more quickly. That's hard to imagine, but it's true. To run well without a wing takes a completely different style, it isn't a matter of having more ability one way or another.

I rode around under caution, feeling the car out a little bit. They threw the green for hot laps, and I drove it down into the corner just like we had a wing on. I couldn't believe that the car could get that sideways. I was out of control in the first corner. The car went sideways and just slid and slid and slid, and I finally stalled out in the boondocks. They came with a push truck and restarted me, and I got my head back on right and made some hot laps, feeling the car and beginning to understand how do to this thing. It was like learning all over again.

When I got back to the pits, they asked me what happened. I said, "Maybe I didn't let the diamond warm up enough." They said, yeah, and you also forgot you didn't have a wing on! Later that night I was running pretty well, running in the top five in the feature. Greg Leffler was right behind me. He was a USAC guy – I had never met him before. There I was with my long hair; maybe he thought I was an outlaw, just a kid. He was pounding on me from behind, and finally his car split my fuel tank. Fuel was gushing out – we didn't run a fuel bladder, which was very dangerous but common for that period. People were waving at me, trying to get me to stop, and finally I did, and we were done. I went down and looked at his car to try and figure out what cut the tank, and kind of mumbled something to him when I left. I'm sure at that time that it didn't mean much to him. I don't suppose he even thought much about it.

At East Bay that year I won the non-qualifiers race, which made me feel pretty good. The next day I visited Robert Smith, one of the really famous Florida racers. I had met Robert earlier through an Ohio driver named Johnny Beaber. Robert and Johnny were good friends. Robert is one of the neatest guys in the world, a genuine country boy that you like as soon as you meet him. He is a guy that definitely marches to his own drummer.

We were at Robert's house, and a kid came walking in holding a big black indigo racer snake. I figured it was his pet or something. I was really afraid of snakes, but I was pumped up from winning the race the night before, feeling kind of macho. I said, "Lemme see that thing." I held it in my hands, and it wrapped its tail around my arm. I started to squeeze it, and that thing squeezed down really hard on my arm. The kid got real excited, yelling, "Don't squeeze it, don't squeeze it!" They started prying on that thing, and finally got it off my arm. It turned out that it wasn't the kid's pet at all, he had just found it wild out in the woods!

Later on, a couple of us were throwing a football in Robert's backyard. When we missed the ball it kept going out into this big patch of weeds behind his yard. We'd just walk out there, find the ball, and go back to our game. A little while later Robert came along and saw us out in the weeds, and he was just horrified. He explained that the weeds were infested with rattlesnakes. Sometimes what you don't know *can* hurt you.

Florida was a great place to visit, though. We made several road trips down there in our earlier days, before we were heavily involved in racing. One day Ed, Jac, and I were sitting around home and somebody said, "Hey, let's go to Florida!" Just like that, we loaded our stuff into this old green Pontiac, and away we went.

Well, sort of. The old wheezer actually quit running before we even got out of Millersburg! But we sat there for a while and let it cool off, and the thing refired, so we just headed on to Florida. Breaking down on the road didn't enter our mind. Besides, Ed was aboard, and he could fix anything. We didn't even hesitate – we were on our way. Ed and Jac had a sister living down there, so we could stay on the cheap. We visited Robert and he snuck us in to the races in the back of his van. He crashed big time that night, and after that he kept hollering, "I knew I shouldn't have snuck those boys in!" He figured it brought him bad luck.

We were gone for a week on that trip, and we didn't realize that everybody back home was in an uproar, wondering where we were. We hadn't bothered to tell anybody where we were going or when we were coming back. Our families just kind of looked around after a day or two and we were gone. They started getting worried. Plus, the car was still in John Haudenschild's name, and it didn't have any insurance. Ed said later that John was bent *way* out of shape by the time we got home. We had no idea it wasn't insured. We were at a youthful stage where it never occurred to us to think about how our actions affected others. Not that it would have changed anything. Ed's sister had a girl living with her that Ed had the hots for, so insurance was the farthest thing from his mind.

On an earlier Florida trip I went down with my family, and Ed and Jac went down with their dad. We hooked up while we were there and went to the old Florida State Fairgrounds in Tampa. This was before any of us had begun racing, but we were fans. We desperately wanted to get into the pits, but we were too young and we weren't with a car. We begged the guy at the pit gate, and he kept saying no. I felt him kind of pat me on the chest and he smiled, and sent us away. We walked away and when I felt my chest pocket, there were pit passes for us. What a great guy.

Getting into the pits that day was important because all the big hitters were there. Opperman, Pancho Carter, Tommy Dickson was in a car that had "Marsh Farms" on the hood, and it was a fantastic race car. Chrome stuff all over, and a clear Plexiglas box on the hood so you could see the injectors. Awesome!

Another time we went to Florida in my old '66 Chevy van, and we slept on the beach until some cops ran us off. Those were great times, lots of fun.

After our trip to East Bay in the 6x car, 1979 was a turning point in my career. I ran the car all season, and it gave me the continuity and the environment that I needed to progress, in terms of driving and understanding the car. We ran Lakeville all that season, and I wound up winning 13 of the 16 feature events they had.

If nothing else, Lakeville taught me how to race through traffic. Our main event was either 15 or 20 laps. We wouldn't know until after we were lined up and the officials would hold up a board that said either 15 or 20, telling us how many laps. They inverted the entire field, so if you were fast you were starting in the back. Basically, the guy who got to the front first was probably going to win the race. That's a pure form of sprint car racing.

I learned a lot that summer. The car was a four-bar chassis, and as I studied the car I began to understand the science, to get a grasp on what made the car work. The torsion arms, the stops, the shocks. Today, guys change torsion bars like they change tear-offs. At that time, nobody understood the cars well enough. So we hardly ever changed the bars – to us that was a big, radical change.

Even though I was winning races, I have to admit that I didn't understand how I was doing it. Later on Lynn Paxton told me that it took him five years to win his first race and another five years to figure out how he did it. I think there is something to that. I won all those races in 1979 and all I really did was drive the car. I didn't know what I was doing that was right, I just drove.

They kept the car at Dave Pope's house, in a little one-car garage that had a funny setup for heat. They took an old wood stove and rigged up a line that delivered used motor oil into the fire, and you could really get that stove hot when you opened the oil line up. It would glow like a harvest moon. I was there bright and early every day (about noon), and I would work late at night on the car. I was by myself a lot in the garage, so I could learn at a slow pace. Dave was a super-nice guy, laid-back and friendly, and his wife Norma was a terrific cook. It seemed like the whole neighborhood would come visit when she cooked dinner.

They didn't keep points at Lakeville, so winning 13 of 16 races didn't give me the championship. Instead, they had a mid-season championship and then a season-ending championship, which was held the last race of the year.

I didn't really know what "loose," or "push," meant, and certainly didn't know how to correct it, either with the driving line or adjusting the car. I did begin to understand stagger and air pressure, but that's about as complex as it got at that time, at least for me.

The season-ending championship race in 1979 at Lakeville was a gem. Naturally, we all wanted to do well in a "championship" race. I got to the front first, beating Ed through traffic, but I knew he wasn't far behind. That always made me nervous. I just raced as hard as I could and kept listening for him. We didn't run ear plugs then, so you could definitely hear a guy coming. Also, I developed a sixth sense about traffic. I could just feel when somebody was coming. I can't really explain it – I would just get this strong feeling that someone was there, even if I couldn't see or hear him. I won that night, and Ed was second. He was far enough behind me that he thought he had won. He was surprised and disappointed when he came to the flag stand after taking the checkered only to find me already parked there and climbing out. But as usual he was gracious and friendly, and he shook my hand and smiled for our pictures. I know how he felt, because finishing second is always disappointing, even if it is to your best friend. Standing on the frontstretch that night for the victory photo, I wanted Ed in the picture with me. I love looking at that picture. Two good friends, getting to do what they wanted. There was a lot of happiness there.

We finished a great season at Lakeville, winning the majority of the races. But I really wanted to swim in a bigger pond. I wanted to get on the road a little bit, to go against stronger competition to try and get better.

By this time Jac had a great ride with Wayne Yerian, the Yerian Coal Company car. The car was top-notch in every way, brand new Stanton stuff. Jac had arrived, or at least was on his way. They traveled all over Ohio, to tracks like Chillicothe and Findlay. They had some range, running with what we figured were the big boys. Compared to Lakeville, they were a cut above.

Dave Pope and I decided to take the car to Riverside Speedway in West Memphis, Arkansas. They called the place "The Ditch." There was a big race down there, and we wanted to give it a try. On the way down the van broke a piston, and the smoke just rolled out of the tailpipe. Dave pulled the spark plug wire off that cylinder to keep the smoke down some. He then took a big piece of rubber hose and ran it from the breather down to the ground, almost dragging the highway. That routed all the blow-by and oil being pumped into the cylinder out the hose, down onto the road, instead of all over the engine. We left a nice little black trail as we went along.

We slowly worked our way to Memphis. The minute we hit town we checked into our motel. There were two other guys and two girls also checking in at the same time. I didn't know this, but these girls were hookers, and the guys were getting them a room to work in that night. But I was so young and dumb I had no idea what was going on.

We had $300 to race on that weekend, and we carried it in an envelope. I paid for our room and put the envelope in my back pocket. I left the office, and headed toward my room.

I got to the second floor, and went to pull the envelope out of my pocket, but it wasn't there. So I ran back outside and tried to retrace my steps. It was dark by then, and I went back into the lobby. They hadn't seen anything.

I was out in the parking lot looking for the envelope. One of the girls from the hotel lobby came walking up with her shirt hanging open so far that there wasn't much left to the imagination. "What 'you lookin' for, honey?" she said. I told her I lost something. She was standing there, and the two guys came over, and they acted like they were helping me look. One of the guys snickered and said, "Well, if we see it we'll sure get it back to you!" Then I remembered that one of them had bumped into me in the lobby, and I knew what happened. I'd been hit by a pickpocket. I knew I'd never see that money again and there wasn't a thing I could do about it.

The money was gone, and the van was blown up. What a great start to our trip. We got to the track, and in hot laps a guy spun out in front of me. West Memphis is a tight, tight little bullring, with no room for error. I hit the guy with my right rear, and it broke our birdcage and the suspension. We didn't have a lot of pre-made parts at the time; there were still lots of fabricated parts on the car. We didn't have an extra birdcage. We had to try and borrow one.

Dave and I were back in the pits working on the car, thrashing, when Jac came strolling up. I didn't even know he had made the trip down. He said, "What 'ya doin?" I looked up and said, "What are you doing here?" He said, "I got a ride. What happened to you?" I said, "Aw, some dumb son-of-a-bitch spun out in hot laps and I hit him." He had this funny look on his face, and he kind of raised his eyebrows, and he said, "What do you mean, dumb son-of-a-bitch...that was me!" I was shocked and surprised, and we all started laughing, and I said, "Well, like I was sayin', some dumb son-of-a-bitch spun out in front of me..." Good old Haud, he can bring laughter to any situation.

Somebody found an engine for the van in a junkyard, but it was a pretty big operation to pull the motor in a van like that. It took us all day to get that done. We had the van parked just outside of turn one and two, and the thing was just coated with mud from the night before. Sometimes, you'd be better off if you stay home.

Later that fall I talked the car owners into letting me go to western Pennsylvania to race at Tri-City Speedway in Franklin. Kenny ran the car there at least once during the previous season, so they knew a little bit about what to expect. I had to run without a wing again. I made the feature at Tri-City, and I was running along in 14th or so, not going anywhere. Tri-City has really long straights, with tight corners. Lakeville never had a cushion, I had never really seen one before. A cushion is a ridge of dirt that builds up on the outside of the racing groove on a dirt track. With just a few laps left in the feature, I got spun out and restarted on the tail. On the restart I got on the outside and hauled it into turn three, way over my head. I was out of control. It was stupidity, really, on my part.

I guess I was frustrated, and a little bit impatient. With the lack of side-bite without the wing, it was not very smart. I really scared myself. I went up and banged the cushion, and I thought it was all over for me. But I picked up the throttle and the car kind of hooked onto the cushion, and I got back on the gas and started blasting past cars. I passed enough cars that I finished third. Maybe with a few more laps I could have won. I was amazed at how the car worked up on the cushion. A cushion artist? Not me. Not yet, anyway.

The following weekend we returned to Tri-City, and their format called for the top four from the previous week to run a trophy dash. I remembered my success from the previous week up on the cushion, so I tried the same maneuver in the dash. It was early in the night, though, and the track was heavy. On the white flag I drove it down into the corner looking for the cushion.

But I went in too hard, jumped the cushion, slapped the wall with the right rear, then the front end climbed the wall, and I was ready for a ride. That was my first flip in a sprint car, and it was a dandy. It all happened so fast, and then it was over. I felt the belts get really tight, then things got quiet, then I heard the destruction. *Crunch, crunch, crunch*. It really hurt my pride, but that was all that was hurt. Other than the car, which was sure damaged. We had bent just about all the bolt-on pieces, but the frame was okay.

Anytime we hurt the car it was bad, because nobody had any money. The three Creston guys owned the car, and a few others helped out. Tim Baird owned a welding truck; after a while we towed the car with that. Donnie Avery and a few other guys also donated time and money to help us. We worried about gas money and tires, so when we had major repairs it was devastating. Luckily, that was the season-ending race, so we had some time to rebuild the car.

During the cold Ohio winter, we began talking about next season. The car owners agreed that since I was going to stay in the car, we could change the number to 28, since that was my old modified number. Later on, when we raced in Pennsylvania Bill Bailey already had No. 28, so we had to change mine to 28d.

The wintertime social setting in our area usually consisted of going to clubs and bars, mostly to listen to music. And, as is probably the norm, there were a few fights. I was never an aggressive guy, but I never backed down, either. I didn't get in too many scrapes, but I remember one incident that was right out of the movies.

A local guy who was recognized as a pretty tough character made it known that he was going to pound me the next time he saw me. I wasn't going to run away, but the truth was I didn't want any part of this guy. His reputation was fearsome. He was a badass.

One night I was in the Corner Bar in Millersburg, a pretty small place. I stopped in even though I knew he hung out there. I couldn't spend the rest of my life trying to stay away from him. I had the flu that night, and I wasn't drinking. I felt pretty lousy. I was sitting at a table with some people, they got up to dance, so I was sitting there by myself. He came over and sat down, and just looked at me. Finally he said, "You know, I never did like you." By this time it was obvious where this thing was headed. I just kind of smiled and said, "Well, I don't like you either." He reached across the table and popped me, knocking me backwards off the chair. The fight was on, and he bailed on top of me. I don't know if it was fear or adrenaline or what, but next thing I knew I was on top swinging away. It was a classic bar fight. People were cheering and whooping and hollering – everybody wanted to see this. We rolled all over the floor, and finally rolled out the front door across these old concrete steps. I can still remember how much that hurt. We rolled down across the sidewalk, and literally out into the middle of Main Street in downtown Millersburg.

We were so spent from swinging that we laid there gasping for breath, hitting each other every once in a while, and covering up. Finally, somebody said the cops were coming, so we managed to get to our feet and get out of there. I'd like to think he looked worse than I did, but at least it was over. After that, we just kind of stayed away from each other and we didn't have any more trouble.

Of course, fighting and Millersburg went hand in hand. It seemed like every weekend there was a fight in one of the three or four bars in town. For a small town, they had plenty of places to hang out. The Castle, the Corner Bar, the Eagles Lodge – they were the popular places. It was the longhairs-versus-rednecks era. Believe it or not, it was actually pretty harmless. No knives or guns – just a punch here or there. I don't remember one person ever getting seriously hurt. In fact, it wasn't unusual to see two guys drinking a beer together after they finished fighting. Nobody took it really seriously. If you got your ass kicked, you got your ass kicked. You forgot about it a couple of days later.

When I look back and remember that I was in the middle of some of those scuffles, I'm kind of surprised. I'm a pretty mellow guy, and later on in my racing career I just didn't get involved much with fighting, even in pretty intense situations. I guess a young guy still has the macho thing to work out, it's something that I evidently grew out of.

Sometime during that winter of 1979 I met a girl who would change my life. I knew a guy named Bob Graham from Wooster; he was a casual friend of mine, a real good guy. He would go to the races now and then, so we knew each other from that. Wooster isn't that big a town, so you kind of get to know who the race fans are.

One night Bob was in Danners, a small bar in Wooster. He asked me to give him a ride home. I wasn't ready to leave yet, so he was hounding me. I knew he also wanted me to meet his sister, but I wasn't sure I wanted to. All night he kept pointing at each girl that walked in, telling me, "See that girl? My sister looks better than that." Finally the bar was closing and I said, "Well, come on, let's go." It was really cold, the dead of winter, probably 2:30 a.m.

When we got to the house, he insisted that I go to the door and meet his sister. It wasn't actually his house, but a house where his sister was babysitting, and his girlfriend was there also. Why I didn't just drop him off, I don't know. I agreed to walk up with him, and he pounded on the door. The house was dark, and it looked like everyone was asleep. He pounded on the door again. The outside light came on, then the door opened. Bob stepped aside and told me to go on in. I walked in and here was this girl in her underwear and a skimpy shirt walking back across the room. Whooops! Turns out she hadn't seen me, she thought Bob was alone. I said something, she whirled around and grabbed a blanket and covered up. She was very embarrassed and not very happy. Her name was Laurie. The four of us – Laurie, myself, Bob, and his girlfriend – sat up and talked for an hour or so.

Laurie and I really hit it off. Actually, I fell pretty hard for her. I called her the next day, and we started dating. I don't think she knew I was a race driver. I was renting a room from a friend of mine, and money was tight. I didn't have a full-time job, all I did was work on the race car. No full-time job, no part-time job. Of course, all I needed was beer money and rent. And since rent wasn't much, all I really needed was beer money.

I was still a young kid, and I guess that was the drinking stage of my life. I was never a chronic drunk. I just drank and partied with my friends sometimes. It was probably more of a social thing than anything else. It was a stage that I eventually grew out of, like most everybody does (some people just take a while, it seems).

My cousin Bud played guitar and sang with a band, and I liked music. That's another reason we went to the clubs and bars, because there were a lot of garage bands that we liked in the area.

But partying was not my priority. I was still consumed by racing. And things were about to get even better.

5

Racing was on my mind every day, every hour, every minute. Each day I would drive over to Dave Pope's shop in Creston to work on the car. By this time I was knowledgeable enough that I put a lot of the car together after our big crash. Dave was an experienced mechanic who taught me a lot, he worked full-time as a mechanic at a Chrysler garage. He was very much a mentor for me. There were people in and out of the shop all the time. Late at night when everybody left, that's when I got the most work done. I kind of liked working by myself, me and that old oil stove.

I never had a big career plan about where I was going in racing. In early 1980, we had the car ready, and a lot of the tracks in Pennsylvania opened earlier than the tracks in our area. Since I ran fairly well over there at the end of the '79 season, we felt like we could be competitive. The non-wing stuff had kind of disappeared over there, and for the start of the '80 season the tracks had adopted a 16-square-foot wing. I was okay with the new wing rule. I didn't think much about it either way.

We decided to make the opener at Lernerville. I had seen the track several years earlier, when I rode over there with Jac. He was driving a yellow No. 34 car at the time, owned by Newt Ferguson. Jac hauled the car on an open trailer, and pulled it with an old pickup truck. He had never been there before, so I was the navigator. I don't even know how he knew about the place. I think he saw the ad in *National Speed Sport News*.

I really have to give Jac credit. He had a lot of nerve and guts to tow four hours and race against people he had never seen, on a track he had never raced on. He was still very young at that time, maybe 18 or 19 years old. There he was, racing against the big boys. I'd watch him run down the backstretch and set the car for the corner, and I was in awe. He was pretty respectable.

On another trip during that period Jac took the car to Lincoln and Williams Grove with a friend of his riding along to help. Jac had no hesitation to go far from home on his own. Maybe it was just that he was so confident, he didn't hesitate to travel far from home to race against guys that were pretty tough.

Jac always seemed fearless. You never saw him back away from anything. When we were teenagers, I took Ed and Jac out to a local gravel pit one afternoon to go swimming. We went to this place because it had a gigantic rock cliff for jumping. It was extremely dangerous, but we were pretty daring at that age. Ed and I had jumped off it a couple of times before, but Jac had never been there. It was probably 80 to 100 feet above the water. When you hit the water it would sting the bottom of your feet. You had to keep your arms in tight or the water would feel like it was going to rip them off. We walked up there, and Ed and I were kind of hem-hawing about who had the nerve to go first. Jac waited a second and said, "Well, if nobody is going to go, I'll go." And with that he just ran to the edge and jumped.

We could have been pulling his leg – he had no way of knowing if we had ever actually jumped off before. But he didn't hesitate. We ran to the edge and looked over, and saw him hit the water. At that velocity you go really deep into the water, so he disappeared for a few seconds. It seemed like minutes, waiting for him to come back to the surface. Finally he popped out of the water, looked up at us and yelled, "What are ya waitin' for? The water's warm!"

Fearless. Always fearless.

Now, a couple of years later, here I was making the trip to Lernerville. The track had an orange clay surface that rarely would get dusty. It would get slick sometimes, but not very often. You'll almost always see a good race at that place, with two grooves that usually are both good. The only difficulty for us was that it was so far from Creston that most of our guys couldn't go because of their jobs.

So they'd kind of take turns. For the opener, Dave and most of the guys couldn't come. There was a local kid, maybe 14 or 15 years old, named Butch Sherwin. He came with me to help carry fuel and change tires, stuff like that. Other than that, I was on my own. We were definitely the underdogs. To come in to a strange track and expect to win – that was asking for a lot.

I was looking at moving up in the food chain. Lakeville was pretty much looked upon as second-class by most of the northwest Ohio guys that raced at Fremont, Findlay, or down in Chillicothe. They were a cut above. Our cars ran carburetors, while they had fuel injection, using four-bar chassis. The next level from northwest Ohio was Pennsylvania. We had seen the central Pennsylvania guys come to Wayne County Speedway and blow the local guys away. Steve Smith, Dub May, Bobby Allen, Opperman – they could pretty much dominate in Ohio. And our perception was that even though the western Pennsylvania guys were not quite in their league, they were still a notch above the Ohio guys.

At Lernerville and Tri-City I raced against Lou Blaney, Ed Lynch Sr., Ralph Quarterson (I had seen him at Findlay – he was an excellent racer), Jack Sodeman, John Lewis in the Simcox Steel car, and Eddie Murphy in a maroon Trevis car with chrome headers that made my mouth water. Lou won the National Open at Williams Grove one year. He was (and still is) a helluva racer.

It was tough competition, especially for a young guy like me. Trevis cars were hot, but our car was a Nance chassis. In Pennsylvania most guys hadn't heard of Nance. A guy walked up to me and said, "Where do you get a 'Nancy' car." I said *Nance*, out of Wichita, Kansas. Our car had three or four years on it, a lot of laps.

The first weekend we ran Lernerville on Friday and Tri-City on Saturday. We stayed in a motel and drove back on Sunday. That was also big step, staying in a motel. It made me feel like a traveling racer!

The first night out, at Lernerville, we won the feature. Wow! Then we ran well at Tri-City, so we were really encouraged.

That Lernerville win was really special. I was a long way from

Lakeville, and this was a serious bunch of racers with serious cars. We had planned on spending the season at Lakeville again, but winning that race at Lernerville changed our plans. Ultimately, it changed my life, but of course I didn't know it at the time. We decided to keep going over there since we were competitive. Western Pennsylvania was like a new world that had opened up before us. I would pick up Butch every Friday afternoon, and we would make the tow to Lernerville. Sometimes Dave, John Harmon, or John Gantz would drive over later to Tri-City on Saturday, but mostly it was just Butch and me.

I began winning regularly. A lot of weekends I won one race, sometimes two. The handicapping made it tough, because as last week's feature winner you had to start in the middle or the back of the field. So repeating was very difficult. I did learn some tricks that helped me. When we would go out for the feature, I would roll up front and wait for guys to come get in front of me. A lot of times, believe it or not, guys didn't assert themselves, and I would gain a couple of rows. I think that since I was starting in the back, people figured that a couple of rows didn't matter. But I wanted to take every possible inch on the race track that I could. Every inch.

One night at Lernerville Jack Lewis got in my face a little bit about that. Jack's son John drove their car, and Jack had figured out my little trick and was upset about it. No yelling, just a pretty intense discussion. He said it was cheating. I said no it wasn't, it's the other guy's responsibility to take his spot. Jack said his driver wouldn't do that, and I told him, "Well, it sounds like maybe you should fire the son of a bitch." Boy, that *really* got him fired up.

I was the new kid, which was bad enough, but I was also winning races, which I think irritated some people. Ed Lynch Sr. was known as the "Apollo Rocket" and for a while he and I had some troubles. One night at Tri-City I got together with someone and spun, and I was sitting there helplessly and along came Ed, who really drilled me. We got out of our cars, and I saw right away that Ed wasn't happy. In fact, it looked like he wanted to tear me into little bitty pieces. He did some shouting and screaming, but then it was all over.

You have to forget that stuff, because it's nothing more than the heat of the moment. After a while Ed and I got through our friction and things were friendly again. I still enjoy visiting with him and his wife Jean and their son, Ed Jr. Ed Sr. was one of the many guys that ran both sprint cars and modifieds, driving in both features.

One incident that I remember was between Johnny Beaber and me. Johnny can be the nicest, most mellow guy in the world, but when he does get fired up he's ready to rumble. He was a good race driver – won a lot of races and was the track champ at Tri-City. Johnny and Kenny Jacobs were really good friends, and that's how I got to know him. One night at Tri-City I got under Johnny to try and pass him. I think he saw me and crowded me down to try and shut the door. We didn't touch, but the next thing I know he's flipping the finger and shaking his fist at me. I couldn't figure that out. So I got fired up, because I felt like he was trying to block me. After the race he came down to my trailer and got in my face. He was pretty hot. No pushing or shoving, just words. Even to this day, I couldn't figure out why he was mad at me. Like I said, it's the heat of the moment.

All in all, most people were friendly and helpful to us. Especially Don Martin, the Lernerville promoter. After I ran Lernerville a few times, Don walked up and asked me where we were staying. I told him the Butler Holiday Inn, and he told me to just have them put it on his tab. I thought, "I've made it. I'm somebody now!" Just getting my motel paid really meant something to me.

Don was truly a premier promoter, and also a premier person. He was out of the ordinary. He really took care of people. It was amazing how hard he would work to make sure everyone was happy. He made you feel special. He made you feel like he was truly glad you were there. It made me wish many times through the years that more people were like Don.

The fact is, our car didn't look like much compared to most of the Pennsylvania cars. Yet we were winning races. I think that made it all the more irritating to some people. We had so little money. Our front axle had been bent plenty of times, and each time we would just get out the hydraulic jack and chains and straighten it. It got so soft from bending back and forth that if I just touched something the damned thing would bend. Finally one night I got into something pretty hard and sheared the thing in two. It was junk. However, we didn't have the money for a new one, and we wanted to race the following night at Tri-City. The following afternoon at the track we tried to figure out how to fix it. The pits hadn't opened yet, so we were sitting in the parking lot. Butch and I rummaged through our junk in the trailer, and we found a spare 10/10 coupler that was normally used on the rear end. As luck would have it, it was just the right size to fit both ends of the broken axle. So I beat it into place and welded the axle up. It looked awful, but it worked. We ran that old axle for a long time like that.

We towed on an open trailer with utility boxes welded on the sides. It was a little bit short of being state of the art! It would rattle and bang as you went down the road. It was what you'd call "used up." Plus, it was built on axles that came from a mobile home. Those tires were built for low-speed, one-trip applications, and not everyday use. We had to keep about half of our tire rack filled with trailer tires, because just about every other week we'd be rolling down the highway on a hot day and blow one out.

I was getting more serious about my relationship with Laurie, but I still hadn't brought her to the track. She had never seen a race or even a racecar, so finally one day I took her to the shop. I'd shown her some pictures of the car, and that was all. I was hesitant to take her with us to the races, even though I was winning. I was afraid I was just on a lucky streak and if she came along I might not do as well, and I wanted her to be proud of me. Plus, I didn't want her to be there if I did something dumb. I guess that's male pride.

Finally she rode with us to Lernerville. I won that night, then won the next night at Tri-City. Hey, Laurie, this is no problem, right? We decided to run Latrobe, Pennsylvania on Sunday night; they only ran some special shows. I was leading the race when we bent an intake valve and it hung open. Every time the piston came up it forced the fuel back out the injector stack, and it blew back on me. But I was leading the race, so there was no way I was pulling in. Finally the car started to slow down, and I was trying to hang on. I took the white flag, and it looked like I'd go three-for-three that weekend. I'd never done that before. But coming down for the checkered flag the car was slow coming off the corner, and Ralph Quarterson passed me and beat me by a half a car length. Damn.

I drove back around to the pits, and when I took it out of gear the flame from the header ignited all the fuel that had blown all over the car. It was instantaneous. The thing was just a ball of fire. I had never been in a fire before, but I knew I didn't like it. It was hot. I got my belts off in an instant and bailed out. Somebody got an extinguisher on it right away and got it knocked down. We were very lucky. It burned the injector filters off, and melted the spark plug wires, but that was the only real damage. So that weekend Laurie saw it all, the good and the bad.

By the middle of the season I began to notice that it was getting harder to win. I figured the other guys were catching up. It just seemed like I had to work harder to win. We ran the same engine for the entire season, which was about 25 races or so. After a while our engine had lost some its sharpness, but I wasn't experienced enough to realize it. Somebody suggested that the fuel pump might be weak, so we borrowed one. We bolted it on and immediately the car sounded sharp, the throttle response was good, and sure enough on the race track we went straight forward. I just hadn't been smart enough to realize we even had a problem. Man, how inexperienced I was.

Of course, things weren't as scientific as they are now. For instance, at that time we kept the same fuel setting every week. We never changed it. Today, teams use a barometer to measure the atmospheric pressure, and also take into account the altitude of the track. They use a computer to tell them exactly which injector "pill" or jet to use that night. It sure was simpler our way…just roll the car off the trailer and strap in.

The typical weekend continued to be Lernerville on Friday, Tri-City on Saturday, and Latrobe every other weekend. One weekend we got rained out in Pennsylvania, so I decided to drive to Portsmouth, Ohio to an event sanctioned by MOSS (Midwest Outlaw Sprint

Series), which was a forerunner to the All Star Circuit of Champions. Portsmouth was about four hours south on a good day. However, one minor problem: our old van had blown a head gasket, and it kept puking the water out. We had to stop every 50 miles or so to refill the cooling system. It was getting later and later, and by the time we got to Portsmouth they were running the feature. We turned around and headed for Creston, four hours north, stopping for water every 50 miles. Oh, well.

Part of the reason I enjoyed this period was that not much was expected of us. We weren't expected to win races, but we won anyway. That feels great. But winning creates pressure. Later on, when I was in a position where I was expected to win, that wasn't quite so much fun. Then when I didn't win, people demanded to know why.

A lot of pressure is internal, and that was always true in my situation. I tried to keep things fun, but deep down inside I always wanted to be professional, and I put a lot of pressure on myself. Later on the money made it more serious and not as much fun, but that was another story. But when I was winning all those races in western Pennsylvania, I smiled a lot.

I got 40 percent of what the car made. A win at Lernerville paid about $800, the same at Tri-City. So when I won at least one race I made $320, which wasn't a bad weekend. I was able to live on that. I was a man of modest means, to say the least. I was still renting a single room at my friend Scott Drown's house. I lived on the cheap.

But the car was just breaking even. Our first sponsor was North Street Auto Supply in Meadville, Pennsylvania, and even though it wasn't a big-dollar deal it helped us keep racing. We were like most other racers at this level: We raced a lot out of our pockets. It's scary, but it's a way of life for most weekly racers.

It might sound greedy for the driver to take 40 percent, but he is the guy with his butt on the line so that probably isn't unreasonable. The 40 percent is pretty standard in the business. Besides, I remember taking less than my cut lots of times because I wanted to put the money back into the car so we could keep going.

Halfway through the season I flipped at Lernerville and bent the car, so we were done. The guys had told me early on that the car had to pretty much carry itself financially. They didn't have the money to make major improvements or repairs. It was up to me to win and find ways to keep the car going. After our crash I heard through the grapevine that some of the other guys were chuckling about our crash. I think they were glad we were finished. But we weren't quite done yet.

In fact, that crash triggered the biggest break of my career.

A guy named Bill Bowser owned a truck repair company in Ford City, Pennsylvania. Bill also drove his own nice Trevis sprint car. I became acquainted with Bill when I first started coming to Pennsylvania. He was a genuine nice guy. After we crashed, he knew we were finished. He knew a guy that had a coal mining operation nearby, a guy who had some money and loved racing. His name was Sam Bowers.

Sam had sponsored a late model that ran at Lernerville. He loved late model racing. Bill called Sam and told him about me, and asked Sam if he could help me out. At that time, business was good for Sam, and he had a lot of money, a lot of cash flow. He had tons of equipment, including a bunch of trucks that hauled coal. His expenses were enormous, but he still had a lot of money.

Early the following week, I was sitting at Dave and Norma Pope's table eating dinner one evening when the phone rang. Sam introduced himself. I had never heard of him. He said he'd been talking to Bill Bowser, and heard we were parked. He offered to help, and he asked me what I thought it would take. Could we be ready by the weekend? I told him it would take about $2,000. We hadn't bought much stuff, so I didn't really know the prices of things. The $2,000 figure was a guess. He told me to see if we could get the parts we needed.

I hung up the phone and I was very skeptical. I mean, I hadn't even heard of this guy and he calls me out of the blue with an offer to buy parts to help us. Yeah, sure. I called Bill, and he assured me, "Brad, this guy is for real. If he tells you to go get the parts, then you go get the parts. I'm telling you, the money is not a problem."

I called Shirley Kear at Kear's Speed Shop in Tiffin, Ohio, one of the nicest people in the entire world. A great, strong-willed woman that you just fall in love with, but you also don't want to piss her off. She is outspoken and honest and I just love that lady. We struck up a friendship that will go on for the rest of our lives.

When Jac and Ed and I started racing we used to drive two hours to Tiffin to pick up a few parts, and would end up spending the entire afternoon just looking around in her speed shop. We were like kids in a candy store…brand new race cars, new parts, chrome stuff…awesome. At the time Kear's was a big sponsor of Rick Ferkel. Shirley was a big supporter of his. We thought Ferkel was right up there with Opperman, in terms of ability and aura. The Ohio Traveler, they called him, and I know a lot of young guys who wanted to be just like him.

I told Shirley what we needed, and she said she had everything in stock. So I called Sam back and he said go get the parts and he would mail her a check.

I picked up the stuff at Shirley's early the next morning. Wheels, axle, shocks, and driveline stuff. We got the good stuff, including aluminum wheels. That was the first time in my career I had aluminum wheels. I explained to Shirley that I didn't even know this guy Bowers, but I had been assured he'd pay the bill. Shirley was wonderful. As I was going out the door she gave me a big smile and said, "Don't worry about it, kid. If he doesn't come through with the money you can pay me back as you win races." What a vote of confidence! I still get goose bumps when I think of her saying that.

Back at the shop in Creston we were in a full-blown thrash rebuilding the car. One of the bright spots was throwing out that bent-up old front axle. What a relief to get rid of that ugly thing. We had our entire crew there at times, everyone working on the car.

Some of the people at Lernerville were surely surprised that following Friday night when we came rolling into the pits. We rolled the car off the trailer, and there were those four new aluminum wheels. People started to gather around and look, and soon we had a real crowd watching us. Then Bob Stauffer showed up. He built wings and other racing products. He pulled right up to our car and set off a brand new wing, and put it on our car. We had always built our own wings, but none were as nice and shiny as this one. Everyone was just standing around staring, and ol' Doty was strutting around like a peacock. We won the feature that night, so I was super fired-up.

I still had not met Sam, but he came down from the grandstands after the race and introduced himself. "Good job, kid!" Boy, that was a great moment for me. Sam had stepped up to help us, and we responded by getting the car back together and winning the feature. He was impressed with that, and surprised that we could turn things around so quickly.

Sam became a very big supporter, and clearly changed the direction of my career. Some people resented that, because they saw Sam as helping an outsider, a kid from Ohio. One night somebody smashed out the back window of his truck with a big rock, and there was a note attached to the rock that said "Why Doty?" We were both amazed that people would be that hateful.

Sam was a high-strung guy, a charismatic, dynamic person who really stood out in a crowd. He was about 32 years old when he started helping me, but he seemed like an older, more experienced guy. For a successful businessman he was very young. At the race track he would tend to keep a low profile, and most of the time he would sit in the grandstands. Later on, when he actually owned the car, he would spend time in the pits and scrape mud off the car, just to be a part of the team. He was kind of a mentor to me, he was solid and experienced at life and was a good person. He wore blue jeans and work boots and was not an overbearing person at all. I liked that a lot.

The rest of the 1980 season went just great. It was awesome. I kept winning races and Sam was happy, and my car owners were happy as well. At that time western Pennsylvania had something called the Cavalcade Championship, which was based on feature wins throughout the area. So as the season began to wind down, I was gunning for three titles: Lernerville, Tri-City, and the Cavalcade championship. I was leading the points at the two tracks, and I knew we had the most wins for the region. I was still pretty concerned, though, because the points were tight.

We won the Lernerville title, and the following night at Tri-City we needed to finish at least one spot ahead of Clark Kothera for the track championship. We started the feature toward the back, and the engine began to vibrate immediately. I had noticed the vibration during the earlier heat race but it was much worse now. We didn't have a spare engine anyway, so we couldn't have made an engine change before the feature. Later we tore the engine down and found that the crankshaft was cracked. But it still ran good that night, but vibrated badly. After a few laps the vibration put my fingers to sleep as they clenched the wheel. But we kept going forward and finally won the feature, and clinched the title. On top of that I won the Cavalcade championship. My first year in Pennsylvania, and I took three titles, won 14 races and had 22 top-three finishes.

As I look back at that period, it seemed like such a blur. I went from obscurity to a little bit of stardom, and it seemed like it happened overnight. I still felt really uncertain; my insecurities were showing. I was afraid the bubble would burst. I wish now I would have paused and savored it a little bit.

Maybe I had too much drive – I don't know. I didn't have blind ambition, the kind where a guy is willing to do literally anything to succeed. But I was consumed by racing, there was no doubt about that.

At the end of the season Sam told me that he wanted to be more than a sponsor. He wanted to own the car, so he bought the old Nance car and the trailer from Dave, John, and John. They didn't get another car – I think they were kind of relieved to be out of the car-owner role. They were truly happy for me, so I felt like things had worked out well for everyone. I'll forever be grateful to those three guys for giving me such a good start to my career.

An explosion was about to happen. Both my career and my life were at a turning point.

6

After two years with the guys from Creston, I had a new car owner. I was still going to play a big role at the shop, though, to help maintain the car and keep it going. At first Sam and I talked about me keeping the car at home, and putting together a race shop in Wooster. But after we thought about it for a while he decided he'd like just a little more oversight. Since he was spending all the money he needed to at least be able to see what was going on. Which was absolutely right, absolutely reasonable. He asked me if I would consider moving to western Pennsylvania.

Personally, I didn't hesitate. It looked like it was going to be an adventure for me, something neat. I thought it was cool, the idea of being a full-time racer for this rich coal baron. He was going to pay my room and board and I'd race for a percentage. Helluva deal. I was ready.

By this time Laurie and I had known each other for about a year, and it was obvious there was something special between us. It was starting to get close to decision time, but I wasn't sure how to approach her, I wanted her to come with me but I didn't know if she would. I was scared that she would say no. We sat down and I told her what was happening with Sam, and would she come along. I don't think she even hesitated. It was a great feeling, knowing that she cared enough to come with me. It was very hard for her, because she was (and is) very close to her family, especially her sisters. I took her away from that, and as I look back I suppose it was kind of selfish of me. But if a guy wants a career in racing, he has to be kind of selfish. That's just the way it is.

When it came time to move, we had an old Mustang and no furniture to speak of. Everything we had fit in that Mustang! We moved into a little two-room efficiency apartment in Kittanning, Pennsylvania.

That was surely a hard period for Laurie. I would go to the shop every day, for 8 or 10 hours, while she stayed in that little apartment, all alone. Laurie is a quiet person, and she keeps to herself, so she didn't get much of a chance to meet people and make new friends. That must have been lonely, being alone so much of the time. You know, she never once complained or talked about being unhappy or homesick. She is such a strong person...that strength would be tested later in our lives.

At first we used Jim Smith's shop, which was a little garage like we had in Creston. Jim drove a late model that Sam sponsored. He might have had some hard feelings about my deal, but he never acted like it. My deal with Sam might have actually taken money from Jim's racing budget, and then on top of that we used his shop. But he was always helpful and friendly, and if there was any friction there he certainly didn't show it. Cindy, Jim's wife, became friends with Laurie and that kind of helped. We had somebody to have dinner with, stuff like that. We worked in that shop through the winter.

We started rebuilding the old car to get ready for the 1981 season. We parked the old trailer back behind Sam's maintenance barn at one of his strip mines. We decided to use the old car as a backup, and we would get some new stuff for a primary car. Sam said to go out and see LaVerne Nance in Wichita, Kansas.

I had never been on an airplane before. My life was changing in many ways, my horizons were expanding faster than I could comprehend. Lots of things were happening. Buying a new race car was a huge step for me, like a dream come true.

I got to Wichita, and met with LaVerne. He was a very nice guy to me, a great guy. I had met him a few years earlier when I rode to Wichita with Kenny Jacobs to pick up a chassis. This time, the minute I walked in the door LaVerne acted like he'd known me all his life. Ken Jenkins was the sales guy at that time. LaVerne showed me around the shop – I suppose they knew I was there with a big checkbook.

But they did seem sincerely friendly. We bought one complete car with lots of spares.

I flew home, then when the chassis was ready I flew back to Wichita and rented a cube van to haul everything home. It was stuffed full with new parts. I got back to Pennsylvania and got busy putting everything together.

I had some help putting the cars together, but it was kind of sporadic. Each day I was in the shop, watching the calendar and trying to have everything ready in time to go to Florida in February. It always goes down to the last day; if you've got two months or two weeks it always comes to the last day. You're never really finished, but you have to at least be close enough that you put the car in the trailer and go.

We left the shop on a February morning, Laurie and I alone in the truck. We got a nice little send-off from Sam and some other folks at a local restaurant. It became a hurry-up breakfast because we heard some bad weather was coming in and we wanted to beat the storm. Too late! We made it about 20 miles and we ran into freezing rain.

We had a brand new black Chevy duallie truck with a matching black trailer with orange stripes. Every tool, every part, every component was brand new inside the trailer. What a moment. I hit a patch of ice on a four-lane highway and began to slide. I was only running 10 m.p.h. or so. We were headed for a big guardrail. I was praying, "Please don't let me wreck this thing." To tear a guy's race car up, that's one thing, but to tear his rig up, that's something else.

We missed the guardrail and crept along for a while, and finally the weather eased up. By the time we got to Pittsburgh it had cleared off and we headed south.

The Florida Winter Nationals at East Bay was the destination. The setup that year called for eight races, four with the wing and four without. I was high point man for the week without the wing, and started on the pole for the main event, but our left-side radius rod fell off (who is the mechanic here, anyway? Maybe the bolt broke...). We finished fairly well anyway, in the top five or so. The

Creston guys had driven to Florida to help me out with the car, so I didn't have to do all the work myself.

We put the wings on for the second week, and one night I was running down the backstretch in hot laps when I passed Steve Kinser. Even in hot laps, that pumped us up. I don't know how we did that night, but I remember passing Kinser in hot laps! Later that night we went to the Bullfrog Lounge just south of the race track in Gibsonton. I was sitting there eating and Steve came over and introduced himself: "Hi, I'm Steve Kinser." I was in awe, I have to admit. He sat down at the table and we began to talk.

He asked me how old I was, how long I'd been racing, where I'd been racing, things like that. He was really friendly, really pleasant. It was a nice conversation. I was very flattered.

We went home after the Florida races and Sam and I started to talk about where we wanted to race in 1981. As a driver, I wanted to keep moving up. Sam had spent a lot of money, and he really wanted us to venture out a little bit. The All Star Circuit of Champions had just been officially launched as an evolution from the old MOSS series and it looked like they would run a lot in our region. So we decided to run their schedule as much as possible, choosing to miss some of their races for some other specials.

We knew we would need a mechanic. Actually, Sam figured we needed a mechanic. Personally, I was comfortable working on the car myself like I had been doing. Sam wanted to get a professional mechanic, though. And I didn't object, because it would take a lot of the workload off my shoulders. But it wasn't anything I insisted on. We somehow got in touch with Gary "Deuce" Turrill. He was living in the Memphis area at that time. Deuce is a very likable guy, and we hit it off immediately. He seemed to really know his stuff. So we hired Deuce, and now I had some company both in the shop and in the hauler.

My first few races with the All Stars introduced me to a new cast of characters. Lee Osborne, Indiana Andy Hillenburg, Fred Linder, Randy Ford, and Jack Hewitt, plus good ol' Jac and Kenny Jacobs, that's who we raced against. It was a tough bunch.

One of the things that made it very challenging at first was that we raced on different tracks all the time. I had to learn how to make the car fast on different types of surfaces. I struggled to learn to read the race track. For any traveling racer, I think that is a required skill. Some guys, like Rick Ferkel and Karl Kinser, they really shined in that area. For me, it took a long time before I could really read a track.

What I mean by "reading" the track is pretty simple. Sprint car racing is mostly about traction. Your rear tires are spinning just about all the time, and the key is finding a way to make the tires grip the track and push the car forward. Picture driving on snow or ice. If your rear tires are spinning a bunch, you're probably not going anywhere. If they spin a little, you're moving forward. It's the same principle with sprint cars on a dirt track. The ultimate is to not spin the tires at all.

Finding traction has to do with setting up the car to gain the proper amount of grip. If you have too little grip, the rear tires spin too freely, and it takes a lot of speed away. If you have too much grip the car is hard to drive, because the torque from the engine seems like it wants to twist the car so much that it literally feels like it wants to turn the car over. Plus, you can't make the rear end slide out to get the proper line coming off the corner. The ideal setup is enough traction to go forward, with enough slippage to let the car "work" through the corner. It's kind of a black art, figuring all of this out to make the car work.

Sometimes you can just look at the track and see if it is wet (sprint car racers call that a "heavy" track) or dry. That tells you a lot about what your setup needs to be. One element of dirt racing that makes it more difficult is that we see a huge variety of track surfaces. Man, setting up for a slick, dry track is just so different than setting up for a wet, heavy track. You change the car completely.

To make it even more complicated, another big change with the All Stars was that they ran 40-lap features. With the longer races, the track changes a lot from start to finish. The track might be nice and sticky at the start of the race, but as the cars dig at it the track might begin to dry out and get much more slippery, even dusty. Of course, you can't just stop the car and adjust the chassis, so the driver has to change the lines the car uses, or change the way he applies the throttle, to try and make the car work. As you race you have to constantly watch the track, looking for patches of dark clay that tell you there is moisture there. Also, you have to watch the other guys, to see who is going fast in other grooves.

The only way you learn all this is to live it. It's very tough for a young guy to be competitive in that environment, because other, more experienced guys have already figured this stuff out. I eventually learned, but it was a humbling experience. When a guy blew past me in a different groove, I tried to remember that and understand what to start looking for. It takes a lot of experience to become skilled at being able to read the track on the fly.

A good mechanic can help you with that. He can stand in the infield and watch what other drivers are doing, and he can give you hand signals. He might motion you to move up on the track, or move to the bottom. He can tell you if someone is gaining on you, or if you have a big lead. At that time Deuce was still pretty inexperienced, just like me, so he could only help so much. We were both learning. But the key was we *did* learn. Both of us.

All in all we were pretty competitive, and we won the season openers at Eldora, Susquehanna, and Sharon, all within an eight-day period. Knowing we were up against pretty good competition, we were really excited. We felt like we had the world by the ass.

But while we did win some races, we were having a lot of engine trouble. We kept breaking connecting rods. Dropping out of races is tough on any night, but it's especially frustrating when you know you're competitive. You can hear the other cars out on the track while you're loading your car up, and in your heart you feel like you could have beaten them. But that's part of it: you don't get paid for first until you finish.

We traveled to McCutchenville, Ohio for a race, and as we were lining up for the feature my right front tire went flat. I pulled off the track near turn four, across from the pit area, and the track owner was standing there. We asked if we could change the tire. He said it was fine, since they weren't ready to start yet. But he also said we'd have to start on the tail. We went to the back and worked through the field and won it, but after the race they informed us that we were disqualified for changing the tire. No black flag, they just let us run the entire race for nothing. I passed a local guy on the last lap to win, and I wondered if it wasn't just a rotten deal all the way through. I appealed to the track owner, but he just said he was mistaken, and that he couldn't overrule his officials. Oh, well.

I was especially frustrated, because that night was my first experience with an aluminum-block motor. It was such an enormous difference, I couldn't believe it. The car felt so much lighter, so much more responsive. I found out right away that I had to use the throttle more carefully because the car would literally lift the front end off the ground. It felt like a rocket...what a feeling.

After you experience something like that, it's very hard to go back to the old way. I was spoiled. Racers always think in terms of progress. I guess that's our nature. Faster, faster, faster. That's why it's difficult even today to rein in the cost of racing, because we all get addicted to progress.

Deuce and I worked well together and we had a lot of fun. But things didn't stay the same very long. About a third of the way through the season, Tom Sanders quit his job working with Sammy Swindell on the Nance house car, which was running on the World of Outlaws circuit. Tom was looking for work. He was respected as a good mechanic and he was very knowledgeable about sprint car racing. He was one of the few professional mechanics in the sport at that time. Tom showed up at Atomic Speedway in Chillicothe, Ohio, and asked me for a ride to the next track. Deuce and I were in the truck, so Deuce laid down in the back seat to sleep.

I slid in behind the wheel of the truck, and we started up the road, when Tom began to talk. He is an assertive, strong-willed guy, and he began listing all the reasons why we should hire him as our mechanic. Deuce was supposedly sleeping in the back, and I felt really bad because here was Tom talking his way into this job and

Deuce was right there, just two feet away. It was an awkward situation. It wasn't like I was trying to hire Tom; it was a deal where he needed a job, and he was trying to sell himself. It was going to be Sam's decision anyway – there wasn't much I could say one way or the other. It turns out Deuce wasn't asleep, he was lying there listening to the whole conversation. Deuce and I laugh about it all these years later. He says, "You know, the guy talked such a good story I was ready to hire him myself!"

Tom eventually talked to Sam, and Sam let Deuce go and hired Tom. I think Sam felt that Tom knew so much about the Nance chassis that he brought a wealth of knowledge and experience. I felt bad for Deuce, because he was a great friend and we had a lot of fun (and success) racing together. He went on to an excellent career as a mechanic, so I guess he recovered all right from our situation.

With Tom on board, things began to change. Frankly, not all the changes were positive. We were still winning some races, but then we began to struggle. That introduced me to something that every professional driver deals with at one time or another: friction between the driver and the mechanic.

Like I said earlier, when we raced locally there wasn't a lot of pressure. As I grew in my career, the pressure naturally increased. Once I got to the level of a touring, professional racer, there was strong pressure to win. More money is at stake, and both the driver and the mechanic feel like they have to justify themselves. If you're not winning, it's easy to blame the mechanic. For the mechanic, the obvious strategy is to blame the driver. Tom, or any other mechanic, couldn't very well go back to the owner and say it was a mechanical issue. That's what we hired him for! So naturally, the driver's ability, or desire, begins to come into question.

I was intimidated by the entire process. I was still pretty young and somewhat inexperienced...how was I expected to assert myself with Tom Sanders, who was known to the entire sport as a talented mechanic? There was no way. So I kept my mouth shut and didn't argue, even at times when I felt like I wasn't the problem. I know my inexperience hurt us sometimes, but not all the time. I didn't mind taking my lumps when I made a mistake, but to assume every time we didn't win a race was because I made a mistake just wasn't fair. Or accurate.

We ran a World of Outlaws race at Lernerville, and I was leading the race when Sammy Swindell passed me. Within a lap or two he drove out of sight – he was way faster than I was. I finished second. I was expected to be in the shop every day with Tom at that time. When I got to the shop the next morning, Tom and Sam were down on their knees on the floor. Tom had a piece of chalk and had diagramed the race and exactly how and where I lost the race. The conversation kind of swings around to be, "Well, the car should have won the race except the driver did this wrong…" You can kind of guess the rest.

Maybe there was something to that, I don't know. But my feeling was that Sammy was so much faster than us there wasn't much I could do with him anyway. But all I could do was drive the car…how could I argue with someone who is considered knowledgeable and defend myself? I not only swallowed my words, but I began to question myself, began to compromise my confidence.

That morning helped me understand why there is so much job turnover in this business. It wasn't that I was not a good driver; it wasn't that Tom was not a good mechanic. I think we were both good at what we did. But the very nature of racing puts two guys into conflict, because there are so many variables on how you get the job done. Only one winner each night, and a bunch of other teams wondering where they failed. That's a lot of anxiety and self-doubt, and there's always plenty of that to go around.

Our schedule took us to a lot of new race tracks. They raced several times at Eldora Speedway, which is one of the toughest and most exciting tracks I ever encountered. I had visited Eldora as a spectator several years earlier. I walked through the back pit gate that day and walked around to the third turn. The track looked like a half-mile bowl carved into the Darke County, Ohio countryside. It was steeply banked, with a big concrete wall ringing the place. They green-flagged a hot lap session just as I walked up to the outside of the third turn, where you can walk down across the track to the infield. Ed Haudenschild was in that session, so I perked right up. The cars went into turn three so fast, it took my breath away. It looked like they were gonna just drive through the wall. Awesome.

When I finally got a chance to race there in the Creston car in 1979, it was a learning experience. When I was preparing to race there people told me, "If you breathe the throttle at Eldora, they'll drive right by you." I started my heat race and got out front, and I was holding the throttle down to the floor with all my might. You have to talk your foot into it, because it wants to lift up when you see the wall coming. But I kept it down on the floor, waiting to hear someone come up from behind. Because of the echo of my own engine off the concrete wall, it sounded like someone was right behind me. In reality, there was nobody close. We won the heat by a straightaway, but my leg was all cramped up from pressing down so hard on the throttle! I guess I took their advice a little to the extreme. My ears had tricked me, but it worked.

In the 1981 opener at Eldora for an All Star race, I was leading the feature when my seat broke, of all things. Actually, the seat didn't break, it was the bolts that mounted it to the frame. I had to hold myself up in the car, and at Eldora you generate unbelievable g-forces that try to push you out of the right side of the car. The seat was just sliding around inside the car, bouncing me around. It was very uncomfortable. I had my lap belt and submarine belt to hold me in, but my right shoulder was against the rock guard, which is the body panel along the right side of the cockpit. My shoulder belt was rubbing against my neck, I was that far to the right. Late in the race I saw Rick Ferkel pull alongside, and I held my breath. I was worn out, but when he pulled alongside it kind of woke me up. He tried a slide job in three and four and got alongside me, but I stayed on the cushion and drove back by him on the outside. I was sure happy to see that checkered flag, because I didn't have anything left, physically.

You might wonder why I didn't pull in, with my seat wallowing around like that. But when you're leading the race, almost nothing can make you quit. Even though you might race a lot, you don't get to win many races. It takes something extreme to make you give up when you're leading. I've kept racing even when my safety belts came loose. Why? I don't know. There is something inside a person that makes you want to win so desperately that nothing else seems to matter at that moment.

The travel changed a lot during this period. In my early years we were just 30 minutes away from Lakeville, then later when we ran Pennsylvania our tow was three hours or so. Now, we would leave on Thursday or Friday and not come home until late Sunday night, maybe Monday morning.

Laurie and Tom's wife Barb traveled with us, along with Tom and Barb's two little daughters. I drove the truck most of the time, with Laurie and one of the little girls in the front, and Tom and Barb and the other little girl in the back seat.

Traveling in the truck with a total of four adults and two kids was pretty cozy. But their kids never created any trouble, they were good little kids. I think Tom and Barb were concerned about us being irritated by the kids; they were pretty strict on them and kept them under control. But Laurie and I didn't mind them, they were good little girls. Besides, Laurie is just a natural with little kids. She loves them and they always love her.

I always felt more comfortable driving the truck. I probably should have let the mechanic drive the truck more, but I just liked to drive. I never worried if I was driving the truck. Plus, I think every driver worries about the perception that he isn't dedicated, so I wanted to make sure I did more than my share. I wanted to prove that I was willing to work hard to make it in this business.

That 1981 season also opened my eyes to the physical fatigue that comes with being a traveling racer. Not only did I drive the race car at night, but I had a full workload during the day as well. Driving the truck, and helping work on the car.

If a racer had a position where he could focus on driving and preparing the race setup without having to do all the physical work, that was an advantage. Mounting and grooving tires, changing gears, changing torsion bars – all the work that had to be done, and you had to help do it. Spending those hours on the hot asphalt of a hotel parking lot, or the dusty ground in the pits, I know it affected my performance in the race car. I'm sure of it. Sometimes by the time the feature started I just didn't have a lot left because I'd been working hard nearly all day long. At that time, that was probably very common, because most other drivers also had to do much of the physical work.

We usually stayed near the track the night after a race, and we would hit a car wash in the morning and clean the car. We would also begin some maintenance work there, such as changing the oil, cleaning the fuel injectors, and washing and cleaning the injector filters. We would also cut open the oil filter and stretch out the filter material, looking for any metal or foreign material that would give us a clue that the engine had a problem somewhere.

Then we'd begin driving to the next track, which was usually at least a couple of hours away. We would try to get there early enough to finish the maintenance work. Then we would begin to work on the chassis setup for that night, changing bars, mounting tires, shocks, things like that. If it was a big thrash to get the car changed over, or a long drive to the next track, sometimes we didn't even get to the car wash. We would just knock the dirt off of it and go.

All this was changed if we crashed. Usually that meant we stayed up all night to rebuild the car. Luckily, I didn't crash much during that first season with the All Stars.

If Tom and I had an argument at the track, it made for a chilly day in the truck the following day. In fact, it was chilly most of the time! We had some good times together, but we also argued some. But if you want to do this bad enough, you just put up with the unpleasant things that are part of the program. If you don't learn to deal with that kind of stress, you can't make it. You have to bite your tongue and let it go, or you go find another occupation.

Tom and Barb rented a house not far from Laurie and me, and we visited them a couple of times. In their basement there was this old wheelchair. Tom would sit in that thing and do wheelies, just horsing around. I sat in it once, and I felt really uncomfortable, really weird.

116

I kind of scolded Tom because I said it wasn't right to have fun with something like that. A premonition, maybe?

We didn't run all the All Stars races in 1981, but we ran enough to win four races and finish fourth in points, winning the Rookie of the Year title. I was very proud of that, because I felt that with the competition we were up against that was a good showing.

It was that fall that Laurie and I decided to get married. Sam was sending Laurie and I, along with Tom and his wife, to Hawaii for a vacation. What a great gift! I came home from the shop one evening and we were planning the trip, and Laurie giggled and said something like, "Hey, while we're there let's....oh, never mind."

I kept prying it out of her, and finally she said, "Wouldn't it be neat to get married while we're in Hawaii?" I said, "Hey, that's a great idea!" Boy, right then she gave me a big hug. Later on I teased her that we probably would never have gotten married if she hadn't asked me!

When we got to Hawaii a limo picked us up at our hotel and took us to a pastor's home. He had a beautiful waterfall in his backyard, and it was there that Laurie became my wife. It was a wonderful moment, one that I am very thankful for. I was such a nervous klutz that I dropped her ring and it bounced off a rock and almost went into the waterfall. But we just laughed, it was too perfect a moment to let anything interfere.

Hawaii was beautiful. Laurie was beautiful. Life was beautiful.

7

During the winter of 1981, Sam, Tom, and I all talked about what we wanted to do for the 1982 season. Sam really wanted us to run with the World of Outlaws. Although I was excited about the opportunity, I have to admit that I was just a tiny bit intimidated. Looking back now I realize that I wasn't completely ready for the series at that stage of my career. I say I wasn't ready because I just didn't understand the pressure that came with racing in that series.

But if our team wanted to move up, the Outlaws were the only choice. I could have kept running with the All Stars, but there was no question that the World of Outlaws was the top series in sprint car racing.

The organization was beginning their fifth year. They were still very new, but already they had established themselves as the dominant series in the sport. Big crowds, big purses, and big stars were the norm, night after night.

Sprint car racing was completing a transition during this period. Through the years, USAC had been viewed as the top sprint car league in the country. And no doubt about it, drivers such as Parnelli Jones, A.J. Foyt, Larry Dickson, Gary Bettenhausen, Pancho Carter, and Tom Bigelow had attracted a big fan following. You're talking some very talented guys there.

But by 1978 USAC had slipped a lot. They didn't have the big national schedule any longer, and they didn't have the household names racing with them. And when Jan Opperman came along, the world of sprint car racing changed. Dramatically.

Part of the aura of USAC was the belief that their guys were better than guys from other series. So people naturally looked at every young driver and figured that if he was going to go anywhere, sooner or later he had to go race with USAC. When USAC traveled to different tracks, the USAC regulars would almost always beat the locals.

Before the World of Outlaws came along, the word "outlaw" was used to describe a sprint car driver who raced outside of USAC. Lots of people looked down at those guys. They couldn't be any good, or they'd be racing with USAC, right?

But Opperman did something that is very difficult to do: He changed people's attitudes. Here was this guy with long hair and a floppy hat, talking about Jesus, traveling around the country running with whomever he wanted. He began racing with USAC some, and he beat them. Not every time, of course, but consistently enough that all of a sudden people starting looking at USAC and wondering if they really were the toughest series.

Plus, it was evident that there was fan support for a newer, larger sprint car series. In early 1978 many of the top "outlaw" teams got together and decided to run a series of races that offered a $2,000-to-win purse. It was pretty much open competition, with very few rules or regulations, and may the best man win.

They hit a gold mine. Ted Johnson was involved from the beginning, and as it evolved he was the new leader for sprint car racing. The World of Outlaws were going places.

For me, the timing was perfect. I wanted to see the country, and I wanted to race against the best. When you looked at the Outlaw roster you saw the names of Steve Kinser, Sammy Swindell, Doug Wolfgang, and Rick Ferkel. Nobody in the country could honestly say that any group of racers anywhere could collectively top those four.

For young guys like me, the World of Outlaws provided a career path. The bridge between sprint cars and the Indianapolis 500 disappeared during the 1970's, so we weren't going to Indy anyway. So if we were going to be sprint car racers, why not try the top league?

During the 1981 season we ran some of the WoO races in the Midwest. Deuce and I took the car to Butler, Michigan for a WoO race on May 13. Butler had an oiled sand surface, and it was really a mess. On one of our trips there they had just applied a coating of oil to the surface, and puddles of used motor oil were literally standing at spots on the track. When the oil splashed on anything hot it would just stick like glue. Headers, brakes, the engine block – it was an ugly, sticky mess to clean up. My uniform, my shoes... what a mess.

For the May race, the track was very slick. I was leading the feature, running the bottom groove. I kept listening for someone to come up and challenge me, but I never heard anyone. I was counting the laps, and they showed us the five-laps-to-go sign. I knew we were going to win this race. Coming out of turn four with two laps to go a tire went flat, I could feel it immediately. I rode around to try and finish, but finally I pulled in.

I had shocked myself. I almost won that race. I had gone from running locally at Lakeville, to one season in Pennsylvania, to almost winning against the Outlaws, all in less than two years. It fueled my desire and made me feel like I could hold my own with these guys.

So when Sam told us he'd like us to run the full Outlaw schedule, I was excited. I didn't hesitate, I was all for it. That was the big time, and I had a chance to go for it. And I felt good that Tom was with us, because he had run with those guys before. He knew how to get to the tracks, he knew the setups, and he knew the series. I figured he would be a big help to me.

Running the All Stars the year before had taught me how to read a new track, so going to new places wasn't really a big issue, I figured.

Really, life was a blur at that point. My career seemed to be taking off, but it was all happening so fast. I had a great ride with Sam, and I was also a newlywed. I was so busy at the time that I didn't really savor what I had going. Naturally, I can look back now and see that, but at the time I didn't take one minute to enjoy what was happening. It was a wonderful period in my life, though.

I've always enjoyed traveling, seeing new things, and I was looking forward to seeing the country and going racing at the same time. What more could a guy ask for? I would see the U.S.A. and get paid for it. And there was never a question about Laurie coming with me. She would be there at nearly every race.

I was so eager to see all the sights and scenes that I didn't want to drive at night, because I was afraid I might miss something. I liked being on the move, the adventure of it all.

Before the WoO season began, we decided to change chassis. We went from Nance to Gambler. Gambler was winning most of the races, and their cars were really fast. This sport is monkey-see, monkey-do. People begin to say, "Well, we need to get one of those." The same thing happens today: Any manufacturer hopes the heavy hitters run their stuff, because if they are winning, the product is going to be popular. That goes for any component – tires, engines, chassis, shocks, anything. Everybody switches fairly quickly, you can't afford to stay with something that isn't winning.

But at the time it was kind of hard for me to make that change because a Nance was pretty much all I had driven. The line of thought is that we have to have the right pieces to compete. There is a loyalty in racing, but it is quickly strained when you don't win. The ultimate objective is winning races, and if you're not doing that, it's kind of a senseless exercise, really.

In our situation we just talked about it and made the choice. It was a team decision. Sam gave us a lot of room to make our own decisions, but I always wanted to make sure he knew what was going on.

One of the factors in the decision might have been that the Gambler shop was much closer to us. They were in Hendersonville, Tennessee, and we could get there in 10 hours instead of driving around the clock to Wichita. At that time, Gambler, Nance, and Stanton were the main chassis manufacturers. Nance was in Wichita, and Stanton was clear out in Phoenix.

By then we had moved our shop from Jim Smith's building to a bigger building located on one of Sam's coal operations. It was a place where they mixed high-sulphur coal with other grades, and then they sold the mixture to utility companies. Later, the cost of low-sulphur coal dropped to where the high-sulphur stuff wasn't as attractive, and that hurt Sam's business a lot. The race car was kept in a big shop right by the plant where the trucks were maintained. The race car was kept in the front, and the trucks were in the back. It was very noisy, and it was hard to keep the shop clean, with all the dust.

The strip mine was about five miles away, and they hauled the coal to the mixing plant in big tri-axle dump trucks. They would dump the coal into a mixing machine, and a conveyer took the mix to a dump truck, and away they would go. Sam probably owned 10 or 12 trucks, and they went non-stop all day long.

Sam bought a small house for Laurie and me in Kittanning. It was an upstairs apartment and the first floor was the garage. They called it a two-bedroom loft home. This was just 2 or 3 miles from the shop. We went home at Christmastime, but we didn't go home much. Sometimes Laurie would go home for a few days, or her sisters would come over and stay with us, but for the most part we were pretty disconnected from our families and friends back in Ohio.

I didn't get home as much as I should have. I didn't see family or friends, we didn't take the time to slow down and think about it. Everything was hectic and fast-paced. During our Christmas visit we'd stay for four or five days, then rush back to Kittanning to prepare for Florida. Even during the time I was back in Ohio I was itching to get back to the shop. I always had a feeling that there was so much to be done, and I felt like I was wasting time if I wasn't working.

After Tom and I got back from our trip to Hendersonville, we put one chassis up on stands and started bolting stuff on. The spare chassis we carried on top of the trailer. If you look at pictures from that era, you'll see that's what a lot of teams did.

I packed as many racing T-shirts as I owned. And blue jeans. I would learn pretty quickly about doing laundry on the road. I'd throw my blue jeans and T-shirts in one load and fire suits in the other. At that time I used Simpson fire equipment. (I liked their Bandit helmet. It looked cool.) Later on I got a deal from Simpson where they provided gloves, helmet, arm restraints, shields, and shoes, and I bought the suits. Sometimes I'd have a deal where our sponsor bought the suits.

We missed a few of the Outlaw races in 1982, but we ran most of them. Those we missed were probably because I crashed and we took a race or two to regroup. We didn't go race anywhere else.

At this time the Outlaws were visiting a lot of new race tracks. It was actually a good time to join the series as a rookie, because everybody else was making their first trip to some of these tracks as well. I'm not sure how much of an issue that is anyway. Some places you just feel comfortable, no matter what you do there. If you're a racer, you learn very quickly to figure out the track. Plus, Tom had run some of those tracks and he was important to me in terms of helping set the car up.

We were racing at Big H Motor Speedway in Houston, when I got word that Dave Pope passed away back in Ohio. He had battled with cancer for a while, and it finally took him. I knew he was slipping away, but I was still so sad when I heard that he had died. He had been a friend, and a mentor to me. I wanted so much to go back to Ohio for the funeral, but because of my commitments on the road I felt like I couldn't.

We ran Knoxville in April and finished fourth. I have to admit that I didn't really understand the heritage there. My Mecca, my palace, was Williams Grove. I didn't know the history or significance of Knoxville. It stood out on the schedule, and I knew it was special, but I wasn't in awe of the place. At this time there was no museum, just a small grandstand and a dinky press box. It was a big race track in a small town. I finished fourth, behind Doug Wolfgang, Sammy Swindell, and Danny Smith.

A month later we were at the Grove, racing against a couple of legends, Bobby Allen and Lynn Paxton. Those guys were very good at Williams Grove. Paxton ran the Boop's Aluminum car, which had a big-block engine. Man, he was awesome fast. Allen won and Paxton was second, and I was third. It was nothing to be ashamed of, finishing third behind those guys.

As we traveled around to all these new tracks, having Tom along really did help me. I wasn't starting from zero. Tom could give me a good basic setup and we could work from there. I had enough experience that I could sense what the car was doing. Whether he listened or not, that was another story. There were times that we debated on what the car was actually doing. That's typical, because we both felt like we knew some things. The key was finding the happy medium. He would work with me, but we had disagreements at times. That's also typical.

But truthfully, things weren't right between us. Maybe it was because we weren't winning races, maybe it was our personalities, I don't know. But by the middle part of the season Tom was talking to Sam about getting rid of me. Some might have said that Tom made Sammy Swindell, that he was the reason Sammy won all those races. So there we were, not winning, so it must be the driver, right? Sam eventually had to make a decision, and he decided to stick with me. Tom didn't want to keep working with me, so in the middle of the season he quit. It was already a really tense situation, so maybe we both needed the relief. Something had to give. Plus, I think Tom was getting burned out from all the travel. He eventually began working for Gambler at their place, which allowed him to get off the road, so it was a good situation for him as well.

So there we were, without a mechanic. We hired Roger Leeskamp because he was recommended to us and we needed somebody quick. I couldn't do it by myself. Roger was from out west somewhere. That didn't work out, so after a month we were looking once again.

Daryl Saucier had worked for Bobby Davis Jr. and had been the mechanic when Bobby won his first World of Outlaws race at Devil's Bowl in early 1982. They had just split up, so Daryl was available. We hired him in September of 1982. Sam believed in me, and we knew we had good equipment, and he felt like if we could get the right mechanic it would be magic. So that's what we were looking for.

In a lot of ways, our situation was like most other businesses. You're always hoping the person you hire is the right person, and that the chemistry is right. And when a person is new to an organization, everyone kind of tiptoes around with each other for a while, learning each other's personalities.

Early on, I noticed that when we would stop and get fuel, Daryl would go in and buy two or three candy bars and a bag of chips, then drink a diet soda. I loved to razz Daryl about that, and he would laugh and say that it was okay, the other stuff didn't matter because he was drinking a diet soda!

I realized right away that Daryl and I were very, very different. Different, both on and off the track. His personality seemed to be very intense, and sometimes he didn't seem to like anything or anybody. My personality is not like that. I'm more mellow, and it's important to me to be happy. He was a highly critical person, and he was outspoken with his criticism of many people, and many things.

Two clashing personalities make things difficult in racing, because you spend hours and hours together. It gets to the point where any two guys probably don't even want to hear each other's voice. We'd ride down the road together, room together, and race together. We weren't making a whole lot of money then, and we didn't have the money to get separate rooms. Plus, Sam expected me to be a key part of this team. He wanted me to be involved in everything. After all, he had said early on that it was my team to run.

Overall, it was very hard that first year. It seemed like I led a lot of races but either broke or crashed. Late in the year at Baylands Raceway Park in Fremont, California, I was leading a feature event when I broke. It had been a very rough weekend; they had flipped 30-some cars in three nights of racing. There had been a lot of rain, and the track was very rough and choppy. I started 18th.

I worked my way up to third, Ron Shuman was second in the Ofixco car, while Wolfgang was leading in Gary Stanton's car. I ran them down, my car was really hooked up. Funny thing was, I was bicycling the car up on two wheels, lap after lap. That's how the car worked best! It wasn't meant to, but the track was so rough, that's what worked. It got routine, to bicycle the car up on the cushion. I'd bounce through the holes, hook the right rear into the cushion, and the car would get up on the right side. I'd turn the wheel to the right and lift to catch it, then mash the throttle and go to the next corner.

I passed Shuman going into turn one on the outside. Everyone was running the bottom because it was smoother, but starting that far back I had to find a groove that nobody else was running. After I passed Shuman I caught Wolfgang on the backstretch and passed him in three and four. I knew there weren't many laps left.

126

Baylands always had a curfew, and we were already way past their scheduled time. Right after I took the lead the red flag came out. Somebody had flipped. I came around just *certain* the checkered would wave because of the time. But it didn't, and after a few minutes we restarted, then got the red again. Still no checkered flag. We were questioning why the race was going on that late after curfew. Finally they said they would go five more laps or until the next red.

I was hoping that we could just get through this thing. I didn't think we could run five laps without a red. Coming out of four, they were waving the white flag, and all of a sudden my engine revved up. The Jacob's ladder had broken, and it allowed the rear end to move side-to-side, and it eventually broke the torque tube off at the center section. I coasted into the infield, and watched Wolfgang win the race. It was a heartbreak. But that kind of summed up my 1982 season.

At the end of the year we were fourth in points and won Rookie of the Year. To be honest, I think I would have rather won some races. It was very hard to adjust to not winning. You know you're in tougher competition, and you have to accept the fact that you're not going to win as many. That makes getting some wins even more rewarding, though, because you know they're coming against the best racers. But not winning an Outlaw race my first season, maybe that's what shook my confidence so bad. I'm not sure if it ever really came back.

Looking back across all those years, the rookie title is more special to me now than it was at the time. I would have probably been more confident if I had won races, but in retrospect it was special to win the rookie title.

1982 was difficult, but 1983 would be even tougher. As it turned out, winning races wouldn't be enough to keep our team together.

8

Whaen Daryl was hired, one of his conditions for taking the position was that he didn't want to move to Pennsylvania. He wanted to live near Memphis, his home. During the winter of 1982 he took the new chassis and supplies from Gambler and began assembling our new cars at his shop in Memphis.

I was too young to recognize it, but when he took possession of the race cars it dramatically shifted the dynamics of our team, and my relationship with Sam. All of a sudden Daryl talked like he was in charge of everything. And each day he would be the one to call Sam and keep him current on what was happening.

In February I met up with Daryl and we headed to East Bay Raceway in Florida to open the 1983 World of Outlaws season. We also ran an event at Jacksonville, a dry, sandy track where it was very tough to pass. The start of the race is crucial on a track like that, because everybody tries to get every possible advantage before the cars get scattered and it's hard to get around people.

We were somewhere in the middle of the field for the start, maybe the third or fourth row. Everybody in the front of the field tangled on the start, and when I slowed Sammy Swindell – he was running the Old Milwaukee car – climbed my left rear wheel and stuck his right front tire inside my cockpit. It broke the corner of the hood and tore off the injector stacks on the engine. It made me mad – we had this brand new car, and already it was all skinned up. It wasn't Sammy's fault, though, it was just all bottled up and he had nowhere to go either.

After Jacksonville, Daryl decided we needed to travel to California. He wanted to spend some time at Ron Shaver's engine shop. We left Florida on Saturday morning, and on Monday morning we were sitting in Shaver's parking lot in Los Angeles when he opened. We drove 48 hours straight through, sharing the driving, stopping only for fuel, food, and bathroom breaks. We hit a big snowstorm in Texas where they got about two inches of snow in 30 minutes. Despite the bad weather, we made it all the way across in pretty good time. From sea to shining sea, in two days.

Daryl began working on our engines while we were at Shaver's shop. We put a brand new hood on the car, and new injector stacks. We decided to run the CRA race at El Centro, a non-wing race. We didn't really go out there to race, but since we were out there...you know the thinking.

El Centro is unique in that the flag stand was way down toward turn one, instead of being in the middle of the straightaway. I went out to qualify and messed up my first lap. On the second lap I wanted to make sure I stayed on the gas all the way past the clock. It was a daytime race, and they had bales of straw piled around the track. The fair was going on at this time on the fairgrounds nearby.

I hauled the car into the corner, past the clock, and let the car drift up into the marbles, thinking my lap was done. But it slid and slid and slid, and got up into the bales. I hit the bales and tripped the car, and did a quick snap rollover. The car came down right on top of the cage, right on top of that new hood. Crunch. It broke the Jacob's ladder off, and smashed that new hood. I crawled out, and Daryl was already there. Boy, was he unhappy! It was a pretty stupid move on my part, a really dumb mistake. We fixed the car, and ran fifth.

By this time Daryl and I had just worn each other out. He had worn me out, anyway. It wasn't just the personalities, either. We had serious differences in philosophy on the race track.

Daryl always insisted on setting up the car very, very tight. And even though I disagreed, I didn't rock the boat. That was a very big mistake on my part. I tried to diplomatically suggest that the car wasn't right, instead of insisting on changes. Maybe it was my inexperience, or my youth, I don't know. But I just kept my mouth shut and tried to adjust my driving to adapt to the car, which I really struggled with. Stupid me, I just tried to run it harder, which isn't the right way to adjust.

Actually, during the previous season Daryl hadn't been with us for a month before we had our first really big conflict. Immediately following our heartbreak at Baylands, we headed for Santa Maria, California. Santa Maria is a beautiful little track, maybe just a couple of miles from the Pacific Ocean. The moist night air rolls in off the water and usually keeps the track really, really tacky. The car was really tight when I went out for hot laps, and the car bicycled in the corner really high. I ran around a few laps and came in, and I told Daryl that it was too tight.

He immediately snapped at me, and said I'm not driving the car hard enough. He said if I'd drive it into the corner harder, the wing would push the left rear corner down and make the car turn. He said that I was getting out of the throttle too much, and that's why the car was so tight.

I went out to qualify, and as I went down the backstretch I was thinking, "Well, he said not to lift..." So I didn't. The car bicycled, dug in and turned right, slamming into the wall. I flipped a couple of times – it was a hard crash.

Later that night we called Sam, and Daryl told Sam flat out that I just drove into the corner and hit the wall. I'm sitting there listening, my heart just sinking. I was eaten up with self-doubt, thinking, "What did I do wrong?" I knew at the time that it wasn't all me, but the inexperience, the self-doubt – I just didn't know what to do about it. I sat there and didn't say a word, my stomach hurting with anxiety.

It wasn't like my phone was ringing off the hook for other rides, anyway. I had a top Outlaw deal that many guys probably envied, so I couldn't very well think that I had a bad deal. Of course, nobody ever knows what's really cooking inside a team. There's almost always more friction and discontent than you see on the surface.

The 1983 WoO schedule resumed in March at Big H Motor Speedway in Houston. On our way back from California we first caught the open competition Springnationals at Devil's Bowl near Dallas, and we won it. That was good for a total of over $4,600. We also ran Little Rock, Arkansas.

From there we headed for Houston. At Big H the car was way too tight, and the instant I got on the throttle the front end would raise up. We made the feature and were running in the top five, and the car came off the corner once and the front end came way up. It was a gigantic wheelie. I tried to ride the thing out and stay on the throttle, riding on the rear wheels. But the stagger will invariably turn the car to the left, and I didn't realize that Ron Shuman had pulled alongside on the left. I hit Shuman's right front with my left rear. My front wheels were in the air, and when my rear wheel hit his, my car just took off. It just launched like a rocket. I flipped end over end down the frontstretch, doing some barrel rolls for good measure. That one hurt, physically. I felt that one for several days.

I wasn't knocked out, and in that situation you just wait until it's over and then you open your eyes. When you're flipping like that, and it's silent, you don't know if you're still in the air or if it's over. You're so disoriented for a moment you don't know if you're on the ground. You just ride it out. The ones that seem to *really* hurt are when the car bounces on the tail section, and you hit the back of your head on the seat or the bars.

My first thought when it was over was, "Aw, shit, I'm in trouble now." I knew everybody would be mad at me for a while. That's what bothered me. The thought of getting hurt wasn't really an issue, but I didn't want to have to face Sam and Daryl.

When I got out of the car and they were cleaning up the debris, Shuman approached me. He told me that it wasn't all my fault. He said he felt bad because he thought he might have moved up. But it wasn't his fault, it just happened. It was just hard racing, and with my front wheels in the air I wasn't fully under control, either.

After all that had happened, with the crashing we had been doing, I knew things were going to be pretty tense. We loaded the car, and Daryl didn't say much. We went back to Memphis. He was on the phone with Sam, and I heard him tell Sam about the crash. "Sam, he just drove it down into the corner and ran right over Shuman's right rear wheel. I don't know what he was thinking."

This time, I knew I had to say something. I couldn't take this anymore, being blamed for everything. And in this case, he didn't even describe the crash correctly. I wondered, was he doing this on purpose to get rid of me? Did he not see the crash? When he was still on the phone, I was sitting on a chair nearby. I got to my feet and spoke up, and began to tell Daryl that he wasn't right, he didn't have his facts straight. He just glared at me.

I said, "Tell him, Daryl, tell Sam the truth." He just glared. I kept saying it, louder each time. Finally he hung up, and he had this killer look in his eye. He said, "Don't you ever talk to me like that in front of Sam Bowers again." He looked like he was ready to explode. He said he'd crush me if I ever talked like that again. I told him that he was crazy, that Shuman would vouch for what really happened.

I was so overwhelmed in the midst of all of this. I didn't know what to do. I didn't know how to handle this. So I did nothing, and just kept my mouth shut in my misery.

Part of my stress was that Laurie was at home expecting our first child. I'd like to say that I wished I was home with her, but I was a selfish racer. My career was so important that I didn't dare think about not being out on the road with the Outlaws. I felt like my livelihood was at stake. Had I quit and gone home, maybe I wouldn't have ever got another ride.

The Outlaws were off until the middle of April, so we went to Pennsylvania to run some local shows. We won at Lincoln Speedway, a very competitive track. All things considered, even though you could cut the tension between Daryl and me with a knife we started going pretty well.

We were back at Devil's Bowl on April 22, and Jac was there in Doug Howell's car. During the feature I was coming off turn four, and Jac came off the corner under me and drilled my left front with his right rear, a side-to-side hit. It was basically a slide job, but he didn't clear me. I don't know, maybe he thought we were back in the old mini-bike days and he was using me for side bite! When he hit my front end it turned me right, and I went head-on into the concrete wall. Man, it was a hard impact. It dazed me. My mind started to clear, and at first I couldn't believe he did that. Then I got mad. He might have been one of my best friends, but I was mad this time.

I went down to his pit and confronted him. We weren't screaming or yelling, but I was angry. I felt that because of our friendship we ought to give each other plenty of room. I was more disappointed in him than anything. He felt bad about it, and I know he didn't do it on purpose. Really, I know for a fact that Jac would never in a million years crash me on purpose. Still, with our race car all bent and twisted, I was mad at him.

We were scheduled to race at Oklahoma Fairgrounds Speedway two days later, so that night we drove straight through to Oklahoma City. We got there early the next morning, when the sun was just peeking over the horizon. We went to Shane Carson's shop, a guy there by the name of Clark Drake was working for Shane. Clark was only 18 at the time. Daryl wasn't a welder, but Clark sure was. He had already built a chassis or two in California before he went to work for Shane.

Clark put new torsion tubes on the front of the car, and new uprights, then rebuilt the front of the frame. He did this in one day, while we worked on other stuff. There was another guy there named Andy Allison. Nobody called him Andy, though – his nickname was "Dad." Sometimes he traveled with us. Dad had a wooden leg, and he worked so hard that day that he blistered his leg where the prosthesis was attached. By the time we quit that day we were all worn out.

The next day called for a daytime race at the Fairgrounds, which was a big half-mile track. I liked that track. We were still bolting parts on the car while we were in line to sign in at the pit gate. During the feature, Doug Wolfgang was leading in the yellow No. 18 Gambler house car. Steve Kinser was second. When I got into third, they had a big lead. I ran down Steve, and he and I raced each other for two or three laps, back and forth. I couldn't seem to make the pass. Finally I got by, and I could see Wolfgang way out front. I reeled him in, and my car was working perfectly.

The laps were running out. I finally caught Doug, and I passed him coming off turn four to take the white flag. I drove on around and won my first World of Outlaws race.

Finally! I did it!

I stopped on the front straight, and when I climbed out of the car the crowd just roared. What a wonderful feeling, hearing those people cheering for me. I was elated. Maybe more *relieved* than anything. Two years earlier at Butler I had almost won one of these, and now I had finally proven that I could win with these guys. We were all so tired, but so happy. There was a big celebration on the front straight, lots of pictures, lots of happiness. But even in the midst of jubilation there was a big surprise waiting back at the pits.

I climbed back into the car and drove back to the trailer. There were tons of well-wishers there to greet me. But I could sense that something was wrong. I could tell that Daryl was upset about something. He wouldn't look at me. I had the trophy sitting in the trailer, and next thing I know Daryl walked past and grabbed the trophy and took it outside and slammed it on the ground. He said, "I don't want to see this f——ing thing again. Get it out of here." I was so shocked I had trouble even thinking of what to say. I finally stared at him and said, "Man, what is wrong with you?" He said, "You didn't deserve to win this race. You f—ed with Kinser all that time, why didn't you just knock him out of the way? He would have you!"

I was amazed. I stammered and stuttered, and said, "Daryl, we won the race." But he said, "Yeah, but you shouldn't have. You tried to give it away."

Looking back, I think maybe he felt I praised Clark Drake too much in the victory lane interview. Maybe Daryl felt like I didn't give him enough credit for setting up the car, and he reacted in anger. That was his way of expressing his hurt feelings.

It was a win, anyway. But what a situation: We won, and we still bickered!

We went back to the Midwest and won a weekly show at Cortland, Ohio. The Outlaws were back at Eldora on May 21 and 22 for a two-day show, and we finished sixth in the preliminary event. We came back the following afternoon for the finale, which was on TV by Diamond P Productions. During the feature event our car was great, and I worked my way into the lead. Jeff Karshner (his parents own K-C Raceway in Chillicothe, Ohio) was giving me hand signals on the backstretch. Finally, after I took the white flag, he walked out to the middle of the track with his arms spread as wide as he could, with a huge grin on his face.

It was special, winning a World of Outlaws race in my home state. The crowd was very loud, and supportive, and it felt good. I always believed that if a guy wins at Eldora he can win anywhere, because that place is so tough and demanding.

From there we went on to Williams Grove, where we ran second both nights of a two-day show. Then we went to Lincoln, where I was running second at the Saturday night show when it started to rain after just six laps in the feature. We came back on Monday and passed Bobby Davis Jr. for the win.

The Lincoln win was part of an unforgettable day for me. I had a nice lead with just a few laps to go, when we hurt the engine. I managed to nurse it home, and when the race was over I went straight back to the pits. We were going to run another show there that night that was unsanctioned, and I knew we'd be scrambling for time to fix our engine. They presented me with the winning trophy at our trailer.

Back home, Laurie was two weeks overdue for our first child. Naturally, that had really been on my mind. I was on the phone a lot, checking in. Her mom came and stayed with her in Kittanning.

After the ceremony to give me the trophy, the guys on the PA said, "Also, folks, we just got a very special phone call. Brad is the father of a bouncing baby girl! Mother and daughter are both doing fine." The crowd cheered, and everyone in the pits came over and shook my hand, patted me on the back. I was overwhelmed with emotion. It's an odd thing, an event like that. Even though I knew it was coming, it was still a shock when it happened.

Now, any good husband would have gone straight to the hospital. But not a racer...we raced the following day at Grandview, Pennsylvania, then on to Bridgeport, New Jersey the day after that. We had a three-day break before the next race at Orange County, New York. I can't even remember how I got back to Kittanning, but I did. I arrived at the hospital and went to the nurse's station. "I'm here to see Laurie Doty," I said. The nurse didn't look up, she just told me to go on back to the room. I said, "Well, what's the room number?" Man, she gave me a look like I was worthless scum. Three days late! I just chuckled and ignored her. I wasn't going to let anything spoil the moment. I just wanted to see Laurie and our new baby.

Brandy had the longest black hair I had ever seen on a baby. She looked like she was three months older than the other babies there. I was so happy, but at the same time I was scared. This was a lot of responsibility, and I didn't know if I could handle it. Laurie was very understanding that I hadn't been there with her. I felt bad. Really, I still do. I wish I could have been there. That was a special moment for us, and I wish we could have been together.

After that short break, it was back out on the road. Even though Daryl and I were personally strained, we were still going very well with the race car. When I analyze those wins at Oklahoma City, Eldora, and Lincoln, it all makes perfect sense. Daryl insisted on a tight race car, which was perfect for a dry, slick track. All three of those races were daytime events, which almost always mean a slick racing surface. Daryl had that setup figured out. Now, if we could just get going on the tacky tracks as well.

Even with the friction between Daryl and me, there were some happy times as well. "Dad" would travel with us, and he could brighten the day for anyone. He could sing, or maybe do Elvis impersonations. He was always cracking a joke and making us smile. He could even make Daryl laugh! I don't know why he had the nickname Dad, because he wasn't much older than I was. He had a noticeable limp with his wooden leg.

At I-70 Speedway they used to have a band playing after the races, and he would get on stage and sing. He was pretty good! People would start chanting "We want Dad!" He just thrived on the attention. He always wore bib overalls.

One night all three of us were staying together in the same motel room, when late that night Daryl got up to go to the bathroom. When Dad took his bib overalls off each night, he would leave his wooden leg in the pantleg. The room was dark, and Daryl tripped over the wooden leg and kicked it halfway across the room. Somebody turned on the light real quick, and the look on Daryl's face was priceless. He was trying to explain how he almost fell, and we were laughing. Daryl finally managed to smile, and he told Dad, "Well, next time pick your damned leg up, willya!"

Another funny episode happened at Huset's Speedway in Sioux Falls, South Dakota, when Daryl and Dad accidentally locked me in the trailer (at least they said it was an accident). We pulled the rig into the infield, and unloaded the car, the tools, tires, and some spares. Then we had to take the tow rig back to the parking area outside the track. I was still in the trailer when I heard the doors close and latch. I thought, "Okay, guys, real funny," and figured they'd let me out right away.

I heard the truck start and felt the trailer move, so then I figured they were just playing with me. It was dark inside the trailer, but there was just enough light leaking in around the doors that I could still see a little bit. So I went ahead and got my firesuit on, and after a minute I felt the trailer stop, and heard the truck shut off. I waited a moment, thinking that the doors were going to open, but only silence. Finally I realized that the guys didn't know I was in there! I started yelling, but nobody heard me. I could hear other tow rigs parking near us, but nobody could hear my shouts. Finally, after lots of pounding on the door and shouting, somebody outside heard me. It was a muffled conversation, but they finally understood to go get somebody with our car to bring the key back, and let me out. The guys told me they had no idea, but I just said, "Sure, guys. Sure you didn't."

By the middle of 1983, things had gone from bad to worse. I started crashing a lot, and looking back I didn't handle the pressure like I should have. Instead of riding around and finishing eighth or 10th like the car was capable of, and taking an ass-chewing, I tried too hard for a better finish and crashed. I didn't have the security to just step up and say that was the best the car could do. Throughout my career I never felt secure enough to say that, but especially not in this situation. Instead, I made myself look bad by crashing.

In early June we ran a two-day show at Lernerville. Sammy Swindell won both while I ran second and third. The Outlaws were off for 11 days, so we ran some local shows. We ran Wayne County Speedway, grabbed a third at West Memphis, and then towed to Greenville, Mississippi, where we ran second. We capped the trip with a win at Little Rock.

All in all, it looked like we weren't running too badly. But the pressure of being in a top car worked on me a little bit. I felt like we were supposed to win all of those races.

The Outlaw schedule resumed at Big H Motor Speedway in Houston on June 22. We traveled to Emery Wisenbaker's race shop in Houston. Rick Hood drove Emery's car at that time. The weather was hot and humid on that day, so stifling that it was hard to breathe. Daryl began helping Emery work on their car, while we needed to change our rear end. Daryl worked quite a while helping them move their fuel tank, and I was aggravated that he was spending so much time helping them when we had so much to do.

I was struggling to change the rear end, and I had worked up a pretty good sweat out in the heat and humidity. I needed a hand pulling the rear end out, because that's usually a two-man operation. The next thing I knew, those guys were sitting in the office in the air conditioning. I walked in the office and sat down, to cool off and to ask Daryl if he was going to come out and help me. He asked me what I was doing in there. He looked right at me and told me he wanted me to leave. I was kind of shocked, and I said, "Huh?" He said Sam would be calling, and he didn't want me in the room when they talked. I got up and stomped out.

Looking back, I can't believe I handled this so wrong. I should have forced the issue, and not let him bully me. But I didn't. I did nothing, and I let the thing fall apart entirely. It was a miserable, insecure time for me. I sometimes look at younger drivers today and wish I could speak to them and tell them not to let things like this bother them. But maybe this is the stuff that molds you into what you are.

To make matters worse, Sam was getting pressure from his

business, and from his family, to park the team. The coal industry was changing, and it had a very negative effect on the high-sulphur coal that Sam sold. He was having a tough time of it, through no fault of his own.

But we stayed on the Outlaw trail, which began a western swing at Raceland Speedway outside of Denver. Then we went to Black Hills Raceway in Rapid City, then to Huset's. We left the WoO trail and returned to Pennsylvania, to sit down and talk with Sam.

Laurie and I met with Sam in the shop, and it was an emotional meeting. Sam decided he didn't want to continue on with the team. It was a difficult moment. Laurie was crying, and Sam and I had tears in our eyes trying to get through this. With the pressure he was getting from his family, and with his business struggling, he knew it was time for him to concentrate on other things and get out of racing for a while.

He was very outspoken that he wasn't doing this because of anything between us. He really felt bad. He kept telling me that he was sorry, and he was very apologetic.

There is no doubt about it, I owe Sam a debt of gratitude that I can never repay. He was a huge boost to my career, and the money he spent to help me race was quite a gesture. The whole episode had been a dream come true for me, literally. He plucked me out of Ohio and moved me to Pennsylvania, put me on airplanes, bought me new race cars, and provided Laurie and me a home to live in. It was like being drafted into the pro leagues.

He said to prove to the world that he wasn't quitting because he was unhappy with me, he was going to give me the race team. I could sell it, I could find a sponsor and race it, whatever, but it was my choice. He was going to give me the equipment to get my start on the next chapter of my career. I was surprised and overwhelmed. Nobody does that sort of thing, nobody. Maybe that was the emotion of the moment talking, I don't know. He told me to load up everything in the shop – the cars, the tools, the welder, the tube bender, everything – and take it to Ohio and start my own team. Then we decided to run a few more events together at the Ohio Speedweek, which was just around the corner. Daryl wasn't there at the meeting, but he was still with us when we went to Ohio.

We ran terribly at Speedweek. I crashed at McCutchenville in a really bizarre episode with Bobby Davis Jr. I was running down the back straightaway when the yellow light came on, so I got off the throttle and rolled in on the top of the track in turn three. I heard a car coming on my left side. It was Bobby – he hadn't seen the yellow. He hit me hard and I flipped, under yellow! It doesn't get any worse than that.

Well, yes it does. We went on to Mansfield to run the big half-mile. I blew the engine going down the front straight, which locked up the rear wheels. It turned the car sideways at the end of the straightaway, and turned it to the right. Somebody hit me on the right front and spun me back to the left, and I hit my legs on the right side of the car. I can still see Jimmy Sills coming at me, wide open, for the second hit. It happened very quickly, but I did have time to see him coming. Jimmy hit me so hard that it bent the car into a u-shape. They told me later the car was so bent they had to take the rear end out to load it in the trailer. It bent everything, and I mean everything.

My legs were all beat up, and they hauled me to the hospital. I was pretty sure my leg was broken, because the pain was intense. As it turns out there were no broken bones, but everything was stretched, strained, and bruised.

That was my last ride in Sam's car. From that point forward some of the details are fuzzy in my memory. Daryl took everything back to Pennsylvania, while I stayed in Ohio. After a few days Laurie and I went to Kittanning to get our stuff. We saw Daryl, and he informed me that things had changed. He was going to take some of the stuff and form his own team, and Sam was going to help him.

I was disappointed, but I had no hard feelings. Hey, after all that Sam had done for me, there was no way I was going to be upset at him for anything. My feelings were hurt a little bit that he wanted to continue with Daryl, but really, I had no complaints.

I didn't care about the equipment or the race cars. But I resented Daryl for driving a wedge between Sam and me. And I was angry at myself for letting it happen. But on the other hand, I had tried to prevent it. I tried to communicate with Sam. But it just didn't work out.

So I was unemployed, on crutches, with a new baby at home. I took some time to recover back in Ohio, because for a week or two I couldn't do much anyway.

I was off for just a couple of weeks when I wound up running Gil Suiter's car, a yellow No. 1az. Jeff Swindell had been running the car, but they split up and Gil needed a driver. In the middle of the season when a car owner needs a driver and a driver needs a car owner, they find each other. It's pretty simple, because there aren't a lot of choices at that point.

The mechanic was a guy named Dennis Weidman, and everybody called him "Flash." They used a Jack Rich chassis, which were kind of unknown at that point. They were pretty popular in Arizona; Jack had built a lot of non-wing cars. It was an adjustment for me, because I didn't understand the geometry of the chassis. So I just sat down and tried to drive the car. Later that season they switched to Stanton chassis.

It was sure a lot less pressure. Flash was a laid-back guy, fun to work with. We ran most of the WoO schedule. Laurie and Brandy stayed home, and it was hard for me to be away from them for weeks at a time. Laurie and I didn't have any money, so I wasn't able to fly home when we had a short break. I really missed them, and I felt very alone.

Even though I missed some of the Outlaw races in the middle of the season when Sam's deal ended, I still wound up sixth in points for the 1983 season. All things considered, that wasn't too bad.

I liked Gil, and I had a good time running his car. As it turned out, though, 1984 was going to lead me to another car owner. His name was Gary Stanton.

9

Gary Stanton had a long history in the sport when we met in the fall of 1983. He was one of the premier car builders in the business, and he also had a very strong car on the World of Outlaws circuit. Gary had spotted me when I was driving Sam's car, and in late 1983 he talked to me about running his car in 1984. Doug Wolfgang had driven the car in 1983.

Gary was a very creative guy. I often thought he could probably build anything, if you gave him enough time to think about it. He had a very keen mind for sprint car racing, and he truly understood the sport. Not just technically, but he understood the nature of the beast, and the personalities of all the different players. He would teach me a lot during our time together, and we built a friendship that remains strong today.

Gil's shop was in Phoenix, which is also where Gary was headquartered. They were friends, and I think that was a factor in Gary and I getting together.

Gil was teaming up with Bobby Davis Jr. and Kenny Woodruff to take over the Gambler house car, so I was sort of a free agent anyway. Gil and I liked each other, and I wouldn't have minded continuing on in his car. He was a nice guy.

I flew to Phoenix in late February to meet with Gary and get things rolling. Gary and Gil were both at the airport to greet me. It was a good feeling that it was such a nice transition from one team to the next.

Gary didn't have a full-time mechanic, so I was once again in charge of taking care of the race car and driving the rig. So I jumped in the truck and headed for Dallas, very eager to race after a winter's layoff.

At the motel in Texas, Doug Wolfgang came by. I think he was going to run Doug Howell's No. 4 that season. I didn't know him very well at the time, and he climbed in our car and sat for a minute or two. He was teasing me, saying that he wanted to make sure it still fit in case he needed to go back to his old ride.

"Better watch yourself, kid," he said. "'Cause if I need a ride, I'll come back and try to get this one out from under you." He was laughing, and I'm sure he was joking with me, but I have to admit it got me to thinking. Of course, that's exactly what he wanted.

That season was a time of transition for Gary. He and his fiancée Beth were in love. Gary will admit that racing was secondary to him that summer. He and Beth made it a priority to have fun and enjoy life. They had a nice motor home in which they traveled to all the races, but he was kind of laid back about life. It was actually strange, dealing with somebody who realized there was a life outside of racing.

Since I took care of the car, I had a lot of stuff to do. I was busy all the time. Gary showed up on race night to help me, but most of the maintenance was my responsibility. One day in Sioux Falls it was extremely hot, and we were rebuilding an engine in a hotel parking lot. There were parts spread out all over the place. Inside the trailer was like being in an oven.

When I'd wash the car each night I would roll it out by myself and spray it, then I'd wait till somebody else showed up at the car wash to help me push the car back in. After a while I got to the point where I enjoyed being alone in the truck, I could listen to exactly what I wanted on the radio, and stop where and when I wanted. I began to get pretty independent! Some of the other guys from other crews offered to ride along and help with the driving, but I turned them down. I actually liked being on my own again, doing my own thing.

Gary Stanton can build or create anything in a shorter time than anybody I've ever seen. In our trailer he installed a rail that went down the center, so that we could pull engines right there in the trailer. To my knowledge, he was the first guy with the Outlaws to do this. You could get the engine out, and roll it along this rail to the front of the trailer. We needed to make an engine swap at Middletown, New

York that spring, and Gary was planning on being there to help me that morning. But he and Beth went antique shopping and got sidetracked, so it was just me. I got frustrated at times, but I was never angry about it. I understood. It was his car, and his money, and he had every right to spend his time and money how he wanted. So there I was in that trailer, all by myself, pulling that engine. Kenny Woodruff came walking by, headed back to the hotel to shower. He had gotten up early to get his work done before it got hot. He poked his head in the trailer, and there I was with no shirt, sweat dripping off of me, and he said with his slow drawl, "Son, all I can say is you must really want to race." I just smiled and said, "I sure do!" Later on, I drove for Kenny, and I sometimes wondered if my working so hard had helped me get the ride.

Gil had switched to Gary's chassis late in '83, so I knew a little bit about the car. It was very simple, very straightforward, very well designed. Gary has a knack for building something that you'd look at and say, "Why didn't I think of that?" He built his own brake pedal assembly that mounted to the firewall with just two bolts. Little stuff like that made the car very simple, but so efficient.

The car was very forgiving to drive. If you could get the chassis close, the rest was easy. You didn't have to be perfect to go fast. Like any good chassis, it would adapt very well to either a slick track or a tacky track, a big track or a small track. Our car was one of the nicest looking cars I've ever driven. A guy named Corky out in Phoenix put a custom paint job on the car: pearl white with candy-apple red, yellow, and blue stripes with fancy scallops that swept back onto the tail tank. It had a light blue No. 75 on the tank, with big numerals. It was beautiful. It had a nice West Coast look, really trick.

The Outlaws were racing in Pennsylvania in late May, and Williams Grove scheduled an open competition event following the WoO race at Lincoln. Gary was going back to Phoenix for his daughter Tammy's graduation. We talked about running the Williams Grove show by myself; I wanted to go but Gary didn't particularly want me to. It didn't pay Outlaw points, but it offered a nice purse. I kept working on him and finally he agreed that I could go over there. But just as he got into his car to head for the airport, he laughed and said, "Whatever you do, don't win it, because you'll make me look bad."

I think one of the reasons he didn't want to run the show was that we hadn't exactly been setting the world on fire. We had some engine problems. In our primary engine we kept getting oil in one of our cylinders and fouling the spark plug. We didn't have a spare that was really up to par, so we kept going with our primary. We just put a hotter plug in that cylinder to try and burn the oil off.

Since Gary was back home, I didn't have any help that night at Williams Grove. I ran into Deuce Turrill, who was walking around the pits. He had just quit his job with Sammy Swindell. I said, "Hey, do you want a job for the night?" He laughed and said, "Sure!" I offered him a percentage of what we made, just like if he were working full-time for us. We rolled the car out and set the wing, and put tires on, and I don't think we changed a thing all night long.

We started toward the back because of their handicapping. The track was very rough, which was unusual for the Grove. I ran all four wheels up over the cushion, out by the fence, and started moving up. I took the lead late in the race, and just drove it home. As a driver it was so fun, because it was a driver's race track. Just get up in the rough stuff, get out by the wall where nobody was running, and "Yahoo!" it through the holes. And the caliber of cars at that time was very strong, so I felt like we had done something.

Deuce and I were pretty happy. He met me on the front straightaway and gave me a high-five. For a makeshift team with a weak motor and starting in the back, we did okay! I called Gary the next day, and I began with, "Hey, I made you look bad, because we won it!"

A few weeks later Gary and I won the WoO feature at Lernerville, giving us our first Outlaw win together. Don Martin, the track promoter, always gave the race winner a huge, huge hoagie sandwich in victory lane. We passed it around to anybody who wanted some – I think it fed half the people in the pits.

Even though Lernerville was once my home track, I hadn't had much luck there for a couple of years. Winning one in front of the home folks was very neat, very special. Steve Kinser finished second, and Sammy Swindell was third. Beating those guys at my home track was awfully nice.

Gary and I headed for Knoxville for the Nationals in early August. On the preliminary night I was running third behind Steve Kinser and Shane Carson. Coming off turn four they got together and spun. As they were spinning, I drove by them and went under the flag stand with the green still out. Going down the back straight the yellow light came on. Both those guys kept themselves going. They came up and tried to get back in front of me. No way! Knoxville used an orange Plymouth Roadrunner for the pace car that year, and I had my front wing just inches from the car's back bumper to block those guys. The pace car kept going faster and faster, it was laying over through the corners. It's a wonder that we didn't all crash in a big pile.

After many laps under yellow, they finally showed us a lineup board and put me back in third. We restarted and finished the race, Steve crossed the finish line first, followed by Shane and me. I immediately went to the office and filed a protest, because the rules clearly stated that if you cause a yellow you go to the tail. They both argued that since they didn't stop, the starter shouldn't have thrown the yellow. It was kind of comical, Steve saying that they threw the yellow for Shane, and Shane saying, no, they threw it for Steve. After further review the officials ruled that they had made a mistake, and they awarded me the win.

Steve and Shane were scored second and third. The guys behind them were probably more unhappy than anyone, because they felt like they should have scored them last. I guess they figured that since Steve and Shane kept going, they would have fallen in place in second and third. So maybe it was right.

On the final night we ran fourth in the feature event. I was getting better at Knoxville.

Right after Knoxville some of us ran the Jackson Nationals in Minnesota. It was a high-dollar event that paid something like $10,000 to the winner. Gary and I were awesome fast there, and we started out with a win on the preliminary night, so we were really optimistic. In the main event we were leading, and I was already figuring out how much money we were going to make. Toward the end of the race our engine blew up. That's what you get for counting your chickens before they're hatched.

In September we made a swing through the West. On September 14 and 15 we were at Santa Maria Speedway, where I had crashed heavily two years earlier in Sam's car. But I still liked Santa Maria. It was a small track, so traffic was an issue, a big issue. Constant lapped traffic. I was leading the feature event on the final day, and Sammy was all over me. He'd show me his nose and get under me, but I was fast enough to keep him behind me. Late in the race we came out of turn four and it seemed like the entire straightaway was filled with traffic. Going into the first corner I put three or four cars between us, and Sammy got bottled up a little bit. There were just a few laps to go, and he couldn't catch me after that. I won the event and made $6,000. More satisfying than the money, though, was beating Sammy in traffic. Man, that guy could drive traffic.

A week after Santa Maria we headed for Silver Dollar Speedway in Chico, California. The event was called the Gold Cup, and it had been a California tradition for more than 25 years. The early races were held at the quarter-mile West Capital Raceway near Sacramento, but the track was closed in 1980. Promoter John Padjen moved the Gold Cup to Chico later that fall. The Gold Cup is kind of a West Coast version of the Knoxville Nationals, because it is a big, multi-day national event with a lot of history. It is an important race that just about every driver wants to win.

Chico is a very exciting place for the fans, but it's tough on race cars. It's a tight, tacky quarter-mile track, and you just can't seem to loosen your car up enough there. We would run something like 20 to 22 inches of stagger there, which was unheard of. You bicycle, you wheelie, you turn over – that's typical Chico action. Because of that, you tend to see a lot of cars torn up there. And when everybody is really trying hard, like at the Gold Cup, it's especially tough. I'm not complaining about the track, because it's equal for everybody. I liked racing there. But when you rolled into town, you knew you were in for a tough weekend.

In 1984 the track was typically sticky and choppy, very rough. There had been something like 33 cars upside down during the course of the weekend.

We finished third in our preliminary race, and Gary and I had a really good car for the main event. Previous World of Outlaws Gold Cup events were always 40 laps, but at the last minute they decided to change this race to 50 laps. Little did I know that was going to have a big effect on my night. Before the race I was complaining to Ted Johnson that they shouldn't have lengthened the race. I wasn't the only one – most of the other guys were vocal as well.

I was leading early, and the car felt perfect. I wasn't trying to hustle the car, I just rolled easily through the corners and stood on the gas on the straightaways. Gary leaned out onto the track and spread his arms as wide as he could to signal me that I had a big lead. He also signaled me to back off, to slow down some. I flashed the "OK" sign, but I was already taking it as easy as I could. The car felt great.

I lapped quite a few cars, and I saw Sammy Swindell in front of me, running third. Steve Kinser was second, and I could see him up ahead, on the same straightaway. Man, I was pumped. I was going to win the Gold Cup.

I just rode behind Steve and Sammy, counting the laps down. There were just two laps to go when I was coming through three and four and I felt the torque tube break. The torque tube houses the driveshaft from the engine to the rear end. The instant it broke I knew we were finished. I just turned left into the infield, and coasted to a stop, turning off my fuel to stop the engine. I sat there for a second, thinking about that $10,000 that had just evaporated. I sure wish they wouldn't have added the extra 10 laps.

When the race was over Steve pulled up out of turn four and climbed out. He was looking around, saying "Where's Doty?" He thought he had finished second, he didn't even know I had broke, because we had such a big lead we were out of his sight.

Total disappointment. Actually, that word is not nearly strong enough to describe my feelings. I was crushed. The Gold Cup would have been the biggest win of my career up to that point. But what can you do? Nobody knows when a part like that is going to break, it's just the way things go in racing. But this one really hurt. People tried to console me, and I was trying hard to keep my composure. I went into the tow rig and tried to hide. After a few minutes Gary Gerould knocked on the door. Gary was the track announcer, and today is a well-known television reporter on ABC. He just came by as a friend to try to console me, to help me get through it. He had interviewed me after the race, so he knew how disappointed I was. Maybe he could tell that I was utterly devastated.

I didn't want to be a big baby in front of everybody, and I was fighting a losing battle in terms of keeping my emotions inside. Gary just sat there and listened, and helped me get through the next few minutes. After I talked to Gary a while and changed from my firesuit, I went back outside. A big crowd had gathered, and I signed some autographs and smiled with the fans.

After everyone had gone, Stanton and I loaded the car. I climbed into the tow rig and pulled from the pit area, and I was still so despondent that I needed to try and clear my head. I drove around Chico for a while, feeling pretty low. Finally in the middle of the night I found a pay phone and called Laurie. It was probably 5 a.m. back home. I just needed to talk to someone. I kept asking, "Why? Why did this thing have to break? What's the reason for this? Why did this happen to me?" It's true that I was feeling sorry for myself, but my feelings at that moment just illustrate how much I cared for all of this. Winning meant so much to me. I had only won a couple of Outlaw races that year, so to have a huge win like the Gold Cup slip away, it was just hard to accept. Sleep came very hard that night.

We headed back east to Syracuse, New York, to the big, fast one-mile track at the State Fairgrounds. Gary wasn't big on doing elaborate setups for one particular track, so we didn't change the car a lot for Syracuse. Boy, that place is so fast. When you are at speed the air wants to literally pull the helmet off your head. The car felt so good to me, with so little special preparation. That weekend was the best I ever felt at Syracuse. We ran our short track wing, which had a thick belly. The amount of dip in the top of the wing was not really for the big, fast tracks. But the package seemed to work well.

I was running third in the feature, when a lapped car and I got together coming off turn four, and I spun. In an instant I was going faster backwards than I usually run at a half-mile track. Cars were going past me at 160 mph on both sides. I was trying to keep the car straight, going backwards. I was concerned that the car would come around and dig in on the left rear and start me flipping. That would be a very bad thing at that speed. We ran very little stagger there, which helped a lot, because the car didn't want to turn so much when I was rolling backwards. But that few seconds really had my attention, let me tell you. You don't realize how fast you're going until something like that happens.

I finally got the car stopped, and restarted on the tail. We immediately started blasting through traffic. My claim to fame that day was that I actually scared Jac Haudenschild when I passed him. You don't do that very often. I was trying to get under Jac to pass him, and we were coming up on another car. The back straight is extremely narrow, especially at those speeds. I had a lot of momentum and passed Jac, but we came up on the other car so fast that I couldn't just get up behind the car and gradually move over in front of Jac. The hole just wasn't big enough. It was big enough for the width of my car, but not the length. So I pitched the car with a sharp turn to the right, which got the back end loose, and squirted in between them and made the pass. After the race Jac came up and said, "That move scared the hell out of me." Who knows, that might have been the first time in his life that he said those words! I got all the way back to third. Jeff Swindell was running second, Sammy was leading but was out of sight. I reeled Jeff in and I could see that his right rear tire was gone, just worn out. I knew I'd be able to drive by him for second, and about that time a red came out. They were able to change tires and we finished third, which was pretty good coming from the rear. I should have had second, though.

Late in 1984 we went to Ascot for the non-wing Don Peabody

Classic, which was not a World of Outlaws event. I had to run the B-main, where I finished second to Jac. Then in the A-main we both went forward, but neither of us could get the win. We had done a total of 75 laps that night, a 25-lap B and a 50-lap A. It was a cool night, but when I stopped the car after the feature I was soaked with sweat. The steam just boiled off of me – I literally had a fog rising above me. Weird! It looked like I was on fire.

We had the car going good, and the bonus was that Gary and I got along very well personally. When we were together we ran well and we had fun. It was a very good period in my career.

10

After a pretty good season in 1984, I was set to run Gary Stanton's car the following season. Gary and I had really clicked, partly because our personalities are similar. Gary doesn't get angry and scream and yell, he's more level, more even.

Gary will tell you that he isn't the type of guy that gets mad and fights, he just calmly takes his toys and goes home. And through the years he had done that. He and Ron Shuman were leading the World of Outlaws points in 1979 when they had some differences with Outlaws boss Ted Johnson. Instead of having a big war, Gary just stopped running the car in the series. It was pretty simple.

The race car had probably never made a lot of money for Gary, anyway. Since he had the chassis business, he had plenty of work to do already. It was important to have a car out on the Outlaw circuit, but most chassis companies have found over time that you don't have to have a "house car" out there to be successful.

Like most of us, though, Gary had a race car because he enjoyed it. When it got to where it wasn't fun, he would park the car for a while. You can disagree with him, but Gary doesn't expect perfection. He doesn't demand that everything has to be his way. He's a guy you can get along with. Even when we disagreed, there wasn't a big conflict. We always found a way to work it out. You knew when he was mad at you, or disappointed in you, but he didn't scream about things.

We continued on the early part of 1985 together, and we were running pretty well. But we weren't able to crack the win column at any Outlaw events. Gary's chassis business was still very successful, but there was trouble back at the shop.

Gary came to me in early July and told me that he was going to have to park the car for a while. He apparently had some personnel issues back in Phoenix, and he felt that he needed to spend all his time back there to address the situation. He was very honest with me about what was going on.

Gary's business was very important to him. It was his financial bread-and-butter, so it was only right that he needed to focus his time where it was most needed. I was disappointed, but I understood completely.

That meant I had to find a new ride, right in the middle of the season. Sometimes that can be very difficult.

We decided to run one last race together, at Paragon, Indiana. I can't remember how it happened, but I flipped down the back straightaway at Paragon and severely bent the race car. Paragon isn't a big track, but I still tore the race car up.

All this was made more difficult by the fact that I liked Gary so much. I wish we could have continued on together. But I certainly understood why he needed to go home. He was my friend, and I felt bad that he had to deal with his business issues.

At this time Kenny Woodruff was the mechanic on the No. 18 Gambler house car, one of the very best cars in the country. I had heard that he was going to talk to me about running that car. I was intimidated by the idea of working with Woodruff, because he had a reputation as a very tough guy. Bobby Davis Jr. had gone very, very well in that car, and the talk was that he was going to leave the car at the end of the season.

I wasn't sure if I wanted to get involved with the team, because I remembered the pressure that comes with a high profile, high-dollar team. At Paragon I talked with my friend Ron Shuman, asking his advice. Shuman said I'd be crazy not to give the car a try if the opportunity came up. His reasoning was that it was such a good car, there was no doubt I could win some races. Even if I ran the car for only a month, just look at the money I'd probably make. Good ol' Shuman, always looking at the bottom line.

After Paragon I went back home to Ohio. I wasn't home very long when my phone rang. Tony Wilson was the team manager for Ron Pack, a guy from Arkansas. They had a race car that had run some regional events, and they didn't run much with the Outlaws. Ron called Tony one day and said he heard Stanton had gone home, and suggested that Tony track me down and see if I'd consider driving their car. Tony said later that he laughed at that idea, because he didn't think there was any chance he could talk a World of Outlaws driver into running their car.

Maybe it was because he felt like they were too small or something, I don't know. But the fact is, my phone wasn't ringing off the hook. So when Tony tracked me down and called me, I listened to what he had to say. We talked several times over the next few days, and ironed out a deal to give his car a try. We agreed to finish out the year together, and see how it went. It was kind of a trial period for both of us. Ron Pack apparently liked to gamble, because his car number was 4a, for "Aces."

They had a Gambler car...literally. And during this period Gambler was building a very good race car. Like Stanton's, it was a simple car to work with, and if the engine was running well, you could do the rest with wing angles, shocks, and stagger. You didn't have to make a lot of major changes to make the car work. I had experience with Gambler chassis when I drove Sam's car, so I knew they made a pretty good chassis.

We hooked up for the first time on my birthday, July 27, at Eldora. We ran sixth in the feature, which was a good start. Then we won our third time out at Granite City, Illinois. We didn't run a lot of Outlaw races.

I think they might have been just a little bit intimidated to run with the Outlaws. Personally, I sure thought they had a good enough car to run that series. They ran engines from Danny's Engine Service in Memphis, which were good engines, although Danny didn't have a dyno. They were steel blocks, however, and just about everybody else was running aluminum blocks by this time.

But this was definitely a bunch of laid back, fun guys. They were good 'ol boys, with an easygoing nature and a heavy southern accent. Tony was the team manager, and he took care of all the paperwork and financial matters. I was in charge of the setup, which suited me just fine. Gary Stanton and I had worked well together and I learned a lot, so I felt like I knew enough to set the car up right. But that much authority also puts more pressure on you, because if you set it up and you drive it, who are you gonna blame when you don't win?

Bubba Harrell (you've gotta love a guy named Bubba) helped us with the car, and I can honestly say he was the most quiet, polite guy I've ever met in racing. Another young guy named Jeff helped us for a while. I rode with those guys, so we spent a lot of time together. They did the maintenance on the car, but I didn't mind pitching in to help them when I was caught up on my stuff.

When I settled on driving their car we agreed to try and run some of the bigger races. I wanted to run as many of the Outlaw races as I could, but we didn't run exclusively with any series. Those guys were kind of in awe about this whole thing, being on the road and having an Outlaw driver in their car. But we were all just a bunch of racers once we got to know each other.

During a trip out west we had some time off, and we visited the Spruce Goose airplane and the Queen Mary ship, both in Long Beach, California. These guys were wide-eyed, and it seemed like it was their first time to the big city. I understood exactly, because that had been me just a couple of years before.

They were always "fixin'" to do something. One night after racing at Eldora we got a motel room, all four of us sharing a room. Ed Haudenschild and his wife Tammy came by, and we ordered pizza. We were just sitting around, and Jeff began rooting around in his suitcase. I said, "Jeff, what are you doing?" He said with his slow drawl, "I'm fixin' to take a shower." I grabbed my stuff and said, "While you're fixin' to, I'm doin!" I dashed to the bathroom and got there before he did, and closed and locked the door. He banged on the door and said, "Hey, I was first!" I just laughed and said, "Nope, you were just fixin' to. I was doin'." After that it was always a running joke, every time they'd use the word I'd say, "Don't just be fixin' to. Be doin'."

After a few weeks together, we had the car going pretty well. We won at Farmington, Missouri in early August, although our steering was messed up. We then traveled to I-70 Speedway for the Jerry Weld Memorial. Since we didn't have a spare, I borrowed a steering box from Doug Wolfgang. Doug was running Bob Weikert's car at this time, and he had been very successful, to say the least. Davey Brown Sr. and Jr. were working on the car. I won the feature that night, and Doug finished second. It was sure nice of him to loan me that steering box! When I took it down there all three of them were teasing me, saying, "Now don't ask to borrow anything again, okay?"

Right after that we went to Knoxville for the Nationals. By then I had run the Nationals a few times, and I understood the meaning of this huge event. It was really growing during this period, and it was already a big deal. The Nationals were very, very special. We usually stayed in Des Moines and drove back and forth each night. There was just the one motel in Knoxville at that time, so lodging was tight even then.

When I was racing I didn't party or enjoy the Knoxville nightlife. With four nights of racing, driving back and forth to the motel, and maintaining the car, I don't know where anybody found the energy to party. The heat alone would wear you down. The fans and the people that can sleep till noon, they must have been the guys doing the partying. Maybe in the old days it was fun for the racers, but it was pretty intense by this time. With the intensity, and big purse, you kind of lose the fun aspect of it. That's just the way it is. But then again, maybe I was just too serious. I looked at it like a business. It was my livelihood. Maybe I should have had more fun with it.

We had trouble on our preliminary night, and we didn't qualify for Saturday's A-main. So we were behind the 8-ball, right off the bat. We won the non-qualifiers race on Friday, though.

Saturday night we were scheduled to start in the middle of the C-main. We had our work cut out for us. I knew we had a slim chance of making the A. Our team was already an underdog with that steel motor, and we weren't a high-dollar team compared to the top guys. A guy named Steve Wolph from Lincoln, Nebraska was in our pit stall when we unloaded that night, and he joked with me about how green and inexperienced we were.

I started in the middle of the C and we won it pretty easily. Ronnie Daniels was second, and Tim Green was in third, very disappointed because he was one spot out of the transfer. I know what that heartbreak feels like, although I always did make it at Knoxville.

You've got to be careful coming through preliminary races like that, but you have to be very aggressive. Don't take yourself out, but don't wait one minute. You've got to make every lap count. You've got to really focus and keep your mind sharp. As the laps were winding down, Steve asked my crew if they had tires and fuel ready. They kind of looked at him and said, "Do you think we'll need 'em?" They scrambled around and got tires mounted and things, and when I came in after the C they were ready for me. We didn't have a lot of time before they started the B, so we had to thrash.

I started dead last in the B, and I knew I was up against tougher guys, guys that could win a feature anywhere else in the country. Everybody's heard that old cliché; "You don't win a race on the first lap." To be honest, I always thought that was a bunch of baloney. To a certain extent, anyway. In our sport you have to get a strong surge at the start and pass as many cars as you can right away, before they get strung out. I've done it, and other guys have done it, but sometimes you have to go to the high side and sweep past a bunch of cars on the start. If you can't get a lot done on the first lap, you're not gonna do it, period. I passed several cars on that first lap, and that was the surge I needed. But it started to rain before very long, and they stopped the race.

I wasn't far enough forward, so I hoped that they wouldn't call the race. It stopped raining and we got restarted, but the rain had changed the track a lot. We loosened the car up during the delay, but it was a guessing game. It was very nerve-wracking. I was afraid I wasn't going to be able to pass. But the car worked enough to pass some cars, I moved into the transfer position with four laps to go, and then took the lead with two laps to go. It was me and the motor, neither one of us breathing much. Every lap, every corner, every pass is critical. You hope for the right yellows, and you have to have some luck.

158

I took the checkered and came around to victory lane, and I pulled up and shut the car off. Boy, the crowd was noisy. At Knoxville people seem to pick an underdog from the preliminary races and root him on. I was the guy that year. Of course, it would have been better to already be qualified, but this was the next best thing. Tony and the crew were so excited about winning the race that once again they forgot to get tires and fuel ready, and Steve reminded them and we were again at full scramble. We had a few minutes to get ready for the main, and I had a chance to catch my breath and get a drink of water. Plus, let the car rest a little bit.

It's nights like that when you feel like you develop a personal attachment to your car. You kind of bond, even though you know it's just a machine. When you do something like this, you just feel like there is something special there, that you owe a debt to that car. I was never really big on that, but I felt that way on that night. Without that race car, I would have been a nobody.

There were heavy hitters that didn't make it out of the B. Jack Hewitt, Robby Unser, Billy Boat, Charlie Fisher, Danny Smith, Terry Gray, and Terry McCarl all missed the show. You know, even while I was elated to win the race, I felt genuinely bad for those guys. Heartache is a big part of racing. But, on the other hand, you are so focused on your job that you don't take much time to think about other guys.

I started the A-main on the tail, but our car was still pretty good. Dave Blaney finished fifth, and I was closing on him at the end of the race. Doggone it, I really thought I could catch him. I just ran out of laps. I wanted at least a top-five finish, and I came close. Wolfgang won it; he was so fast that he lapped me. Sixth place wasn't bad under the circumstances, but I felt like I had one more position in me. I wasn't really disappointed, though, because it had been a great night. Like the saying goes, they knew we were there. And those trophies are still among my most prized possessions.

From Knoxville we followed the World of Outlaws out west, where we finished second and fourth at Baylands in a two-day show.

We finished third at Petaluma, which is one of the smallest race tracks that you could ever run. The cars hooked up so tight you'd wheelie all night. We just couldn't keep our front end on the ground. There was a red flag later in the race and during the delay Tony took great big clods of mud and packed them around the front of the car to try and get weight on the front end. We ended up running third, so it must have helped.

At Santa Maria we went from 13th to eighth and 14th to sixth on both days of their two-day event. At Chico we started 19th and finished fourth in the prelim, and went from 21st to fourth in the finale. If I could just start toward the front! We ran fifth at San Jose, and ran fourth at Knoxville for the Outlaw finale in early October.

From there we went to Little Rock, Ron Pack's hometown. He had a bunch of friends and business people there for the two-day open competition show at I-30 Speedway. We came from 11th to win on the first night, and then in the final we won it from 12th. So we were definitely able to make the car go forward.

Our last race together was at Baylands for an open competition show that attracted most of the Outlaws. We ran fourth both nights.

It was during the late 1985 California swing that I finally talked to Kenny Woodruff about running the Gambler house car in 1986. Quentin Bammer owned Moeller Brothers Body Shop in California, and he owned the No. 18. Gil Suiter owned the car in 1984, then Quentin bought it and ran the car in 1985. They had a nice big shiny yellow rig, and they were one of the top teams that year. Bobby Davis had been in the car for a long time, and had been very successful. But it sounded like everybody felt like it was time for a change. Two or three years together in this business, and everybody gets stale. That's the nature of the beast. And it's the same for everybody: drivers, car owners, mechanics, even sponsors. There needs to be a little rotation because everybody wears each other out.

I liked running Ron Pack's car, and I really liked working with Tony, Bubba, and Jeff. But from a career standpoint, I couldn't pass up the chance to get into the No. 18. I mean, this was clearly one of the top race cars in the country. So even though we had been successful, I knew I was going to be leaving Ron's car. They were disappointed, but they seemed to understand. We parted on good terms.

Later on Tony began to build race cars, and today does some driving himself. I'm proud that he tells me that years after we worked together he still uses stuff that I had taught him. That makes me feel good that I had a positive influence on someone.

I was very nervous about getting in the No. 18. Bobby had enjoyed great success, and it was tough to try and fill his shoes. Plus, I wasn't sure if I could work with Woodruff, I had heard that he could be tough and gruff. But we raced together at the Gary Patterson Memorial, which was Bayland's season finale. And it seemed like Kenny and I got along just fine.

But in the off season that followed, Kenny received some distressing news. As it turned out, he was going to assume a lot more responsibility than he had the previous season.

11

Of all the cars on the World of Outlaws circuit, probably none were as high profile as the No. 18 Gambler house car. The car had a history that dated back almost to the start of the series in 1978, and everybody knew that it was one of the fastest cars in the country.

Gambler has built a lot of chassis over the years, and early on the company decided that they wanted one of their cars to be very visible on the WoO circuit. C.K. Spurlock is the guy who owned Gambler, and the race team, and he was a high-profile guy himself.

C.K. was the road manager for Kenny Rogers, the country star. Somehow Kenny got involved, because his name was on the car. This was in the very early 1980s, during some of Kenny's peak years as a star. He was very famous, and a lot of people were excited that his name was on a sprint car. Danny Smith drove their car at the time.

After Danny left the ride, the team hired Bobby Davis Jr. Bobby did very well with the car, and in 1984 they finished third in the World of Outlaws points behind Steve Kinser and Sammy Swindell. One year later they were second in the final standings.

So this was obviously a car that could run well. Although Gambler sponsored the car, by then C.K. no longer owned the team. When I got involved Quentin Bammer was the car owner. Although Kenny Woodruff actually hired me, Quentin was the car owner.

After the Baylands run that previous fall Kenny and I shook hands to work together in 1986. I thought I had hit the lottery: the Gambler house car, Kenny Woodruff, Bammer paying the bills, and Coors Light sponsorship.

The car had run really well in the past, so naturally I felt a lot of pressure. I didn't want to look bad. Who would?

Even though I had won races by this stage in my career, I still had a lot of self-doubt. I always questioned myself. But the only way to know for sure was to run the car and see how I'd do. It was surely an opportunity that I couldn't turn down.

During the winter, though, Quentin was going through a divorce. He let Kenny know that he didn't plan on running the car that next summer, because he obviously had a lot of things going on and certainly didn't need to worry about the race car.

But when Kenny told me about Quentin's situation, I thought I was going to be out of a ride before I'd even gotten started. But Kenny reassured me. He said he had promised me a ride and he was working on finding a way to provide it. He told me that he was going to try to proceed as the car owner. I didn't mind that, because he definitely knew how to make the car go. The only question was financial. Kenny wasn't a rich guy, and it's very scary to think about the financial risk you assume when you're trying to keep an expensive race car going. But he was optimistic, because with Gambler and Coors on as sponsors, we should be able to make it. I was optimistic, too.

Kenny spent much of that winter in Tennessee at the Gambler shop, getting the cars ready. I came down once or twice during the winter, but Kenny did nearly all of the preparation.

I spent the winter chopping firewood and enjoying time at home. It was nice, staying home and relaxing with Laurie and Brandy. It was one of the few times in my career that I didn't have a race shop nearby, and I didn't have any responsibilities to help with the car at all.

We lived in a home in the woods, and we supplemented our propane furnace with a wood-burning stove in our basement. To stay in shape I cut and chopped firewood. It was cold, but I could still work up a good sweat. I enjoyed being at home, relaxing.

Kenny and I both figured that the Coors money could help us keep the car going. But it turned out that there was a lot of mystery surrounding that money. We quickly found out that not all the money was coming to us. It was a very mixed-up deal. I eventually got stuck for some appearance fees that I had been promised, and I never saw a dime. The deal had been put together by a third party, and it was constantly a question of where the money was going and who was supposed to do what. Coors said they sent the money to the third party, and it was our responsibility to chase it from there.

That whole episode turned out to be one of the most aggravating and frustrating in my life. I don't blame the Coors people – they paid the money and fulfilled their obligations. To this day I still have a really good relationship with Coors, they have been very good to me. But all of the money didn't filter down to the team, and that made it very tough on us because Kenny needed that money to keep the car going. There just seemed to be lots of people with their hand out, and when the pie got to us the slices were just about gone.

Coors also sponsored Steve and Karl Kinser. A lot of people through the years figured we were teammates, but that wasn't the case. Karl always owned his own car. We were competitors, just like all the other guys, even though we both had the Coors name on our cars.

We went to Florida in February for the All Star races. At that time they didn't allow aluminum engines, so we had to put a steel-block engine in the car. We only had one steel motor, and that turned out to be a problem. We won the first race, but on the last lap we burned a piston. Without a spare, I headed back to Ohio.

I had just enough time at home to load our motor home for the first swing of the World of Outlaws season, which was set for February 22 at Ascot Park in Gardena, California.

Kenny kept the car at the Gambler shop in Hendersonville. He actually lived in Sacramento. What an arrangement: He lived in Tennessee in the winter, then traveled all summer with the race car. Man, he paid the price in terms of being away from home.

On the first day of the Ascot opener I came up on a lapped car and he moved over in front of me. I ran over his wheel, and my car just launched like a rocket, flipping along. It tore the car up, but we managed to thrash around and get the car fixed for the second day, and we finished sixth.

A few days after Ascot we ran Kings Speedway in Hanford. Sammy beat us fair and square that day, but he was disqualified because his muffler had fallen off. I climbed out of the car thinking we had finished second.

Sammy was not going to get paid for first, or get the points, and they gave me the trophy. Sammy came over and asked if he could at least have the trophy. I kind of debated, and I decided to keep the trophy. Maybe I should have given it to him, but in hindsight I'm glad I kept it. It's the tallest trophy I have. All my trophies have meant a lot to me over the years.

We qualified third and won our heat at Devil's Bowl on March 8, then finished second in the main. We came back a day later and finished fifth.

We finished third at Oklahoma City on March 16, then qualified second, won our heat, and finished fourth at Lanier, Georgia on April 4. We came back to finish second there the next day. We ran third at Granite City, Illinois on April 11. But the following day we blew the motor, and didn't start the feature.

I won the dash that day, and during the race the crankshaft broke. The engine was rattling big time, so I shut it off. I tried to tell Kenny what kind of a sound it was making and I just couldn't quite describe it to him. He finally said, "Well, let's start it up so I can hear it." I kind of winced and asked him if he was sure, and he said, "Yeah, let's see what it's doing."

We refired it and it made a very big noise. And it wasn't a healthy noise. So that engine was done, it wiped the block out and everything.

Kenny and I both knew that we couldn't crash a lot or hurt a lot of engines, or we would have been finished. Ron Shaver was building our engines, and I'm sure he went out of his way to try and help us. He and Kenny had a really good friendship.

I had always heard that Kenny was a gruff, tough character, but we hit it off right away. I liked him. Naturally, we had some disagreements, but it was never a big deal. I never felt like we had any big issues. I'm sure there were nights that he wasn't happy with me, or I wasn't happy with the setup, but we didn't really have the tension that I expected. We seemed to develop a mutual respect.

I always believed in keeping my family away from the race car, because I didn't want the team to feel like I was allowing my personal life to interfere with my focus on racing. You have to understand that a lot of mechanics and car owners sneer at race drivers, and make fun that they aren't really very committed to the team. You know, they just show up and drive the car, screw things up, then they go home. This was a time when motor homes were still pretty rare, so a lot of guys didn't have their families with them.

Laurie and I felt that women, kids, and race cars didn't mix. When she was pregnant for Brandy, we were afraid to tell Sam Bowers because we were afraid I'd get fired. We thought maybe he would feel like my focus wouldn't be on the race car. Of course, Sam didn't do any such thing, but that was my perception.

That season with Kenny, I had a motor home and Laurie and Brandy traveled with me. I wondered if Kenny would resent them being along. As it turned out, it was just the opposite.

Kenny became fairly close to my family, and he liked to joke with Laurie and Brandy. It was surprising, I thought, because here was this guy with a gruff, tough reputation who was like a teddy bear around Laurie and Brandy. I sometimes wondered if maybe Kenny felt good being around kids, since he had spent so much time away from home all those years.

Sometimes he was full of surprises. We were headed for Eldora one afternoon, and we had just gotten off I-70, headed north on Ohio 127. I was following the tow rig in my motor home.

All of a sudden the tow rig slowed down and pulled off on the side of the road. Kenny came walking back with that serious expression, and I figured the tow rig must have broken down. I rolled my window down, and Kenny walked up to my door.

"Hey, Brandy, how about you riding with me for a while?" he said. Brandy kind of cuddled up to her mom, acting shy, and Kenny said, "Well, there's an ice cream place up the road a little bit, let's go up there and get some ice cream."

Well, Brandy thought that sounded all right, so she went to Kenny, and he carried her to the truck, and off we went to the ice cream stand. I was amazed, I must admit. Here was gruff, tough Kenny Woodruff, in a role that I had never even imagined.

We stopped for ice cream, then headed on up the road. After a mile or two the tow rig stopped again, and here comes Kenny carrying Brandy back to our motor home.

"Well, she used me," he laughed. "She's had her ice cream, and now she wants to ride with mom and dad again." That was a nice memory, and I still smile when I think about it today.

I was really pleased that Kenny would listen to my input on the setup. He wanted my suggestions. He had the final say, but it was an open discussion. He tried hard to give me a car that I was happy with.

The thing about Kenny is that he is very meticulous, and he keeps things neat and organized. Look at any deal he's been involved in, and you'll see that it's well organized and clean. He is a professional. As a race driver, that's a big, big deal. You can look around at your surroundings, and if things are clean and well maintained, you think, "Well, a wheel is probably not going to fall off this thing."

We headed for Knoxville in April, where we won our heat and finished second in the preliminary feature. We came back the next day to run fifth. On May 9 we were at Santa Fe Speedway in Chicago, and we qualified second and won our heat, then finished fourth in the feature. But we blew the engine the next day at the Indiana State Fairgrounds. We were rained out at Eldora on May 18, then went to Lernerville on May 21, where we crashed. Things weren't going all that well, and they were about to get worse.

We went to Williams Grove the day after the Lernerville event, and it was a day that nearly cost me an eye. We were running down the front straight, and something flipped up and knocked my visor open. Before I could get the visor back down another object hit me directly in my left eyeball.

Whenever you crash, you know it's coming. There's a split second where you know something bad is going to happen. But in this case there was no warning of any kind, just...shock. And pain.

Try to imagine having somebody hitting you as hard as they can with a ball peen hammer right in the eyeball. That's a pretty accurate description.

It was probably a rock, or maybe a clod of dirt. Whatever it was, it was big enough to instantly break my nose and eye socket. We were running along at 120 m.p.h., and when it hit I didn't feel the pain for maybe a second. But it just knocked me silly; I lost my bearings for an instant. I lifted off the throttle, and blood was spraying everywhere. My helmet, my fire suit, the cockpit, it looked like somebody had used a spray can.

The blood got in my right eye as well. So I was completely blinded, and I rolled to a stop in turn one. It looked like the car had just broke, so nobody was in a hurry to get to me. I sat up there, and they threw the yellow. When the track was clear somebody ran up to the car, and I heard them scream, "My God, my God, get an ambulance."

I thought to myself, "Oh, shit, this isn't good. How bad is this, and what has happened to me?" By then, the pain was very intense, just indescribable.

They threw the red and got an ambulance to me. I didn't really know what had happened. I never lost consciousness, although I wished that I had, because that would have spared me some of the pain.

They got me out of the car and loaded me into the ambulance. It had been a rough night. Larry Christie was a WoO official at that time, and he had been hit by a car in the pits earlier and broke both his legs.

Richard Brown helped on our race car, and he borrowed somebody's passenger car real quickly and took Laurie to the hospital. He tried to keep her calm by telling her, "Oh, he probably just needs a couple of stitches."

The hospital was very busy that night. I laid on the gurney for three hours, and I kept trying to sit up. I was swallowing blood because of my broken nose, and I tried to tell the nurses that I was going to be sick. I finally threw up and made a huge mess all over the room.

My eyeball swelled up the size of a baseball. My nose was laying off to the side, and my cheek was broken, with my eye sticking out of my socket. That night I got up at about 4 a.m. to go to the bathroom, and I glanced at the mirror. What a mess. I was so shocked I was dizzy. It took my breath away. The eyelid was shut, but the eyeball was so big it looked like someone had popped a baseball under my eyelid. I wasn't able to sleep all night because of the pain. They gave me some medication but it didn't help much.

They contacted my family doctor at home, and they agreed to release me if I promised to go to my doctor back in Orrville. That was the condition. They couldn't observe the eyeball until the swelling had gone down, anyway.

Kenny drove our motor home to the hospital to pick me up. When I walked out of the hospital he literally did a double take, and it looked like he was going to cry.

As Richard drove us back to Ohio, I had six hours to think about my career, and wonder if I was finished. I kept trying to force my eyelid open, not with my fingers but with my facial muscles. Laurie really got after me to stop. Finally, after about four hours it opened just a tiny, tiny crack. I could see Laurie. She was fuzzy and blurred, but I could see her. I knew I wasn't totally blind, which meant I could probably continue racing. She looked beautiful.

My doctor told me that we'd have to wait and see before we knew much. I waited four or five days before I had my nose looked at by a specialist. He was immediately angry that they hadn't treated my broken nose earlier, because it had started to heal improperly. So he had a lot of work to do, including surgery.

After the surgery I saw the doctor and he pulled the packing out of my nose, and it was very, very painful. It felt like pulling a golf ball through a garden hose. I yelled so loud, they could hear me in the waiting room.

In the days following the surgery I kept having this intense pain in my chest. They finally figured out that while I was in surgery they had accidentally over-inflated my lungs with the respirator. It stretched my lung tissue, and that was causing the pain. The whole thing turned into a big mess.

They made a plaster cast that set my nose, and it was taped and stuck to my skin along my face. They reinforced it with surgical tape.

But the important thing was my eye, and it was coming back. I wanted to race the next weekend, so Simpson built me an oversized helmet with extra padding, and I was going to try to race.

I returned to racing in the Nichols Brothers car at Fremont on June 7 at an All Star race. I ran second in my heat, but the feature was rained out. I felt pretty good in the car, though.

I rejoined the World of Outlaws at I-70 on June 11. Danny Smith had driven the car for a few races while I was out. I finished third in the feature, and that was a big relief. I was grateful to be racing again. And I finally made some money! I had been off for a few weeks, and that's scary when you race for a living. It seemed like I had gone forever without a paycheck.

Although everything came out okay, I still have some slight problems with my left eye. If I close my right eye and try to focus sharply on something with my left eye, I notice a little difference in vertical lines. But my vision is back to 20/15, which is way better than average.

Through all of this stuff Kenny was having a hard time keeping the car going. Money was extremely tight. We finally sat down at Lincoln, Nebraska in late June to talk about things.

There were some changes coming. Les Kepler and Fred Marks had been running a car on the WoO circuit with Jimmy Sills driving, a red No. 9. They split with Sills at Oklahoma City on June 22. I ran into Jimmy that night at the hotel parking lot and he told me he had just been fired.

As it turns out, there had been some discussion about what Gambler wanted to do as far as their house car. They told Kenny that if he didn't want to continue, they could move the Coors paint over to the Marks & Kepler car, and that I could move over there as the driver if I wanted to.

At Lincoln Kenny sat me down and told me about all this. I felt really bad for Kenny, because at that time in our season it's tough to adjust to changes like this. I was uncertain about what I wanted to do.

While Kenny and I sat there we made some phone calls, and one of the calls was between Les Kepler and me. I told him that I needed a couple of days to think about it, and I wanted to go home for a couple of days. The Outlaws were off that week. Les was very supportive, very willing to give me a few days to think it over.

After the phone call Kenny and I stood up and shook hands. It was an empty feeling, and I didn't like that moment at all. We kind of looked at each other, not knowing what to say.

The schedule picked up at Colorado National Speedway in Erie, Colorado on July 2. I had the flu, and I still wasn't sure I wanted the ride. I was actually thinking about maybe running closer to home, so I wasn't sure what I wanted.

I called Les and told him I was sick, and that I needed a little more time. But he felt like they were in a bind, and he talked me into taking the trip. I thought I was going to puke on the airplane, I felt so rotten. Laurie stayed home.

When I got to the motel they were still switching body panels, getting the Coors signage done. We qualified eighth and ran fifth, then the next night we qualified first and ran seventh.

They had Jimmy Thorpe working on the car, and he had a guy named Bob "Cowboy" Carter helping him. Fred Marks' son Dave also helped out on the car. They all seemed like good guys, so it looked like this deal was going to be all right.

Change. It never stops coming. I now had a new car owner.

12

Fred Marks and Les Kepler had raced against us for some time, with Jimmy Sills driving their car. I knew they had good equipment. I felt comfortable that they could give me a car that could win. Fred and Les were real estate developers and builders in California. They built a lot of subdivisions, laid out the streets and built the homes. The general feeling was that these guys had some money.

Les was the more assertive of the two. Fred was more laid-back, more calm. Sometimes I didn't understand their relationship, because even though they maintained their friendship for a lot of years, it seemed like they argued and fought a lot. Les' wife Susie was a very nice, kind person, and sometimes when Les was hard to get along with Susie was the unofficial mediator. Everybody liked Susie. Everybody liked Fred's wife, Bobbie, too.

Fred and Les had survived a plane crash in Mexico a few years before they got involved in racing. That was kind of a catalyst, because they vowed to stop working so hard and to have fun with life. So they bought a race car. Some fun! They raced around California for a couple of years before they started following the World of Outlaws.

All in all, I was optimistic. And happy to have a ride, because you always fear being out of work during the middle of the season. Even though I felt bad for Kenny Woodruff, I knew he'd be okay. I knew he wouldn't be out of a job for long, because the guy is a talented mechanic.

Jimmy Thorpe was very meticulous, and he was an excellent welder. Sometimes, though, Jimmy was hesitant to use duct tape and bailing wire to get the car together, because he wanted it to be perfect. I remember once we were thrashing to get the car going, and he spent a lot of time trying to get something to fit just right. Finally I said, "Man, just stick it on there, we've gotta go!" But we got along great. He was a really nice guy. Later on he started his own very successful welding business.

We ran pretty well together, we had a lot of top-five finishes. Actually, though, we were going about the same as Kenny and I had gone.

During this time Laurie and I were expecting our second child. She was at home, waiting on her due date of July 18. We raced at Kokomo, Indiana on July 20, then I hurried home. We went to the hospital the evening of July 21. She had experienced labor pains that day, so it looked like it was time. But the hospital said she wasn't that close, so they sent her home. But she was certain that it was time. So we sat in our car in the parking lot for a few hours, listening to the radio.

At 11 p.m. that night we walked back into the hospital. Now we were ready. They put us in a birthing room, and it had a big recliner, and I sat in that recliner and fell right to sleep. While Laurie was lying there suffering, I was snoozing. She's still mad at me about that. Finally when the time was at hand, one of the nurses kicked my recliner to wake me up, telling me that I might want to pay attention while we had this baby. At 5:40 a.m. on July 22 Braden Lee was born, and I had a son. I was becoming a regular family man. I wasn't sure I was ready for the first one, and now we had two!

On August 4 Jac's uncle, Dick Edwards, promoted an All Star race at Buckeye Speedway (now Wayne County Speedway), and they asked me to come. J.W. Hunt put up $1,000 for a special dash between Jac, Kenny Jacobs, Jack Hewitt, and myself. You always want to do well in front of your hometown people. I had never had much success at Buckeye, though. But on this night we set fast time, won our heat, won the dash, and won the feature. We hauled just over $5,000 out of there. It was a great night for me, winning at home like that.

J.W. Hunt was a neat guy. He owned a strawberry operation in Florida, and he was apparently very wealthy. He was just a big, friendly sprint car fan. He'd show up at the track with a wad of money and a big smile, and he usually gave away both. He made everybody around him feel good. He would put up extra money for races, or help a guy that was down on his luck. He helped a lot of people through the years, that's for sure. He died a few years ago, and I don't think the sport will ever see anybody quite like him again.

I had a few days before we went to Knoxville for the 1986 Nationals. I ran second in the heat and won our qualifying feature on Friday. I was feeling very confident, I felt like this was one I could win. Rain washed out the non-qualifiers features, so they did that program on Saturday afternoon. They reworked the track that evening and we were pretty late getting started for the final event.

During the practice before the main event our birdcage broke, so we had to replace it very quickly, while they were running the B-main. The birdcage is part of the rear suspension, and when it breaks you've got to replace it. To change the birdcage you had to move the weight bolts, and when we put it back together the weight bolts didn't get put back in place. As soon as we fired the car and lined up for the main event, I could feel that something was bad wrong with the car. If I pulled in I'd have to restart on the tail, so I just tried to drive the car and hang in for the best finish I could. We came home eighth, and I was very disappointed.

Right after that we towed all the way back across the country to race at Syracuse. Then it was all the way back to California for the last three races of the season. That kind of scheduling just drove us crazy, because it was just stupid. All the way across the country, for one race, then all the way back.

Of course, we all bitched about it, but the funny thing was, we all made the trip. That's an example of how you get so caught up in the thing that you feel left out if you don't stick with it. You feel like everyone is leaving you behind.

The Pacific Coast Nationals at Ascot Park was new to our schedule that year, and it would be the last race of our season. That was a big race; it had a long history before the Outlaws came along. It had always been held without wings, but in 1986 with the Outlaws sanction it was now a winged event.

Bobby Davis Jr. and I had a heck of a race that night. We swapped the lead back and forth, maybe three or four times in two laps. We were really racing hard. Our car was good, and I really wanted to win this race. When you pass somebody and they pass you right back, it usually means that your cars are equal, and it's up to you as a driver to make the difference.

I could pass Bobby, but it was tough to keep him behind me. Finally I changed my line just a little bit and that helped, because after that I stayed out front. Naturally, I was worried about breaking, but I tried not to think about it. I just focused on driving the race car.

When I took the checkered flag, it was euphoria. That was the biggest win of my career. The money, the prestige, the history, it was a tremendous package. We won over $10,000, along with a new aluminum block, and a wheelbarrow full of merchandise. It seemed like it took a half-hour to give us all of our winnings in the victory circle. Ascot always had a big production at their victory circle, with pretty trophy girls and a big podium.

What a great way to close out the season. I went into the winter months on an all-time high. That kind of thing motivates everybody, from the drivers to the crew members. They maintained the car out in California, so I was able to go home to Ohio and not worry about working on the race car. So it was another winter of cutting wood and enjoying life at home.

During the winter Jim Thorpe left the team, and they hired Kelly Pryor to work on the car. Kelly worked really hard and did a great job keeping the car together. Sometimes I felt bad because he got caught up in the pressures of the team and got his butt chewed for things that weren't really his fault.

A guy from Pennsylvania named Andy Preist rode with us for a couple of months, a guy who worked hard for little or no pay. We always had plenty of people to help with the car, that was never a problem. There was always somebody willing to hop in the truck and ride along.

We opened the 1987 season back at Ascot on February 21 and 22 with a couple of daytime shows. The track got hard and dry both days, almost like asphalt. That's tough on tires, and guys were blowing tires right and left. You have to change your style a lot on a track like that, you've got to keep the car straight and be smooth. We won the opening day race after a really good duel with Johnny Herrera, who was just a kid at the time, driving his dad Joe's car.

There was a controversial new development in sprint car racing at this time. Gambler had created a driveline setup that employed CV joints and a torque arm instead of a torque tube. The setup used an open driveshaft running through the cockpit to the rear end. The problem was that the CV joints would break, and that was like having a sledgehammer with you in an 8000-rpm washing machine. Very dangerous. Several guys had broken legs caused by CV joint failures within the first couple of weeks. Kenny Jacobs had his leg almost torn off from a driveshaft. I saw that incident, and it was very scary.

After we won on the first day at Ascot, when I stopped on the front straightaway our right side torque arm was broken in half, and the left was cracked about halfway through. My shoes were covered in grease from the CV joint that was burning up. They covered up the broken torque arm with a coat, and as I walked to the podium for the victory celebration I told Les that I wanted the CV joint setup out of the car.

Obviously, I was concerned about getting my legs mangled. That first day at Ascot a couple more guys got hurt that way.

Right after the race, several people walked up to the car and asked to see the torque arm setup on our car. "Cowboy" Bob Carter told them it was still a secret development deal, and that he had to keep it covered up. Jerry Bryant, who was the General Manager at Gambler at the time, walked up and asked Bob why he had the torque arm covered up. Bob lifted the coat and showed him, and said, "That's why." Jerry was shocked.

Les didn't really want to take the CV joints out of the car. He felt like they kept the thing maintained, and that it wouldn't break again. We argued and talked through that evening and the next morning. Finally, at the track, Les agreed, and he walked over to Kelly Pryor and Cowboy Bob and said, "My driver doesn't think it (torque arm) is very safe, so get it out of there."

So Kelly and Bob started taking it out, and Jerry came up and told them that if they took the torque arm out, they would never work on a sprint car again. Remember, Gambler had thousands of dollars of these CV joints and torque arms sitting on the shelves back in Tennessee. How was it going to look if their house car wouldn't even run them?

That set up a very interesting conversation between Les and Jerry, to say the least. They walked off as they were arguing about who was really the car owner, and who was the sponsor. The bottom line was that Kelly and Bob kept working, and we put the old torque tube back on for Saturday's Ascot finale.

When I rolled out for the finale, I felt like my ass was really on the line. After forcing the issue on those CV joints, if we went out and didn't run well I was probably going to get fired. But it turned out that changing back to the torque tube didn't hurt us at all.

On the second day I drove the car the same way I had the day before. I could lift the front end in a wheelie almost all the way down the straightaway. I would lift off the throttle to set the front end down, then smoke the tires through the corner. I was leading the race with just a couple of laps left when the yellow came out. Tires were still a problem on the hard race track, so I pulled the rock shield back a little bit to look at the right rear tire. I saw the cords showing on the tire, so I knew this one was gonna be close. I just hoped the tire wouldn't go flat. We got the green, then took the white flag, and then saw the caution flag again. I was very anxious, and when we re-started I was hoping we could just hang on. We won the race, then pulled up in victory lane for another $10,000 celebration. Ascot was turning into my favorite race track!

While we were celebrating, the tire went flat. Sometimes you just need a break.

After that, you didn't see much of the open driveline any more. We proved that you could still win on a dry slick track with a torque tube setup, so there weren't any advantages to the CV joint setup. In terms of driver safety, the open driveline was just a bad idea.

We were really starting to run well together. We had lots of seconds and thirds, and we won again at I-55 Speedway in April.

Since this was still the Gambler house car, we had a deal to get all the good stuff. Every so often we put new cars together, and Gambler sold our older ones. We had very good equipment. At that time Gambler was the car to beat.

For a driver, that's pretty important. It helps you with your confidence, because you figure that equipment is not going to be an issue. There are also no excuses, because you can't complain that somebody has more equipment than you do.

On July 17 we won the feature at Santa Fe Speedway after a real battle with Steve Kinser. I led the race early, and it looked like we were in line for another win. Santa Fe was a little quarter-mile track, and it seems like you're in traffic all the time. With just a couple of laps left I came out of turn two and there were three lapped cars, running three-wide. I stood on the brakes to try to keep from hitting them, and Steve caught me.

He showed me his nose; I was running the top. He almost put a slide job on me, but he wasn't far enough forward to steal my line. I slipped between him and the wall, and took the lead for good on the last corner of the last lap. I had been tempted to move to the bottom to try and block him, but I stayed on top and that worked.

The next day I won the feature at Martin, Michigan at U.S. 131 Speedway. There were lots of rocks in the track, and several guys got parked because rocks were breaking things on the cars. There were dents in the roll cage tubing, and holes through wings. We won the first night, and the second night nobody wanted to run because of the rocks, and they canceled the show.

We went to Hawkeye Downs Speedway in Cedar Rapids, Iowa for a non-sanctioned race on July 21. The event was sponsored by Coors Light. The local beer distributorship had set up a big promotion that weekend. That's when Coors sponsored both Steve and me.

The night started off with Les Kepler making a complete ass of himself when we pulled in. It was early, but right on the frontstretch a security guy pointed where he wanted us to park in the infield. Les got out of the truck, and was screaming at the guy, using bad language, right in front of the few people who were already there. He didn't want to park back there, and he was really giving the guy a bad time. Les could be like that. When he decided to raise hell, he went at it with both barrels.

During the race, Steve Kinser and I were running hard for the lead on a restart, and he slipped over the cushion. I could see he was losing it, and I went for the inside line. Well, he saved it and came down off the high groove, and it looked like I was going to ram into his side. I did everything but spin the car to avoid him, really turned the car hard to the inside to miss him. He got back alongside me and ran me all the way to the bottom, going in to the turn. I just about spun.

After our tangle there was another yellow. He was in front of me, and he shook his fist at me out the side of the car. I banged into the back of his car, giving him a little nudge, and I pulled alongside of him and flipped him the finger. Steve's a big guy, and I was concerned about that, but I was just as mad as he was. What made me mad was that I felt like I'd done everything I could to avoid him, and he was still mad. If he was going to raise this much hell about it, maybe I should have leaned on him and tried to take the lead.

He ended up winning, and I was second. They set up a big victory podium, with Coors Light signs all over the place behind us. Steve got right up on the stage and had his finger in my face, talking pretty mean, and he told me in real plain terms that if I ever touched his car again he would tear my head off.

I had my finger in his face, too, yelling at him, when we both realized that all of this didn't look very good, both of the Coors Light drivers fighting on the Coors Light stage after we had swept the Coors Light feature!

We had all the anger out of our system, though, and we were

all done. We probably stayed mad for a little while, but we kind of made up and forgot about it.

A couple of days later I crashed really hard at Eldora. I was going into turn one when I peeled the right front tire off the wheel. I must have caught the cushion too hard. At Eldora, you try to drive with the right front, because it pins the wheel hard and helps run the car straighter, which is faster at Eldora. If your car is right, you're very neutral. When I hit the cushion and peeled the tire, I hardly had time to flinch before I hit the wall. I flipped very hard. Sometime during the flip I hit my head. It didn't knock me out, but it sure hurt. I didn't sleep that night, because of the concussion.

After the race we went to Mike Streicher's in Findlay, Ohio, to rebuild the car. I drove up there in my motor home. I was worthless to help them, because I was still so stunned. I was junk. Every time I'd lay my head down the room would start spinning. I stacked pillows up so I could try to rest sitting straight up. I never did get to sleep.

The following night we raced at Millstream. I shouldn't have raced but I did anyway. I didn't see a doctor. I wound up running second to Steve Kinser that night. Gordon Johncock was there, and he watched the race from our trailer. They had to help me in and out of the car that night because I was still all messed up. After a while I began to get concerned because the headaches just wouldn't go away.

At Knoxville that year Steve had everybody covered, and he lapped almost the entire field in the main event, including me. Really, he was just starting to get on a tear. He and Karl dominated the series in late 1987.

From Knoxville we went to Memphis. That night there was a crash, and Lee Brewer Jr. was in Daryl Saucier's car. All I remember about the crash is that somehow on the back straight there was a tangle, and I had to maneuver real quick to miss it. Lee wound up running up over the back of my car, and he flipped. Daryl was angry with me – he thought it was my fault. I was sitting in my car during the red flag, and I still had my helmet on. Daryl came walking up, screaming at me, and telling me, "I had to fix race cars when I worked with you because of your carelessness, now I'm still fixing cars because of you!" I told him to get away from me, and he leaned into the cockpit and slapped me upside the helmet. I saw stars and felt a flash of pain. I immediately knew something wasn't right, likely it was a lingering problem from my Eldora crash two weeks earlier. I was already concerned about my headaches, and now this really startled me. They finally got Daryl out of there, and we finished the race.

A few days later in Albuquerque, New Mexico we were sitting at the motel. Laurie was with me, and Brandy and Braden were riding their little toys in the parking lot. I saw Daryl coming. He was walking at a fast pace right toward me. He walked up and started yelling at me, right in my face, "I'm gonna whip your ass," stuff like that. I kept telling him to get away, that I was already hurting, and backing up from him. I don't like to think that I just backed down from him, because nobody wants to back down when someone is in your face. But I was nervous. Nervous because I knew something was wrong, I knew I had some bruising or something with my head. I didn't know what was going on with that, and that is a very unsettling feeling. I was scared that if he hit me hard in the head...I didn't know what could happen. I kept backing up from him, until I'd finally had enough. He is a big guy, so I was looking for something to hit him with. Right by me was my kid's ride-em toy, a little plastic thing with big plastic wheels. I grabbed that dude and – *wham* – hit Daryl right upside the head. He had a look of complete shock on his face, and he backed up a step, mumbled something, and just walked away. That was it.

My headaches eventually went away, and we followed up with several third-place finishes over the next couple of months. At Chico in late September we set fast time, won our heat, and won the feature. For the finale we finished second, and you can probably guess who won. Yeah, Steve Kinser.

I finished second to Steve Kinser a whole bunch of times in 1987, something like 30 times when you count heat races and everything. It seemed like I was always behind the No. 11. I don't care who you are, that messes with your mind. It shakes your confidence. Your car owner starts questioning you, asking you why you can't beat that guy. You have the same car, the same horsepower, why can't you beat him?

Of course, most of us figured that if we had Karl Kinser working on our car, we could have won most of those races, too. Of course Steve is a great race driver, one of the greatest ever. He's a very talented race driver. He would have won races, and championships, and Knoxville Nationals titles. But to dominate, it takes more than one component. You can't dominate with just a great driver, or a great mechanic, or a great car. You've got to have all the pieces in place, and Steve and Karl did.

They really showed it in the 1987 season. They had always won a lot of races, but that season they went crazy. They won 46 World of Outlaws events, and a total of 57 feature events. After our win at U.S. 131 Speedway in July, they won 24 of the next 26 races, including the Knoxville Nationals, the Pacific Coast Nationals, and the Western World Championship. It's hard for people today to understand just how dominating they were that season.

Maybe that was one of the reasons that our team was wearing a little thin on each other. We finished second in World of Outlaws points, and had a very good year, but we were really stressed. I liked Les, but his volatile moods made him a difficult person to be around. I was always trying to be careful not to press his button.

When the season finished up I had the winter to think about things. Les' car was a good ride, but the stress was getting tiring. It wouldn't take long before things blew up completely.

Looking back, 1987 was my most successful season in racing. It was the most money I had ever made, and I should have been on a real high. We should have been elated with our season, but we weren't. It was just the opposite. There we were, so very close to the top, and we were bitterly unhappy about finishing second.

Of course, you never know what life has waiting for you around the next corner. I've had a lot of years to reflect on 1987 and what a great season it was. I had no way of knowing about the huge changes that were in store for my life in the months that followed.

13

Fred Marks left the team at the end of the 1987 season, so that made Les the sole car owner. I felt like Fred's leaving was a blow to our team, because he was a guy that I could talk to about any issues or problems. Les was a lot harder to communicate with, and Fred had been my go-between. Now he was gone, and it was me trying to work directly with Les. In addition to Fred, Kelly Pryor left the team as well.

Les and I had a couple of heated discussions over the telephone that winter, mostly about T-shirt deals, stuff like that. I arrived in Florida the following February and a friend told me that Les was still upset at me, and was pretty vocal about our disputes. So there was friction before we ever ran a race that year.

I didn't realize it at the time, but Les had created some resentment among some of the other teams. Les had a lot of money, with a first-class car, and the biggest, shiniest tow rig. He picked up the nickname, "Mr. More." I was later told by some of my rivals that they took special relish in beating Les' car, because their perception was that here was a rich guy who didn't care about the sport as much as he wanted to show off.

I do know that it was sometimes hard to reason with Les. He could get defensive, or emotional, and it was hard to have a civil discussion from that point. Then another time he might be the most wonderful, charismatic guy you could ever meet. The difficulty was that you didn't know what his mood was going to be.

Les tuned all the engines on our car, and he took a lot of pride in our horsepower. That meant if there were any engine issues, he took them personally. One night at Eldora in 1987 the engine started missing late in the feature. I still finished second, and after the race I pulled my helmet off and told them that we lost a cylinder. Les got really mad, and said, "Oh, don't you tell me that *my* engine laid down! Don't you even try to say that!" Man, he was pissed. We walked around the right side of the car, and there was one of the spark plug wires dragging on the ground. I pointed at it and said, "So, it couldn't have been the engine, right Les?" I just stomped back into the trailer, I was so disgusted.

I probably should have quit during the winter, but I just hated to leave a good race car. And, to be truthful, I didn't dislike Les. It was a combination of his moodiness and the fact that we were together so much that wore on me.

Our sponsor had changed from Coors to Kodiak smokeless tobacco, with a green-and-white paint scheme.

We ran Florida together, and then headed for Manzanita Speedway in Phoenix, Arizona. Jac and Elayne Haudenschild were traveling with us; they followed us in their motor home. We'd go down the highway, talking on the CB radio, having a great old time. We didn't even use "handles," it was just "Hey, Brad!" and "Hey, Jac!" Sometimes we'd switch to one of the side channels to keep from bothering other people.

They knew the stress I was under, and they had seen firsthand some of the friction between Les and me. I remember them telling me that they didn't understand why I stayed around, if Les was going to treat me like that.

Jac was driving Gary Runyon's car at this time, a red-and-white 7R.

We ran the Manzanita race, and in the feature the car started to run out of fuel. Late in the race it began to falter and blubber through the corners, and I was trying hard to keep it running to the finish. I was running second, but I slipped to third right at the finish. After the race I stopped on the frontstretch so the officials could check our car, since we were in the top three. When I climbed out of the car, I could see that Les was angry with me. I could tell from the look on his face that he wasn't happy. He was mad about losing second right at the finish.

I told him the car ran out of fuel, and he immediately raised his voice. "Don't you use that excuse," he yelled. I just shrugged my shoulders and said, "Les, the car is out of fuel. If you don't believe me, stick the tank," and walked away. He was still yelling, and I just went to my motor home to change clothes.

Ever heard that expression, "the straw that broke the camel's back"? For me, getting yelled at for running out of fuel was the last straw. After changing clothes I finally decided that I'd had enough.

I walked back to the car, and Les started to say something about going on to California. I just said, "Les, this isn't going to work, and it's time to do something different. I quit."

The next morning I was waiting in the motel parking lot and he came walking out, and he asked me, "Hey, can we talk about this?"

I said, "No, there just isn't anything to talk about. Let's just go our separate ways and be done with it." I could tell that if we tried to talk we were just going to have a big blowout. I didn't want to deal with that. So we just settled up right there on our finances, and I got my stuff and left.

That was the end of my ride in the Gambler house car. It seems bizarre that such a good run, and such a good opportunity for everyone, ended like that. Just quietly split, and it's over.

My timing sure left a lot to be desired. Actually, I'm surprised that I had the nerve to quit like that, because I was very uncertain about where else to go. But I'd reached a point where something had to give. It didn't have to make sense; but something definitely had to change. I didn't want to go through another season of stress and unhappiness.

I was supposed to meet Jac and Elayne at the Laundromat across the street from the hotel. We did our laundry, and I told Jac that I had just quit the Kepler car. I told him that I was nervous, because now I wasn't sure I could get another ride.

Jac is always the guy that doesn't worry, no matter what. He kind of chuckled and said, "Don't worry about it. You'll get a ride. You worry too much."

But I still agonized over my future. I didn't know exactly what to do at that point. I could drive home to Ohio, or I could go on to California and hope to find a ride. I decided to go west.

I stopped several times on the road to use the phone, calling car owners I knew in California. But the seats were all full, and it looked bleak.

Jac and I were supposed to hook up on the highway to make the trip, but I didn't see him again until I got to California. Boy, was I in for a shock.

When I got to Los Angeles I found our hotel. I pulled into the parking lot, where I saw Kelly Pryor in the parking lot working on Gary Runyon's No. 7R car. I climbed out of my motor home and walked over to Kelly, and he had this funny look on his face, kind of like he was shocked to see me. I asked him where Jac was, and he said, "You're not going to believe this. Are you sure you want me to tell you?" I said, "Yeah."

Kelly said, "He quit us. He's driving for Kepler." You could probably see the blood drain from my face. I said, "What!!?" He said, "Yeah, he definitely quit us, and he's driving for Les."

By chance, within a minute or two Les came driving up in the truck, and he had his new driver with him. Good 'ol Haud, smiling, with his elbow resting on the truck door, as happy as can be. I was just stunned. My best friend, slipping right into my old seat. He climbed down out of the truck and just grinned at me, and said, "Hey, Doty, what's happening?"

I was truly at a loss for words. I was hurt, I was mad, all the emotions were there. Les was standing there grinning from ear to ear, and that didn't help any.

Wow. It's still hard to talk about that one, and how much that stung. The funny thing is, I know Jac as well as any person on earth, and I know that he didn't do it to hurt me. He probably didn't even realize that it *would* hurt me. He's so happy-go-lucky, and avoids thinking about conflicts, that he probably didn't even think about it.

When I was thinking about quitting the team, I talked with a lot of people whose opinions mattered to me. Haud and I talked about it, and he basically helped convince me to make the move, to quit the ride. It strengthens your resolve, when you have people that are lifelong friends who agree with what you're already thinking. It strengthens me, anyway. Jac told me straight out that I shouldn't put up with everything that was going on, all the stress, and all the unhappiness.

All of this was really hard to swallow, because I didn't know quite how to take it. Did he encourage me to quit so he could get in? Or was it just the circumstances, him willing to try it to see if maybe things would be better with a change of chemistry? Either way, it hurt, way down deep in my gut, to see him smiling as he stood there with Les.

Laurie was as shocked as I was. Elayne came out of the motor home and tried to talk to Laurie, but there were tears on both sides. It was just awful. It made for an awkward moment, and for a while it strained our friendship a lot.

With Jac leaving Runyon's car, that left a seat open. I started driving the 7R car. Looking back, Jac probably did me a favor, because the whole episode resulted in the start of a lifelong friendship between Gary Runyon and me. I like him, and I respect him a great deal. He is a truly good person who has shown me that he treasures our friendship.

I got going fairly well in Gary's car, but I knew right away that this deal had a ways to go to be as strong as the Kepler car. And that's when the good old confidence goes straight down the toilet, when a guy sits in the dark of night and questions his ability to make the right decisions.

Naturally, for the next few races I quietly paid attention to Jac and Les, and kind of watched their progress. It wasn't really hard feelings, because I truly didn't dislike either of them. But you tend to wish they wouldn't be as fast as you, because that salves the wound a little bit. But it didn't matter, because they were pretty strong. We would still be friendly, and smile and shake hands, but damn, I wanted to beat those guys.

We headed for Ascot for a practice session, and it turned out to be kind of a tit-for-tat deal. I was pretty fast, and I'd cut a good lap and pull in. Les would look at my time, and would send Jac out with just a little bit of tweaking, and he would be just a touch faster. Back out I'd go, and (you guessed it) somehow manage to get under their time. I was motivated! Then it would be Jac's turn, roaring around that 'ol black race track, somehow finding a fraction of a second here, a fraction there, and he would be quicker.

After a while, things eventually got back to normal between us. The strains in our friendship eased up, and before long we were back to our old selves.

I was trying to focus on how I could help Gary's car go faster at Ascot. To be honest, I began to think that the car wasn't fast enough. I had been running a Gambler chassis for a long time, and Gary's car was a different chassis. Plus, they were doing some experimenting with the heads on the engines, and they were down on power while they were working this out.

We finished ninth in the main event at Ascot, and Jac finished 11th. So it was a personal victory, anyway. But I was very frustrated with ninth. I knew I had to do better if I was going to make a living.

I knew a guy named Dave Brewer who had a Gambler car with Shaver engines, so I figured that would be very close to what I was used to. Somehow that seat came open, so I made a deal with Dave to run his car at Hanford, Baylands, and Chico. The car felt pretty good, but we didn't run all that well. We were in the top five, and we finally blew up his last engine on March 5 at Chico.

After that I returned to Runyon's car on March 18 at Devil's Bowl Speedway in Texas, but we got rained out. We crashed the next day in the feature, adding to my frustration.

I finished sixth at Oklahoma City, then traveled to Bloomington, Indiana, where we dropped out with engine problems. At Eldora we fell out of our heat, won the B-main, and ran ninth on the first day of a two-day show. We came back the following day and ran fifth.

We ran ninth at Memphis, then ran I-55 Speedway in Pevely, Missouri. Our engine problems had become so severe that within a couple of laps of firing the car, it felt like the car was pulling a plow. The engine builders were trying heads with bigger ports, and there was too much fuel getting into the cylinders. The longer you ran the car, the slower it would go. We literally had raw fuel coming out of the headers, it was running so rich.

We decided to stay closer to the Midwest while we got our program working better. Gary is from Carmel, Indiana, so we weren't far from each other in terms of geography.

On May 7 we won a USAC race at Paragon, Indiana. It was one heck of a race, and it was a very satisfying win. It was one of those races where it was a driver's race track. It was very rough, and it took some skill to get around there. You really had to sit up in the seat and drive the car. We were running three wide, and I'd stick my nose between two cars and bounce through the holes and pass people.

Steve Butler had won a lot of USAC races at Paragon, and I beat him that night (he finished second). In fairness to him, this was early in the year that USAC had gone to running wings for a little while, so they were probably still making the adjustment. We made $4,000 for the win, but I felt like it was a million bucks. It felt really good to win again.

But there was a downfall coming. We went to Wilmot, Wisconsin, where I was leading when I tangled with Jack Hewitt and eventually finished third.

We hooked back up with the Outlaws at West Virginia Motor Speedway, but the first day was rained out. The second day we finished 13th. We then traveled to Lernerville, where we finished sixth. From there we went to Williams Grove, where we did poorly both days. We made just $10 on the first day, and on the second day we finished fifth in the B-main and missed the feature.

That was the first time I'd missed the show in a long, long time. It was a real downer. Coming off the year I had in 1987, to miss the show – I knew I had to do something different.

So I started looking for another ride. The fact that I didn't go well in Gary Runyon's car was as much my fault as anyone's. I should have been more outspoken about the motor situation, things like that. But instead I kind of went along, and we just didn't have it together at that point. Gary always had good equipment, so I don't want to knock what they were doing. Maybe I wasn't the guy that team needed at that moment. I wonder now if I wasn't also still kind of distracted after my falling-out with Les Kepler.

We followed the Outlaws through their New York swing, and we ran out of motors at Canandaigua. We blew an engine early, and we didn't have a spare. So we put it in the trailer, and we were basically done.

I walked over to Gary Stanton's trailer. He had Doug Wolfgang in the car, but it was common knowledge that they were preparing to split.

It's hard to explain why that happens, but sometimes it just doesn't click. You can work really well with someone, but if you don't perform well the rest doesn't matter. That's when it gets tough, when you're driving for somebody you like a lot but not winning. So you have to break the package up, mix things around and try again, hoping to hit the right combination.

I saw Stanton standing there, and we started talking about getting back together. I knew I'd have to work pretty hard again, but he had good equipment. Like I said earlier, in the middle of the season when a driver needs a ride and a car owner needs a driver, they somehow find each other.

Stanton and I talked for about two minutes, and we decided to give it a try. I asked him if he was going to stay out on the road or go home, and he said that if I wanted to run the car he'd stay out. We shook hands and smiled, and walked to his motor home. He knocked on the door and his wife Beth opened the door, and he said, "Hey, I've got my new driver," and she said, "Oh, who's that?" Then she turned around and saw me and smiled, and said, "Hey, Brad, are you our new driver?" And we all laughed.

Beth is a bright, cheerful person, and she makes you feel good. I was glad to hook up with Gary again. I forgot about going home. If Gary was willing to stay out on the road and race, so was I. We were back in business.

14

One of the things that makes racing with the World of Outlaws unique is the traveling. Unless you've experienced it, you can't imagine just how grueling and boring the traveling can be. Mile after mile, day after day, week after week.

You might tow for two days to get somewhere, break on the first lap, then tow all the way back. Sometimes it seems futile, and it gets depressing.

We once towed all the way to Winnipeg, Canada and ran the first day of a two-day show. But they paid off that night in Canadian money, even though they had promised to pay in U.S. dollars. So everybody refused to run the second day. Going through customs on that trip was an adventure, with the agents prowling through the trailers. They counted all the fuel bottles, because you had to pay a tax on the fuel you brought in. But it was amazing, towing all the way up there for one race.

In my early days with Sam Bowers, we always had motels. Some teams slept in their truck, so we figured we were pretty lucky to get a room. We'd finish racing, go to the motel and sleep. There was Tom Sanders and I, doing everything. It wore us out, or at least it wore me out, I don't know about Tom. It varied based on our schedule, but we'd often get just four or five hours of sleep a night for days at a time.

It was a tiring routine. We'd go to the car wash that night after the races, and that took at least one hour. To do it right you've got to take the side panels off the car, jack the car up, take the tires out of the tire racks and wash the mud off of them. You get sick of car washes; it seems like that's all you do. Weary. Then on to the motel, and sleep. Shower before bed, then collapse. Next morning we'd get up early if we had a long drive to the next race. If the track was some distance away we'd try to get work done on the car and roll it on the trailer. Then head down the road.

At first, I didn't mind the travel at all. I wanted to see the country. But even in the first year, it started to get tiring. And you'd get physically drained, working in the heat sometimes. You start to wonder why you're doing all of this, but after a while it becomes a way of life, and then you don't even question why anymore.

You get so caught up in it. You know there are other things to do, but it's not what you really want. "Racing is my lifestyle," you tell yourself. Sometimes on big holiday weekends we'd drive past a lake and see people out there boating and skiing, grilling out. If the mood was right, you had some envy for them. But you look back up the highway, and think about going to another race track. Sometimes I thought it would be nice to have a more normal lifestyle.

But racing was never something that I regretted. I never got to the point where I didn't want to do this. If we were home for more than two weeks, I was ready to go again.

I really did want to see the sights around America. Eyes wide open, I used to say. It amazed me that the other guys weren't excited about the scenery and the areas we visited.

Once in New York, in my first year, Karl Kinser and Paul Elrod passed us on the highway. Steve Kinser's feet were sticking out the window; he was asleep in the back seat. Elrod was driving, and he had this big grin on his face. They honked and waved at us as they passed. That night I asked Steve how he could sleep through all that beautiful scenery, and he laughed. "I've seen all of that before," he said.

Elrod was a neat guy. He helped Karl and Steve for a long time, and he drove the tow rig a lot. He was a nice, friendly guy, and he had a serious hearing problem. One time they were going down the road in the tow rig and the engine started rattling real loud, and ol' Elrod didn't even hear it. He just kept his foot in the throttle. Karl and Steve woke up from the noise and had to holler at Elrod before he'd stop.

Of course, it got monotonous sometimes. We had to stop for gas

194

a lot in the early years, because we used a 454 Chevy dually truck to tow with. We had to stop to fuel up every two or three hours. We used a lot of gasoline.

When I started driving for Gary Stanton in 1984 everybody was towing with trucks like that. Everybody was burning up transmissions, pulling 24- or 30-foot trailers, and the load was too great. It just burned the trucks up. So Stanton built his own tow rig, which people referred to as a "roll-your-own." Gary used a bigger chassis, like a two-ton F-600 series Ford. That was a lot bigger than those duallys. He built a full motor home on the truck chassis, and it was heavy enough to support the motor home and pull the trailer.

He cut the back out of the cab and built living quarters on the length of the chassis. It had one over-the-cab bunk, a table that folded into a bunk, and two bunks on top of one another on a back wall. You could sleep four or five if you needed. It was a very neat setup.

When you travel away from home for weeks at a time, you have to plan with the race car much more. When you don't have the luxury of getting back to your shop a lot, you have to bring as much with you as you can. You can usually find other guys' shops when you need big repairs, or maybe the motel parking lot. I've seen some major rebuilds done under the hot sun, with guys lying on the hot asphalt in the afternoon.

All kinds of logistics are an issue when you live on the road. You can only take so many clothes, so you're in laundry mode every so often. Early on it was just Laurie and I, and that was pretty easy, with just two people. No kids, no dogs, just us.

Car washes and Laundromats, you're always on the lookout for car washes and Laundromats. If you found a facility that had both, man, you had hit the lottery.

A lot of the time you're just bored. It's far better today with the large motor homes the guys use, with satellite TV and stereos. In our pickup trucks, we didn't exactly have all the luxuries. So we'd just sit around, maybe watch TV at the motel. That was only if the car was ready to race. If you had back-to-back races you didn't have any spare time, but we had a lot of times where we had a couple of days between races. So you kind of bounce between dog tired and worn out to being bored with nothing to do.

Sometimes we played cards. There was a kid named Red who helped Daryl and me for a while, and we got in the bad habit of playing blackjack while we went down the road. One weekend I won $800 from those two guys. Another time I remember winning $300 at Oklahoma City during a rainout, when everybody wound up in our trailer playing "guts." Of course, I can't recall the times that I lost money!

Everybody always thought about different ways to get back and forth from the races. Some guys tried flying, because that would allow you to get home more. But flying commercial was tough, because it was expensive and a lot of our tracks weren't near airports.

One night in 1988 I flew with Kenny Jacobs to a race in Wisconsin, where I was going to run Gary Runyon's car. Kenny had his pilot's license. That night I tangled with Jack Hewitt. Jack was leading, and I passed him, and he got into the back of me and I slid off the track and turned over. We fixed our car, and I got back to third and Jack won, which pissed me off. But the bad night was just beginning.

We got back to Kenny's plane, and got ready to take off. Corky Otte was in the right seat, Kenny in the left. I was in the back seat, along with Kenny's dad Jake. We headed for home, but we ran into thick, dense fog. Kenny didn't have his instrument rating, and Corky was unfamiliar with the right seat. Corky had actually trained Kenny when he was learning to fly. With the fog, Corky took over the controls, from the right seat. Things began to get pretty grim. We kept missing the Wayne County Airport, which is basically an airstrip. But it had closed for the night, which was common, and no lights were on. Plus, the fog was just so thick you couldn't see anything. We tried several times to find the airport, and we just couldn't. So they decided to search for another airport, with no luck. We finally ran low on fuel, and it looked like we were going to crash. I had accepted in my mind that it was over, that we were probably going to die. Finally, we flew to Akron, Ohio, which was a commercial airport. The fuel needle was on empty.

196

Akron had a guidance system that beeps in the cockpit when you're on course, for weather situations like this. We were on our approach to land when we somehow got off course again, and we lost the signal. I could tell by the look in Kenny's eyes that things weren't good. When we lost the signal they were concerned that we might be flying into light poles, or trees, or buildings, so they tried to climb really fast. The stall alarm in the plane began to go off.

It was very quiet in that airplane. Corky and Kenny were very focused on what they needed to do. It was starting to get light outside. At one point I looked out my window and saw a break in the fog, and I could see an open field below us. I shouted to Kenny and Corky that there was an opening, and that maybe we should try to set the plane down there. They were so focused they didn't really pay any attention, but I was serious. I liked our chances of landing in the field better than running out of fuel and dropping from the sky.

We had to circle around once again. We got back on course, and we approached the runway. The ceiling was so low that we couldn't see the ground until we were just a couple hundred feet up, and when the fog opened we realized that we were too far down the runway, we were going to run off the end. Corky wanted to pull up and go around again, but Kenny took the controls and brought the plane in really fast, at a steep angle, to get down as quickly as possible. We were so short on fuel that he figured our best chance was to take what shot we had and try to make it. But we were coming in too fast, and he pulled up on the stick when we were just 100 feet above the ground, and the stall buzzers began to go off again. He kept working with the plane, right on the verge of stalling, and after a few seconds we were on the ground. We bounced hard, and he got the plane stopped.

I'll admit that it scared the hell out of me. The whole episode shook Kenny up as well, and I don't think he flew for several months after that. They later checked our fuel tank, and as it turned out Kenny was right, that was our last chance. We didn't have enough fuel for another approach if this one hadn't worked.

When we climbed out of the plane, we were so euphoric to be

alive that we didn't care about anything. We all literally kissed the ground. It was a feeling unlike anything else I have ever experienced.

I didn't get a motor home until 1985 or '86. Actually, it was a mini motor home, basically a Ford van with an overhang on top. It was pretty nice, but primitive by today's standards. I bought it for the 1986 season. I paid $26,000 for it, and I was scared that I couldn't make the payments. Today guys spend that kind of money on paint schemes.

Motor homes changed the World of Outlaws in a lot of ways. For one, it allowed the driver and the team to get some space between them. At first, I spent every minute of every day with Tom Sanders or Daryl Saucier. We worked together at the race track and we rode together in the tow rig. I don't care how well you like someone, if you spend that much time together you're going to get tired of one another. That's a fact.

When you get a motor home, you have most of the day away from each other. You can think things through privately, and then at the race track you're a little more productive.

It also helps in terms of having your clothes and stuff with you, without having to carry suitcases in and out of motels every night. It's as close to having a home away from home as possible.

And motor homes changed the dynamics of the sport in another way: It allowed families to travel with the driver.

During the early 1980s, most of the World of Outlaws guys were pretty young. There were always girls hanging around, and some of them made it pretty clear that they would like to get to know the drivers, if you know what I mean.

This isn't to say that all the guys were chasing women, because that wasn't true. It's probably like anything else: A certain percentage of guys were looking, and another percentage of guys pretty much avoided the groupies.

When the wife and kids came along, people sure changed their lifestyle. I can think of lots of funny stories related to this subject, but no way can I talk about 'em. Most of those guys are respectable family men today, and that stuff was a long time ago.

Sometimes funny stuff happened on the road. Well, kind of funny. One time Danny Smith came wheeling into the pit area somewhere, and the back of his motor home had dozens of tiny bb holes all over it. Danny was apparently messing with somebody out on the highway, and he must have pissed them off pretty bad. They pulled up behind his motor home and blasted the back end with a shotgun!

Sometimes things were downright strange. We were running at Ascot one night, and they were introducing the drivers. There must have been 1,000 fans pressed up against the fence on the front straightaway. They announced my name and I waved at the crowd, and a few people called my name as I walked to my car. One was a very attractive blonde woman. I said the usual, "How ya' doin'," something like that. After the races several people came by our pits, and said, "Say, I met your wife!" That's nice, I said. When did you meet Laurie? They said, "Why, just a few minutes ago." I was kind of startled, and I said, "Hey, my wife is in Ohio!" They said, "Oh, that blonde woman, isn't she your wife? She said she was!"

Some people. I just can't figure them out.

Going to California always fascinated me. As a kid, I had this idea of California...I figured it was beaches, babes, and hot rods. Seeing it in the movies, and in magazines as I grew up, California had a powerful allure for me, a mystique. It was someplace that I wanted to see. We read about Ascot and the CRA guys in *National Speed Sport News*, and our gang – Jac, Ed, and I – we were hoping that someday we would get a chance to race there.

Our first trip west came in 1978 when we went with Kenny. When we finally saw Ascot, it seemed like downtown Los Angeles. Bright city lights, palm trees, surrounding one of the most famous race tracks in the world. And they always had the best-looking trophy queens, too.

You could see Ascot from the 405 and the 110 interchange, but how to get there! The roads curved and turned, it was like a bowl of spaghetti. But once you found your way in, you never forgot.

The thing that stands out most from that first trip was the race cars. Custom paint, lots of chrome, just awesome. And some of those guys had beautiful trailers and custom trucks to tow with, and they'd pull in and open the doors and there was nothing in there but one car and a few tires. And compared to my schedule later on, they didn't really run that much. But they definitely had the equipment, both to race with and to tow with.

One of my first trips to race at Ascot came with Tom Sanders. The traffic was intense, and we were right in the middle of it, towing the race car. We broke down on the highway, and had to jump a cement wall to walk to a gas station to get some repairs going. The traffic was unbelievable. No place to get off, no place to slow down, it was intense. Pulling a trailer in that environment, and not knowing where you were going, was a challenge.

I consider myself very lucky to race there, and win, before it closed. The whole Ascot thing – the whole California thing, really – overwhelmed me. The sights, the sounds, the aura. Billboards, the big white wall with all the ads, the big Ascot billboard, and the celebrities. You might see television or movie actors hanging out in the pits, even.

I remember driving past the LA Forum, and I had a Three Dog Night album that was Live at the Forum. I don't know if it was the same forum, but it sure seemed exciting. It was a sensation.

Eyes wide open.

In 1983 I heard through the grapevine that Sam Bailey wanted me to run their car at Ascot for the Pacific Coast Nationals. That was a famous car – the Bailey Brothers No. 01 – and a very famous event. Sam and I hooked up and made the deal, and I flew out there for the event in October.

Some of the guys there that night, wow. Dean Thompson, Bubby Jones, Eddie Wirth, Jimmy Oskie, Lealand McSpadden, Ron Shuman, Brad Noffsinger, Mike Sweeney...guys that I had read about in the racing papers. All the West Coast stars were there.

This was a non-wing race, so I was kind of out of my element. I was pinching myself to be there, under the palm trees racing with the

CRA in California. Wow. Even the push trucks were pretty. Some were custom Ford pickups from the 1950s, just awesome.

We ran our heat and got a transfer to the main. After the race Shuman came over and said, "Doty, does that thing feel all right?" I was kind of sheepish and said, "Well, I don't know...what's it supposed to feel like?" Shuman shook his head and said, "Well, it's gonna bust your ass unless they fix it." He had seen that the car was laying over too much in the heat race, and he knew that wasn't right. It was pretty good of him to look out for me like that.

Sam and Fred Bailey were standing there when Shuman said this, so they figured that maybe they needed to look at the car. They decided to change the car around a little bit and were talking to me about what it was doing, this and that.

Whatever they did, it worked. During the main I felt really good in the car. I still wasn't sure I was doing this right, because I wasn't sure what the car was supposed to feel like without a wing. I was probably spending too much time looking for those California guys to come up any moment and drive by me, this Midwestern winged guy, and make me look silly.

One problem I had was that the steering box was mounted high on the roll cage, instead of the frame rail, like most other cars I had driven. It wasn't what I was used to. Me being a shorter guy, I couldn't reach the top of the steering wheel very well. So we put on a smaller steering wheel to help compensate for it. But on Ascot's busy, smaller track, I was constantly moving my hands on the steering wheel to chase it a little bit. It was really different, more slanted like the angle of the steering wheel in a passenger car. I was struggling to get used to that.

I was running second, and had worked on a lapped car for a few laps. I just couldn't get past him. I got nervous, worried that time was slipping away and that Dean Thompson, who was leading, was getting away from me. I just got impatient. I put a big slide job on the guy and slipped up and banged off the cushion. At that time we weren't allowed to run a wheel cover, and when I hit the cushion it packed the right rear wheel with mud. It was like having a cement block

201

inside the wheel. It shook the car so badly that I finally had to pull in. I was totally disappointed. It was truly one of the most disappointing moments of my career. Who knows, maybe I could have been a winner of the Pacific Coast Nationals with and without a wing.

It was a very prestigious race, one of the top three or four in the country. And since it was a non-winged event and not a World of Outlaws event, I was concerned that I'd never get a chance to run it again. But as it turned out I did get my chance, and I'm glad of it.

California. To this day I wouldn't want to live there, but it was an awesome experience to visit. A limo might pull up beside you on the freeway, with tinted windows, and you'd wonder who was inside. Was it somebody famous? One night Jac and I were driving on Sunset Boulevard in Hollywood, when I glanced down a side street and saw a bunch of bright lights. Hey, they're filming a movie! We did a U-turn and went back, and we walked on the set like we were somebody important. I was amazed that we could get right up close to the set. They were working on a scene for one of the Halloween movies, as I recall. That's not the kind of thing you'd see driving down the street back in Millersburg, that's for sure.

At the movie scene there was a bed in the middle of the street with a girl in it; they were filming a scary scene. We stood there for at least 45 minutes, and they didn't film a thing, just setting things up. They would sprinkle dried leaves on the bed, move the actress, move the camera, on and on. No wonder it costs so much to film movies.

Another time the bus for the rock group Dire Straits pulled up beside us at a stop light, we just looked over and there they were. You never knew what you were going to see in California.

Another thing that was an adjustment for me, besides the travel, was dealing with all the people at the race track. When I started racing at Lakeville, it was mostly family and friends that came to the pits after the races. But as I ventured further from home, I raced in front of new people, so new faces would come by and say hello.

In 1979 my younger sister Ami and Dave Pope's daughter became friends, and they made up my first T-shirt. They made two of them!

Brad's No. 1 and No. 2 fans, the shirts said. They were 12 years old or so. Those were the first shirts with my name on them.

In 1981 or so we put together our first T-shirts to sell. You have to buy 144 at a time, and at first we wondered if we would ever sell that many. We sold them out of the trailer, had them with us in the rig. It evolved from there. We hung one on a hanger at the back of the trailer, and more people asked. Laurie took care of most of that stuff.

It made me feel kind of funny, seeing strangers wearing my shirt. I didn't quite know how to take that. I was flattered, obviously, but also a little bit insecure about the whole thing. I felt that way about autographs, too.

When I started running in Pennsylvania, more and more people started visiting the pits after the races to say hello. It was strange, total strangers coming up knowing my name. It was a good feeling, but it took me off guard at first. Even today when I'm not at the environment at the races, if someone recognizes me it still catches me off guard. You don't expect it. But it's a warm feeling.

It can irritate you, too. If people are somebody else's fans, they tend to see things their way. You're not going to change their view. Especially if they've been drinking. So every now and then you'd get somebody loud in the pits, bad-mouthing you, complaining that you ran into so-and-so, and there isn't much you can do about that kind of thing. Some people just don't have any manners, I guess. But it's part of the package, part of being in the racing game.

For every jerk, there are 10, 20, 50 nice people. Racing is full of terrific fans, people that are loyal and patient and warm and friendly. Man, do they have strong feelings about their favorite sport.

I always wondered, why do those people want my autograph? I always thought of myself as just a farm kid from Ohio, and yet people wanted my autograph. I thought that was amazing. I still do.

15

Racing with the World of Outlaws put me up against some of the very best racers in the history of sprint car racing. It's probably hard for people to understand just how competitive it is, night in and night out, with the Outlaws. You've got all the travel issues and the personnel issues and all that, plus you've got to belt into the car and fight for every inch, every lap, every night. It's grueling.

Through all the years I raced, I never had the killer personality. I was aggressive, but I think I worried a little too much about being a nice guy. I probably should have been a bit meaner, and less nice.

There was a core of guys in the 1980s that raced together every night, and we sort of became a loose-knit family. But, at the same time, I'm not sure any of us really knew each other. You see the competitive side of a guy every night, but that's only one dimension of the person. We rarely got a chance to go to somebody's house and see what they are really like. That's a completely different side of a man.

Early on, when most of us were just getting started, I think a lot of us were hesitant to show our real personalities. We were worried that people might see the human side of us, and think we were less dedicated. There was a lot of emphasis on being strong, and tough. I think most of us were hesitant to let down our guard with each other. Maybe we were afraid somebody would see that we were human, and not really all that tough and mean after all.

When I look at a list of guys that I raced against, I don't see any enemies. But I also can't say that I was good friends with most of those guys, either. It was more of a working relationship. Later on, when I was no longer driving, it became a lot easier to be friends with people, because we were no longer rivals.

When I first joined the Outlaws, I felt like Steve Kinser and I had begun to build a nice friendship. He helped me a lot. But when I started to get better, and I started passing him sometimes, and beating him sometimes, our friendship seemed to cool for a while. I couldn't understand that, but looking back I think it was because Steve is such an incredibly competitive person, that maybe he has to look at his rivals with some intensity. Maybe that helps him stay "up" every night. And trust me, the guy shows up *every* night ready to race.

There are two things I can say about Steve Kinser: He is a big-hearted, good guy; and he is absolutely, positively one hell of a racer.

I once kept our car at Steve's shop when we ran in Indiana. He had this small house that now sits in front of his current home. Steve had purchased the original house and some land, then later built his shop. He lived there with his buddy, Jeff Smith, early on. I stayed at the house with Steve and Jeff for a few days once when we ran Bloomington, or Paragon, one of the nearby tracks.

Steve was a bachelor at the time. His house was the ultimate bachelor pad, or at least the ultimate racing bachelor's pad. He had trophies in just about every available space in that house. He even had this huge trophy in his bathroom, with a roll of toilet paper hanging on one of the eagle's wings on the trophy! That was by far the most impressive toilet paper holder I've ever seen.

One night I was sitting alone in Steve's house when somebody knocked on the door. It was Larry Crane, who was a big part of John Mellencamp's band. In fact, Larry was with John from the very beginning. I had met Larry once before at Dallas, when we hung out for the weekend during the races. That weekend Larry had a demo tape of the soon-to-be-released Lonesome Jubilee album. I listened to the tape for the weekend, long before it was released. I remember hearing the song *Cherry Bomb* for the first time, and thinking, "Wow, that is a great song." As it turns out, just about everybody else thought the same thing.

Even though I like Steve a lot, I still feel like he's a hard guy to really talk to. I always sense that he's reserved, or that he doesn't like to let his guard down. That's funny, because I know him well enough to know that he is a very big-hearted person.

Steve is a great guy, and I mean that. I consider him a friend to this day. I respect him tremendously as a racer, and as a person. Who doesn't respect him as a racer, after all he's done in the sport?

I remember one time Sammy Swindell and I were talking, and something had gone on between him and Steve. Sammy was really upset at the time. He said something like, "Hey, that guy wants it *all*. I just want a little bit, but he wants *all* of it."

For a while, it seems like he *got* it all. Boy, when he was on, and Karl Kinser had the car right...*whew!* They had everybody covered. Like I said earlier, in 1987 I finished second to those guys 30-some times. I can't describe how that plays with your mind, always following the No. 11 car.

I got tired of finishing second to Steve, but I never got to where I disliked him or Karl. Maybe I would have been a better race car driver if I had taken it personally. And I really did get sick of watching them win. But what was I going to do about it? I was already racing as hard as I could.

To dominate in racing takes all three pieces: car, mechanic, and driver. For a while we might have thought that it was Karl Kinser's car that won, and not so much Steve. We could see that he was pretty good, but you always wonder.

Then late one year Steve made a deal to run Kenny Woodruff's car at the Western World. For some reason Karl wasn't going to make the trip, so Steve was on his own. Steve won the race, and I think he made a big statement. I've wondered sometimes if that didn't help his confidence, because he clearly proved he was capable on his own.

But it didn't matter. Steve and Karl were so effective together; it would have been silly for them to split. They had a great thing going. I'd see them argue and fight, all the time, but they always kept it going. Once at Lincoln Speedway I was leading, Steve was second, and we had yellow after yellow. With every yellow I was more nervous, because I knew he was back there. Finally with two to go we had a red flag. We added fuel and put a new 40-compound tire on. We figured a new tire would hook up better on the restart.

During the red, I could see Karl and Steve over by their car, arguing. I could see the tension, and the gestures, and I could catch little bits of them yelling. I didn't know until later that it was a heated conversation about what their car was doing. I heard later that Steve was angry and thrust his helmet at Karl, saying something like, "If you think this sumbitch is so fast, you drive it!" When we restarted, our new tire did nothing but spin for two laps. Steve drove past me and won the race.

The next day I saw Karl in the motel, and I kidded him a little bit, and I asked him what the argument was all about. He laughed and said, "Hell, Steve told me the car was so good that even I could drive it!"

I guess it's all in how you look at it. It makes me laugh today, thinking about Karl and that line. That was a classic.

They didn't hide their arguing and fighting from anyone. Maybe that was Karl's way of showing everyone that their team was strong, that they could sustain themselves even through the tension. They didn't hold it inside, that's for sure. And once they yelled a while, they seemed to be able to forget about it the next day.

Karl could have been a great coach in any sport. He knows how to work his driver, and get them to follow his lead. It's kind of amazing, really. A lot of people figure he's had great success because he knows a lot about race cars, but I've sometimes wondered if his real gift is that he knows how to motivate his driver.

Even now, you'll see him and his son Mark arguing and fighting about how to set up the race car. Then they'll go out and whip everybody, and they'll be as happy as can be after the race.

I've wondered sometimes if maybe Karl takes a dim view of his driver becoming too friendly with the other guys, maybe thinking that it would take some of his competitive edge off.

Karl was always very friendly to me, though. We never had any problem getting along. Like everybody else, I imagined that the No. 11 car would be an awesome car to drive. If he and Steve had split

The late J.W. Hunt shakes my hand in
1985. Mr. Hunt was a wonderful guy.
(Linda McKisson photos)

I ran just a few midget races, but I had a good run in this
car at I-70 Speedway in 1985. Of the five races they held
that weekend, I won four and finished second in the fifth.
(J.R. Photos)

I won the season opener in Florida in 1986 in Kenny
Woodruff's car. Bad news, though...we burned a piston,
and went home the next day.
(Don Bok photo)

My son Braden is helping me fix the brakes in June 1986 at Oklahoma City.
(Paul Hammack photo)

It's great to have buddies...I'm all smiles with Jac Haudenschild and Kenny Jacobs in July, 1986 at Sharon Speedway in Ohio. Gee, we sure look happy. *(Cyndi Craft photo)*

Ready to race at the Pacific Coast Nationals at Ascot in 1986. I'm among some heavy hitters in this picture, including Sammy Swindell, Steve Kinser, Bobby Davis Jr., Ron Shuman, and Doug Wolfgang. *(J.R. Photos)*

*This was my biggest win, at the Pacific Coast Nationals
at Ascot in 1986. Steve Kinser is clowning around with
me on the podium. Anytime you beat this guy,
you had a great night.*
(J.R. Photos)

Above: Coming off the corner at Santa Fe Raceway in 1987.
(Ken Coles photo)

Opposite, top: On my way to winning the 1987 World of Outlaws season opener at Ascot.
Opposite, bottom: Those California trophy girls sure didn't wear much. Leslie Bremmer made the Ascot victory lane a very happy place. Sammy Swindell (left) seems at a loss for words, while Keith Kauffman sure isn't looking at the photographers.
(U.S. Photographics)

Feeling the front end of your race car raise up coming off the corner is a real rush. It takes a lot of horsepower, and a lot of forward bite, to pull a wheelie like this. (Joe Orth photo)

Racing isn't always easy, or glamorous. Sometimes you get just plain tired.
(Dennis Kreiger photo)

Qualifying for the Kings Royal at Eldora, 1987. I set quick time.
(Ken Coles photo)

There are very few pictures of me in this car. I ran it only a couple of times before leaving the team in early 1988.

Top: Passing Jeff Gordon at Knoxville, 1987. You make a lot
more these days when you pass Jeff. (Pat Taylor photo)
Bottom: Beating Steve Butler in a USAC race at Paragon was
tough. But we got it done in May, 1988 in Gary Runyon's No.
7R. (John Mahoney photo)

*This was a happy night, winning at Paragon, Indiana in 1988.
That's Gary Runyon's son, Jack, on the left.*
(Pat Taylor photo)

Running Gary Stanton's car against the wall at Eldora, 1988.
(Ken Coles photo)

Jeff Gordon visited Millstream Speedway in 1997, and talks with Shane Carson and me.

This was a magic night, when I got behind the wheel again at Eldora in 1998. (MSPN photo)

My buddy Jac Haudenschild gives me a wave.
(Quick Time photo)

One last ride: Steve Kinser pulls alongside in the No. 11, while Sammy Swindell moves up to give me a tap. Kenny Jacobs is moving up on the outside. What a moment this was.
(Rex Staton photo)

Ed Haudenschild has been my friend for my entire life. Thanks, old buddy!

Television has been a blast, mainly because I get to work with people such as Ralph Shaheen. (TNN photo)

Top left: Being unable to walk doesn't mean I'm unable to work. It's all a matter of attitude.

Top right: My early days as a farm boy stick with me. I still enjoy being around animals.

Bottom: This is my family: Laurie and I are in front, with (l-r) Brittani, Brandy, and Braden.

up, there would have been a long line of applicants at the back of Karl's trailer, with helmet in hand.

If they had split, that would have blown things wide open. I still believe that a major factor in their success together was that they made up the entire package: driver, mechanic, and car.

Today, more people have caught up technically, but Karl and Mark will still be a force to be reckoned with, for a long time in the future if they choose to. It would be really tough to win 10 in a row today like Steve once did in Pennsylvania, because the cars seem to be more even now. Yet, I suspect Karl's cars are always going to be up front, as long as he wants to keep doing this.

I raced against Mark some during his first few years. I figured he had a lot of potential, but at the time I figured it had to be tough for Mark to watch his father and Steve dominate those races. He was known as Karl's son, not Mark. That's got to be very hard on a guy. When you're young you always struggle, yet people set a higher standard for you. That's just not fair, but that's the way it is.

When Brandy was very small, she was in love with Mark. She called him "Mach". He'd come by the motor home and tap on the window and she'd pop up, and he'd talk to her through the window. He was a really nice kid.

We had words once when I kidded him at a drivers' meeting about something and he got steamed. I had no idea, but it sure pushed his button. Later I was parking my motor home and he came walking up to my window and started in on me, kind of jumped me about what was said. I lost my cool, and jumped down out of the motor home, and we had words for a second or so. For a while after that I sensed that we were kind of tense, and when I saw him I'd think of that night. But that's a long time ago, and I've forgotten that today. I hope he has, too.

Of course, just beating Steve and Karl, or Mark and Karl today, doesn't mean the rest is easy. There are a bunch of fast guys to deal with.

Even if you have Steve covered, don't blink, because Sammy Swindell is probably right there with you. Sammy is another guy who night after night comes to race.

Sammy is a very quiet guy. When we competed against one another all those years, we never really had the opportunity to socialize a lot. Now, doing TV, I approach him more with questions, so we're able to talk a lot more.

He's probably one of the best mechanic/driver combinations I've ever seen. I've always had a lot of respect for him because he could do both exceptionally well.

I think Sammy has mellowed some, and it seems like his career isn't as all-everything as it used to be. That's very good if that's true, because a man ought to be about more than just being a great race driver. Maybe having a child changed his feelings about things like that. Regardless of the reason, Sammy seems happier today than ever before, and I'm glad.

Sammy and I once had a run-in at Lawton, Oklahoma. Or maybe I should call it a "run-into." When you race 100 nights a year with these guys, year after year, that's a lot of opportunities to bang wheels. About 90 percent of the time it's overlooked, just written off as good, hard racing. Every now and then, though, it tends to be remembered for a while.

At Lawton that night Jeff was leading, and Sammy was having a tough night, getting lapped. That was very, very unusual for Sammy. Steve was second, and I was third. Jeff lapped Sammy, and it looked like Sammy was holding Steve up a little bit. Steve finally got by, and when I got to Sammy I raced for maybe a half-lap and I got too impatient. I thought Jeff and Steve were getting away from me. There were no infield markers, just a nice grass infield. I dove into the grass to try and slide him. I hit that grass and it was like ice. I shot right up into him, right into his side. It spun him sideways and I bicycled. I kept going, and I'm not sure about Sammy. I don't even remember where I finished.

Somebody had a picture of our contact, with him sliding sideways and me completely out of control. I heard later that Sammy hung that picture up in his trailer with the words "My hero" written on it.

I felt like he should have given me more room, but I shouldn't have driven over the top of him. But after a while I just forgot about it. Which is what you have to do. If you hold a grudge forever, it's going to eat you up.

Another big star when I first started was Doug Wolfgang. He was a guy that I really looked up to. He was already a legend in the sport, and had won races all over the country. I always felt like he was a bright, smart person. Doug was articulate, and he knew how to say things. When he spoke, people listened.

He was probably the smoothest driver I ever saw. He could make it look easy, like there was no effort. When he was right at Eldora, for example, it didn't even look like he was turning the steering wheel. That takes some skill, to make it look that easy.

He could probably run a loose race car better than anybody, because he ran the car so straight. His laps were always very consistent. There was a reason he was one of the Big Three: Steve, Sammy, and Doug. He was a super, super talent.

One time I saw a World of Outlaws ad for an upcoming race, and they had four pictures in the ad: Steve, Sammy, Doug, and myself. That gave me a rush that you can't believe.

Bobby Allen was a guy that had a big role in the sport at the time as well. Bobby originally came from Florida, and he led the pilgrimage to central Pennsylvania in the late 1960s. What a great collection of racers that was. Van and Dub May came from Texas, Steve Smith came from Florida, Jan Opperman from Nebraska, Kenny Weld from Kansas City.

When Bobby came to Pennsylvania he was a very progressive influence there, with his chassis work and his ideas. He was innovative.

He would help anyone, even when he knew it would take money out of his own pocket. He would tell you what tire, what gear, what line to drive, then you'd go out and beat him with his own information. He was totally unselfish.

Bobby has a wicked, warped sense of humor. He used to gross you out in a funny way, just doing silly, dumb stuff. Lots of sight gags. He had these false teeth he'd play with, just to make people laugh. He was always fun to be around.

You'd always find him on the bottom groove. He was the best I ever saw at running the bottom. Even when there was no groove there, he could be fast. He won a lot of races in his time.

Bobby Davis Jr. is another guy that was very quiet, very private. He was very focused on his career. You never saw him out partying after the races – he would keep a very low profile.

He shocked me once at San Jose. I was in the motel parking lot trying to square the rear end of Stanton's car. That's hard to do by yourself, and Bobby saw me struggling from his room and came outside. He walked up and grabbed one end of the tape measure and said, "Looks like you need some help!" That was truly a nice thing to do, and I've never forgotten that day.

Bobby was very mechanically able, and very meticulous. He could work on a car all day long and not get a spot on his jeans. He was very knowledgeable about setups, and I think he had a lot of input on the cars he drove. That's impressive, because I think he made a lot of cars go faster with his knowledge and his driving skill.

He and Sammy reinforced my belief that at this level you better be able to understand what your car is doing. That's a key element to success.

Bobby was just very quiet. We never really had a tight friendship, but I guess that was true with most of my competitors. But Bobby was a guy that clearly was a top-caliber driver.

Jeff Swindell came on the scene at about the same time I did. I remember my first trip to Syracuse, New York, and Jeff and I were both running on the big mile for the first time. We were parked in the back waiting for the pits to open, and Jeff and I walked up to the fence and looked out at this huge track. We were in awe.

Jeff ran really well that weekend, and had a top-five finish. I was very impressed, and from that moment I knew that Jeff had a lot of skill.

I always thought it was tough for Jeff, because he was compared a lot with Sammy. They are as different as night and day, and Jeff has proven that he's a good race driver in his own right. Jeff's also a good TV commentator.

You can't think about the Outlaws without talking about Ted Johnson. Despite anything you might think about Ted, he had the staying power to make this deal happen.

I don't know how the World of Outlaws got started, because I wasn't there. But Ted definitely came away as the leader, no matter what happened early on.

I've had run-ins with Ted, and been so mad at him at times that I figured I'd never speak to him again. But he is actually a pretty likable guy. He did frustrate me at times, because he is very hard to pin down on an issue. He always left himself some room, whenever you were dealing with him on any issue. He is a tough negotiator.

Part of the thing with Ted is that he's in a very tough job. When I raced, I thought being an official was easy. After I got away from the driving side, and became more involved with television, I began to see things from a different point of view. For example, we all screamed about the scheduling, but when you have 20 or 30 promoters wanting certain dates, when you make the schedule somebody isn't going to be happy. It's not as simple as I thought it was.

Ted can be as charming, or as abrasive, as he wants to be. I've seen both sides of the man. I think life has hardened him because he's survived being in a tough business, and he's survived two bouts with cancer. He's a guy that never opens up and lets his guard down. That's just his way. He's had plenty of people through the years who tried to take things from him, so maybe that's why he seems hard and distant sometimes. I think I understand him more now, and I understand why he's developed such a tough shell around him.

I like to tease Ron Shuman. I've told him the he probably still has 90 cents of every dollar he raced for! Really, he was one of the first guys I met who knew how to look at racing as a business. He was a very responsible, sensible person, probably ahead of his time in the sport in that respect.

A car owner once told me that Shuman could roll in off the race track, flip up his shield, and tell him exactly how much he owed him from the race. That's probably an exaggeration, but I like to laugh when I think about that description.

Looking back, Ron was very supportive of my career. He once helped me get a midget ride at I-70 Speedway, and I won three out of four races, and finished second in the fourth one (naturally, I was disappointed I didn't win 'em all). He walked over and asked me, "Doty, where in the hell did you learn to drive a midget?"

He was a thinking race driver. If you gave him a chance, he was going to outsmart you. There are many different ways to win races, and Shuman knew 'em all. He was seldom spectacular, but that's definitely a compliment. He was good on equipment and he knew where the pay window was. He was a proven winner, and a good guy to race with.

When I first saw Danny Smith coming over to Ohio early in my career, I had him figured as a cocky, arrogant guy. Because he always seemed so distant, for a long time I thought he didn't like me. He was fast on the race track, though, and I learned that he was a guy that you had to work at to beat. Like a lot of us, he went through a period early in his career where he learned how to crash. But I'll bet some of that was the pressure of being with a top-flight team, and being expected to perform.

But he was always a good, solid racer. Over the years we began to cultivate a friendship, and in early 1999 I spent a day or two with him in Australia, driving around the country sightseeing on the Great Ocean Road along the southern coast. We had a great time. Sometimes you'll find that people away from the race track are very different, and Danny is like that. He's got a big heart, and he's a very friendly, pleasant guy.

Even though we were both from Ohio, I didn't race a lot against Jack Hewitt. We seemed to be on different paths. He's probably a guy who's had equal success with and without a wing, and you can't say that about many people. He won a ton of races with the All Stars, and today he's still very successful with USAC, running without the wing. That's pretty impressive, really, that he's been able to stay fast for so long.

Jack is the kind of guy that can make you really mad, but you can't stay mad. You might have a big blow-up with him, and he's even settled the score with a punch or two. But when it's all over, he might walk in your trailer a few days later to ask you a question, like nothing ever happened. When he senses that you're still mad, he might put his arm around you, and say something like, "Aw, you're not still mad at me, are you?" Then he might give you a kiss on the cheek. Can you imagine?

Just a year or so ago, a bunch of us went down to do a fundraiser for the Make-a-Wish Foundation at St. Henry Nite Club, near Eldora. Jack was his usual, very colorful, funny, wonderful self. He just stole the show.

When I was racing all over the country, I always thought it was cool that Jac Haudenschild was out there as well. Jac is a fun, great guy. You'll never find a more easygoing, laid-back guy than Jac. I've known him all my life, and I've never once seen him going off on somebody and talking bad about them. One of his biggest assets as a person is that he doesn't get caught up in trivial arguments and stuff like that. When Jac left a team, he'd just unbolt his seat, take his steering box, and be on his way.

Some people probably had him figured as a wild, rough driver, but he's fooled them. He's matured so much, he's become a smooth, tough racer. His record at Eldora speaks for itself. When the track is slick, he's got better throttle control than anybody I've seen. He's far from a stab-and-steer guy. He's shown the ability to use all the finesse you need to go fast.

He runs the car straight, and can keep the tires under him, to keep them from spinning. He's as good as anybody in that respect.

Even when he makes you mad, you can't stay mad at him. It's impossible. He just grins at you, and it's all over.

I was always amazed that Jac, Kenny Jacobs, and myself all managed to reach the top level of sprint car racing, from our little area in Ohio. Ed Haudenschild could have been out there with us, but Ed was the kind of guy that was very responsible, and when he started a family he wanted to stick close to home. But for three or four guys to come up together and all make it in the sport, I was always proud of our little group.

Early on, Kenny wanted to quit his job and go full-time racing. We used to play basketball on Wednesday nights in the winter to stay in shape, and I remember one night when he was agonizing over his decision. Should he keep his job, or quit and race full time? He was driving for Ed Reno at the time, who was like a second dad to Kenny. They were very close.

The money he made in racing was "mad money," as he called it. He had the income from his job, so the racing money was like a bonus. I tried to tell Kenny that when you're doing it for a living, and you get to the next level, the pressures are much greater. I don't think he realized that at the time. But he made the commitment, and quit to race full-time. Later on, we talked about the difference, and he agreed after being there that a full-time guy sees things from a much more tense perspective.

Kenny is a very patient racer. He's never torn up much equipment. He has always been a bright, thinking race driver. Of all of us kids, he was the most patient racer. He is a guy with strong opinions, and he doesn't mind sharing them sometimes! He would have been a champion debater in school, let me tell you. He's very persuasive in getting you to share his point of view.

He's had a great career. He's won more All Star races than anyone in history.

The neat thing about our group of guys is that we never let competitive pressures harm our friendship. All four of us are as warm and pleasant with each other today as we ever were. Our wives are even friends. It's a good group of people, and now as we grow older we appreciate each other a lot more, I think.

Sometimes when I look back at my driving career I think about the money I made, but the reality is that money comes and goes. It's the memories that stay with you. The scenery I saw, and the people I met – those memories will stay with me for the rest of my life. Sometimes it was a grind, and I wondered why I kept doing it. But I'm glad that I did.

16

By the middle of the 1988 season, I was glad to be back racing with Gary Stanton. The season hadn't been very successful for me up to that point, but I was confident that Gary and I had the right combination. Gary had changed car numbers: Instead of No. 75 he was now running No. 40.

We didn't have much luck to begin with. Our first night back together we raced at Knoxville, where I spun out in the feature and everybody was scrambling to miss me. It's nerve-wracking for a few seconds in that situation, sitting there listening to the cars go past, wondering if somebody has your number. That night, the very last guy coming past nailed me. It knocked me goofy, and I had a serious concussion. I told the emergency crew I was all right, and I walked back to the pits.

I asked Gary what happened, and he told me I spun and somebody hit me. Two minutes later I said, "Gary, what happened?" Gary told me again. I was sitting there with a goofy, empty stare. Another minute or two and I asked Gary what happened. I think he figured out by then that I wasn't quite right, so he put me on his four-wheeler. We drove back through the parking area looking for my motor home, where Laurie and the kids were staying. The problem was, I couldn't remember where I'd parked it.

We finally found the motor home, and I went in and sat down on the couch. Laurie and the kids were there; they didn't know I had crashed. I sat there and looked at these two little kids playing on the floor, and I realized that I couldn't remember their names.

Obviously, by then we all figured out that something was definitely wrong. They took me to the local hospital, and they sat me down and started to examine me. The doctor would come in the room, and talk to us for a minute, then he'd leave for a short time and return. Each time he came back I'd say, "Hey, don't I know you from somewhere?" I guess it was kind of funny, but maybe you had to be there.

He was trying to test my short-term memory, and my brain functions, and he asked me to remember the sequence: apples, oranges, and bananas. He kept asking me to repeat the sequence, apples, oranges, and bananas. I had trouble with bananas. Maybe I *was* bananas. I told them I was going to leave, because I couldn't remember why I was there! But Laurie took my firesuit, leaving me with no clothes for my escape plan. So I was parked for the night. I think Laurie wanted me to stay just so I wouldn't ask her all night, "What happened?"

By the next day I was a little better, so they released me. I was still goofy, but my memory was coming back. The deal was that if I could remember apples, oranges, and bananas, they would let me go. After considerable work, I finally got it down. Maybe that's tough for me on a good day!

We drove to Eagle Raceway in Lincoln, Nebraska, where we raced a couple of days later. We blew the motor the first night, then came back to finish fifth. So we felt like we were close, we were competitive. Maybe things were going to turn around.

We went to Colorado National Speedway, where we ran second in our heat, won the dash, and finished fourth in the main event. Then we came back the next night and finished 10th.

Black Hills Speedway was the next stop, which was one of our favorite trips. We loved the South Dakota scenery, and driving through the Black Hills. We looked forward to that all year. We usually visited Mount Rushmore, and took some family time. It was nice. At the track we ran eighth, then it was on to Jackson, Minnesota, where we finished ninth.

We drove on to Fargo, North Dakota, where we ran eighth on the first night at Red River Valley Speedway. The second night we fell out with mechanical problems. In early July we headed back to the midwest.

My dad and I were driving to Eldora Speedway to run a USAC event (I ran third), and I saw a short-bed Chevy pickup on a used car lot in the little town of Bucyrus, Ohio. I had been looking for a truck to customize. I was going to be one of the first guys in Ohio to have a lowered, custom truck, like I had seen in California.

The next day we won a USAC event at Millstream Speedway in Findlay, Ohio, and then we had a few days off before the Kings Royal at Eldora.

We went home for a birthday party for Braden, who turned two years old on July 22. Laurie was expecting our third child in a couple of months, so our family was growing. Life was pretty good at that stage. It looked like my racing season was improving, and I had a truck to work on. I was a pretty happy guy.

July 23, 1988. That was a day that changed my life, for sure. Laurie stayed home that night. I made the drive down to Eldora by myself, and it felt kind of unusual to be traveling alone again.

I was very optimistic about Eldora. Gary had put together a new car which he had only raced a time or two with Wolfgang. It was a car that Gary liked a lot; he liked the geometry and figured it would work well at Eldora.

On Saturday night we were awesome in our heat race. It was one of my best races of the year, so I looked toward the feature as maybe my best shot ever to win the Kings Royal. And winning $50,000 is enough to motivate anybody. In the heat I moved into second and Ricky Hood had a straightaway lead, and at Eldora that's usually too much to make up. But I ran him down and passed him on the outside on the last lap, just squeezing between him and the wall. I felt great, the car was fast, and we were ready.

Gary had won the Kings Royal the year before with Jac in the car. So I felt some added pressure, because I felt like I should be capable of winning as well.

They lined the cars up on the front straightaway for driver introductions. I lined up next to Jimmy Sills. They were giving away a watch to each of the drivers. The funny thing was, the watches said "Knoxville Raceway." Jimmy had crashed somewhere a day or two earlier, and had rung his bell (apples, oranges, and bananas...). Jimmy was looking at the watch and I was teasing him, saying, "Man, you're probably really confused now. What track are you at, Jimmy, what track..."

We laughed, and I climbed in and belted up. It now seems so dramatic, looking back. I've seen pictures of me standing by my front wheel that night, and when I look at the picture it kind of takes my breath away. I had no way of knowing that in a matter of minutes my life adventure was going to take a new direction.

We fired the cars, and I found my starting position. I could tell that the track was still wet from the water truck, so I hoped everybody would stay on their toes and get through the start. We did the parade lap, then we were ready to race.

I still remember it very well. The car had a full load of fuel, so I didn't really know exactly how it was going to handle at first. The green flag came out, and I drove down into turn one and tried to run the car straight. It took a big push, and slid all the way from the bottom of the track to the outside. Several guys got past me while I was pushing across the track, including Jeff Swindell. Jeff drove past on the outside, in the middle of turns one and two, and I tucked in behind him. Coming off the corner, right up by the wall, there was a slick spot, and Jeff hit that spot and slipped sideways.

I had nowhere to go. I remember thinking, "Man, this is going to be a good one." I jumped his left rear, and started flipping. When the car was shooting up toward the sky, I knew it was going to be a hard ride. But I'd always walked away, so surely this would be okay, right?

There were four or five cars involved in the crash. Everybody was piling in very hard. On the start everybody is so close together that if there's trouble, it usually involves several cars. Doug Wolfgang was driving Les Kepler's car, and he plowed into the mess, flipping very high in the air. There were actually three or four cars flipping at one time. It was a very violent accident. I was coming down on my top, upside down, when Dave Blaney hit me very hard in the back of my roll cage. I flipped two or three more times, with the car coming apart all around me, until it was finally over.

When Dave hit me, it kind of knocked me out. I don't remember any of this, but when the emergency workers got to the car I was moaning in pain, and telling them I couldn't move my legs. They began prying me out of the car, while I came in and out of consciousness.

Of all the things I say in this book, I want to make it very clear that I don't blame anyone for the accident. It was just a part of racing that happens sometimes, when an unfortunate set of circumstances adds up to someone getting hurt. In this case, I was the one who got hurt. Other drivers have told me privately that they felt bad, that it might have been their fault, that kind of thing. But that's silly. It really is. Looking at it very honestly, nobody did anything wrong. It just happened. There are still days that I wonder why it had to happen, but I don't blame anyone personally.

They were having a very hard time getting me out of the car. A piece of tubing had penetrated my helmet, breaking both the outer shell and the inner liner, stopping about a quarter-inch from my head. Yet, I didn't have a head injury. I've often thought that maybe I was fortunate that the tubing penetrated the shell, because otherwise it would have been a massive blow to the head.

Another piece of tubing looked like it had penetrated my chest. They had to take a hacksaw and cut it off – they thought it had impaled me. When they cut the piece off it just dropped harmlessly to the ground, with no wound.

Gary Stanton had arrived on the scene, and he was shocked. He said later that he had never seen anything like it, with pieces of tubing looking like they were stuck through me. He said he had never seen a car come apart like that.

There was a lot of talk later on that the tubing was too thin, or at least that was the rumor. I asked Gary about that, and he said it wasn't an unusually light car, only the geometry was changed. The roll cage and frame were built on a jig, and that isn't something that can easily be changed for one car. In my mind, I wonder if it wasn't just that the crash was so violent, nothing could withstand it. Plus, Gary was not necessarily a guy who was real aggressive about cutting weight, so I don't think he would have built a thin-tube car to save a couple of pounds. It just wasn't worth it.

I think everyone at the scene was in a state of shock. A lot of people were scared, because it looked very bad for me. They finally got me out of the car, and loaded me into an ambulance. They started up Route 118 to Coldwater, Ohio, where they stabilized me and waited on the helicopter that would transport me to the trauma unit in Dayton.

Right after I arrived, an ambulance brought in a kid that had been in a car accident. He was also in bad shape, and they decided to send him to Dayton first. Ed Haudenschild had arrived in Coldwater, and as they prepared me for the flight he drove back to the track to pick up his wife Tammy. Ed had to find the keys to my truck, which was parked in the infield. He went on to Dayton and they got there earlier than I did. I was at Coldwater for a while waiting on a second helicopter.

I was wearing a brand new driving uniform, and they cut it to shreds that night. But that was the least of my worries.

I had fractured the thoracic level vertebra between T-4 and T-5, which is about the middle of my back. I've looked at pictures of the car, and I still can't figure out exactly what hit me that broke the vertebra. I figured my seat would be all bent, but it wasn't. I flipped another time or two after I was hit, and everything was destroyed on the car, and I didn't have any belts on. So we figured that maybe I whipped around on that last flip, and maybe that did it. It was actually amazing that I didn't have other injuries.

From the track, Elayne Haudenschild made the telephone call to Laurie. The two of them had made a deal a long time ago that if something happened to the other's husband, they would call one another and be as truthful as possible. Elayne told her it was pretty bad, and laid it out for her.

Laurie didn't really know of my exact injuries, but she knew it was serious. She called her mom and they made the trip to Dayton, a four-hour drive through the night. She was almost eight months pregnant. What a miserable ride that must have been.

Laurie is a very smart, intuitive person. She knew from Elaine's call that something very, very bad had happened. She was offered a private airplane to make the trip to Dayton, but she looked at our little kids and said, "They might not have a dad anymore, and I'm not going to leave them without a mom as well." So she and her mom loaded the kids in the car and headed for Dayton, driving through the night.

Sometime in the early morning hours, the helicopter delivered me to Miami Valley Hospital in Dayton. I was stable by then, but we didn't know about the severity of the back injuries.

I was in and out, but I kept saying, "My back, my back," and "I can't move my legs!" So I was kind of aware of what was going on.

At around 6 a.m. Laurie was allowed in to see me. They were doing x-rays and using a scope to check for internal injuries. What a shock that must have been for her, seeing a hole in my stomach and this cord inserted into my body, with someone looking at the internal images.

That morning they did surgery. It took eight hours for the surgeons to insert rods and wires to try and put things together. While they did surgery on my back they had me lying on my stomach. All the fluids collected in my hands and face, and they swelled to grotesque proportions. Unbelievable proportions.

When Laurie walked in and saw me, she nearly fainted, I looked so grotesque.

After the surgery a doctor walked out to address a group of about 15 people who were waiting. My family, Ed, Kenny, and others were there. He said straight out that I had a one-tenth of one percent chance of walking again. I know that many of my family and friends took that news very, very hard. It was an emotional, intense moment in that room. Strong, tough men were crying.

Outside, the hospital parking lot was full of motor homes and race car haulers. They asked the racing people to move their vehicles before 6:00 a.m., because there was no room in the parking lot for the next shift of employees. Their switchboard was lighting up with calls from all over the country, people concerned about me. Some of my fellow drivers and friends were waiting downstairs. There was nothing they could do, but it was wonderful that they cared enough to show that kind of support. Today, looking back, that means more than they will ever know.

People were calling from all over the country, asking to talk with Laurie. She just wasn't up to all of that, so Ed fielded the calls. We couldn't have made it those first few hours without Ed.

Right after the surgery my lungs collapsed. I was slipping away, slowly but surely. The crash had bent me backward, and badly bruised my lungs. My chest cavity kept filling with blood and fluids, until the pressure finally just collapsed my lungs. I couldn't breathe. They had huge tubes inserted through my back to try and drain my chest cavity, and big oxygen hoses running through my nose in an attempt to keep my lungs inflated, and allow me to breathe.

The medical people at Dayton were fighting to keep me alive during those first few hours after surgery. I knew none of this, but people were working hard to allow me to see Laurie again, to hold my kids, to live.

Something deep inside of me responded, and kept me fighting for life. A force I wasn't even aware of, a feeling I didn't know I had within me. But as I lay there with machines connected to me, knowing only a foggy, groggy haze mixed with intense pain, I wanted to live. That's all that mattered. I wanted to live.

17

For the first few days it was me and my thumb, pumping morphine. They had a delivery system that I could apply with my thumb, and I kept it working. God, I was hurting. It was a pain that was intense and constant.

I had hallucinations from the morphine. I kept seeing cobwebs all over the room, and smelling paint fumes so much that it made me sick. It was all my imagination, but it seemed so real. I looked at Laurie one time and she looked like she was about 80 years old. It was frightening.

It was almost a week before I began to wake up and comprehend my surroundings. By then my condition had stabilized, and my survival seemed assured. They had me on so much morphine that I remember only bits and pieces from that period. I had a recurring dream that I was looking through plastic, trying to talk, and nobody could hear me. Years later I think that was when I still had my helmet on, and was still in the car, and I was trying to communicate with the emergency workers.

They had me on a respirator, and I felt like I was constantly choking for air. They kept telling me to relax, to let the respirator work. I kept trying to pull it out, but supposedly it's impossible to remove when it is inflated. But finally in the middle of the night I pulled the thing out, and I could breathe on my own. So they figured I didn't need it, and they didn't reinsert it.

Four days after the crash, on July 27, I begged Laurie to let me see the kids. It was my 31st birthday, and they brought a birthday cake in. I hadn't eaten any solid food yet. Laurie tried to prepare the kids. She told them that Daddy doesn't look like Daddy, and she tried to keep them calm. I was aware enough at the time that I really wanted to see them.

Brandy was five years old, and Braden was just two. The nurse put some icing on her finger and allowed me to taste it, but I gagged from the taste. Brandy picked up a small sponge from the cup beside my bed, and handed it to me, saying very soft and gently, "Here, Daddy, you can wipe your mouth." I still get emotional when I think of that scene.

It was a watershed moment in my life. Maybe it would have been better for them if I had died, because their burden would have been gone. But I wanted more than anything to see my kids grow up. Maybe I couldn't race, maybe I couldn't walk, but all that was okay. I was thinking only of living. The only thing that mattered was seeing those kids grow up. It motivated me in a major, major way. That was the point where I said that I had to get through this. Somehow, I had to survive. There were no options.

We had a lot of friends and family there to help us and support us. Ed was a saint. He kept everyone calm, and got things organized. He stayed for days at a time, talked with the press, and he just handled the things that were needed. What a friend.

I was in ICU for about 10 days. Ed stayed at the hospital for four or five days. They had a room there he rented, like a dorm room. Laurie had a room, also. Everybody stayed close. One night some of them went out to eat but they got too worried that something might happen to me, so they hurried back to the hospital.

We all got a good look at how the system works. Or doesn't work, depending on how you look at it. Some of the social workers were incredibly callous and insensitive to Laurie and our family. They just didn't show much compassion.

One woman in particular really got on everyone's nerves. Ed finally told her, "Look, you've already written him off. Three days after he leaves here, you won't remember his name. We're going to spend the rest of our lives with him. If you're not going to help us, just leave us alone."

After three or four days they began weaning me off the morphine. I began to wake up, but I didn't fully understand my environment. I just didn't know what had happened. Laurie did not leave the building during my stay in ICU.

One of the visitors during that time was Ted Johnson. Ted told Laurie that many years earlier when he had cancer they told him he didn't have much of a chance to survive. He beat the odds, and he told Laurie not to give up. She says today that Ted's words stayed with her for a long time.

From the time they were cutting me out of the car I knew I couldn't move my legs. I knew, but I didn't comprehend.

When I'd wake up early in the morning, I'd ask for Laurie. The nurses would call her, and she'd come in and stay for the rest of the day. I needed her desperately. I battled with my emotions, some days wanting to live and the next day wishing I could die.

Laurie's ankles swelled up from being on her feet, and her pregnancy, and she'd try to keep her legs out of sight of the doctors. She lost weight during this period, maybe walking five miles each day, between walking down to see me and walking back to see the kids.

After one week, they had me sitting up in a chair. I wasn't happy about it, because it hurt. It hurt a lot. But they were trying to get me moving around, because that's what I needed.

They were arranging a transfer to a rehabilitative facility in Chardon, Ohio, near Cleveland. I don't know how they chose that facility, but it was a disaster for me, and for my family. It wasn't a hospital; it was a nursing home for old people. They had no idea how to deal with my condition. They didn't have the equipment, the personnel, or the knowledge. It was a complete mistake, sending me there.

Our insurance would only pay for one transfer, which was used up from the track to Coldwater. So the ambulance company wouldn't take me unless they were paid up front. By this time people were already trying to raise money to help us, and somebody brought Laurie some money from where drivers had passed the helmets at a track somewhere. Laurie counted out 700 $1 bills to pay them. They were kind of crappy about getting paid, so maybe it was justice to pay them in small bills.

They loaded me into an ambulance, and we began a difficult, painful trip. As we headed up I-71, I could lift my head slightly and get a tiny glimpse through the window. I saw us roll past a big truck stop where I used to stop and fuel our motor home. All of a sudden I realized that I would never do that again, jump down out of that motor home and run inside to pay. I began to cry, the kind of tears that come when the stark reality of the situation makes it impossible to ignore.

At Chardon my situation began to sink in. I was severely depressed, and my environment made it worse. All around me old people were screaming or moaning, constantly.

I couldn't sleep at night because of the noise. It was miserable. I couldn't cope with what had happened, and then they put me in a place like this. Laurie went home to regroup for just a day, then came on to Chardon. She brought me a little Walkman stereo so that I could try to drown out all the surrounding noise and sleep at night. One night I heard the John Mellencamp song *Cherry Bomb*, and I woke up thinking I was tapping my foot, but of course I wasn't. I was so bummed. I lay there, remembering that weekend in Dallas, hanging out with Larry Crane.

I remembered going to see them in concert at the arena in Columbus, where so much beer had been slopped on the floor that my leather-soled cowboy boots soaked the liquid up to the point of getting my feet wet. I lay there thinking that I'd never get my feet wet again, never stand at a concert, never get to walk backstage. Hearing that song reminded me of all that I had lost, and I cried out in anguish.

My room didn't even have a TV. Bob Murden had been involved with Gary Runyon's car, and he and Gary drove all the way over from Indianapolis to bring me a new TV for my room, because they found out I didn't have one.

Along with Laurie, Ed and Tammy came up to see me, and every day I was upset when they left. I didn't want to be alone.

244

I told them that I wanted to die. Ed just wouldn't let me give up. He continued to work on me, and told me that dying was too easy. Anybody could die. It took a man to keep fighting, to keep trying.

After four or five days Laurie and I had enough of Chardon. She arranged for a transfer, but before she did she wanted to see where I was going. She and my dad visited Dodd Hall in Columbus, at Ohio State University. She felt like it would be an improvement.

That was a lifesaver for me. I had a pressure sore from Chardon, on my tailbone. So they couldn't do much right away. But at Columbus I had much better care. The nurses came in every few hours to make sure I was moving around, to prevent other sores.

When the nurses walked in and out of the room, I would study the muscles in their legs, watching them walking so easily, so effortlessly. God, I resented them. As I looked down at my legs wanting desperately to move them, how could anyone else understand how I felt?

At Columbus I was around other people who had similar injuries. Some of those guys were very active and already moving around in wheelchairs, and that bugged me. I wasn't recovered enough to begin therapy, but they would roll my bed down to the therapy room so I could watch how it was done.

They first put me on a board that sort of stood me up. After just a minute or two they had to put me back down because I was so light-headed. I had been flat on my back for more than two weeks, so it was a big adjustment to moving my body to a vertical position.

There were four guys in the room with me; two paraplegic and two quadriplegic. A paraplegic has the use of the arms; a quadriplegic cannot use any of the limbs. When I'd complain about my situation, one of the quad guys would tell me that I had nothing to complain about, saying, "At least you've got your hands." I didn't care, though, because that wasn't enough. I just felt sorry for myself.

Actually, if my injury would have been a tiny bit higher, I wouldn't have had my hands. I'm really, really lucky.

One of the first days that I was to go on my own to therapy, I had to wheel a big heavy chair down a hall of about 100 feet. But I couldn't do it. I was too weak. That was about three weeks after the crash. I could only go a few feet before I had to stop and catch my breath. In ICU you're pampered, and everything is brought to you. So when I began rehab, it was a big adjustment.

I started out wanting it all back. That wasn't going to happen, but I was sure I was going to be one of the lucky few to regain everything. That was simply being in denial, and eventually I began to realize that there would be no miracles. This was it.

While I was in Columbus, Jac came to see me. He sat by my bed and we began to talk. He broke down and sobbed, and I was trying to console him, telling him that things would be okay. I was thinking to myself as I talked to him, "I hope this doesn't slow him down, I hope this doesn't affect his career." At the same time, it showed me that many other people were in this with me, people that cared about my life.

Everything seemed so hard. Watching your friends cry is painful. It took a long time before people stopped crying.

I had a lot of visitors those first few weeks. It was nice seeing everyone, but at the same time it was very painful when they left.

Jimmy Sills came to see me. They were racing in the area, and he had Bob Weikert's rig parked outside. He pushed me outside, and I hadn't been out in the sun for so long, it just killed my eyes. I was so weak I could barely sit up. Maybe Jimmy saw the desperation in my eyes, I don't know. But I know it really affected him. Jimmy quit racing for a while after that. I know he wasn't happy at that point in his career, and the combination of that and seeing me probably influenced him a lot. He probably had that private conversation with himself, saying, "I could wind up just like Brad; is it worth it?" Maybe for a while, it wasn't. But fortunately he came back later and was better than ever.

It really bothered me that my accident might have influenced Jimmy to quit. I didn't want what had happened to me to affect others, darn it. I knew how hard you have to work, and stay focused, to be successful as a race driver. I didn't want guys looking at me and losing their focus. Especially a guy like Jimmy, who was such a great guy to race with. He is a good, clean racer you could always trust. He was a gentleman racer. You never had to worry about him. I wanted him to continue to be successful. I didn't want anyone to slow down because of me.

I was in Columbus for 30 days. That's how much our insurance would cover. You have to pass different levels of doing things, such as being able to cook dinner, things like that. The normal program is 90 days, but since we only had 30 days coverage they crammed everything into the shorter time period.

For my injury, there wasn't really any rehabilitation. My spinal cord was damaged, and that was that. You can't rehabilitate that like you can a broken arm or something. My program consisted mainly of them teaching me how to adjust my lifestyle, and learn different ways of doing basic things.

All the time in Columbus, I remained very, very depressed. It got so bad that when people visited, they probably felt better to get away from me, because I was totally negative about everything. I felt like nobody understood what I felt, what I had lost. I really didn't appreciate that my situation had affected all those people around me.

Brittani was born on September 7. I was still in Columbus. I wasn't there for the birth, but the next day Kenny Jacobs drove me up to Orrville to visit Laurie and the baby in the hospital.

That was my first day out in the big bad world in a wheelchair. I found out that I couldn't even get into the bathroom at the hospital, because it wasn't accessible. If it's going to be this hard, I thought, there's just no way.

Laurie had gone through Brittani's birth without me. Laurie had so much to deal with, but I was still selfishly leaning on her for support. But she needed me, and I should have been stronger for her.

When she had Brittani, she vented all of the emotion that she had held inside her. She had been incredibly strong, through all of it, and was very tough. But when I came wheeling in to the hospital, and I wasn't even strong enough to sit up and hold my child, she began to realize that this was how it was going to be.

She broke down and cried, and cried, and cried. And there wasn't a thing I could do but listen. I couldn't make anything better. She was just overwhelmed with everything, and she couldn't deal with it any longer.

That moment was probably the bottom. I was wrecked, my wife was wrecked, our life was wrecked. Even Brittani's eyes looked tired, as a newborn. Maybe it was all the stress Laurie had undergone, the sleepless nights, the missed meals. I don't know. It was a hard, painful period.

But from the bottom we gathered ourselves up and started to inch our way back.

I got some false hopes along the way. I got goosebumps on my legs, and sweat below my injury line. That was very unusual. So I thought maybe the use of my legs was coming back. But it just led to more depression.

With a spinal injury, they really don't know what you might get back. You just wait, and wait, and wait. When I'd sweat pools of liquid at night, I was miserable, thinking it was going to be like this forever. And the doctors couldn't tell me if it would quit, or why it would quit. So we were very, very frustrated. After a while, though, the sweating gradually went away.

I had already started the customizing process of my Chevy truck when I got hurt. While I was in Columbus, the parts arrived that I had ordered to lower the suspension. Ed and Kenny installed the parts, then to cheer me up, Kenny brought the truck to the hospital.

That fall Kenny won the National Open at Williams Grove. When he got out of the car the first thing he asked for was a telephone, because he wanted to call me and tell me that he had won. I was truly happy and excited for him, but when I hung up the phone, I sat in the quiet, lonely room with my empty feelings, flat on my back. I couldn't help but think, "Well, I'll never do that again."

From the time I left ICU, I cried almost every day. I went through periods where I couldn't hold back the emotions.

While I was in Columbus they wheeled me in to visit with a psychologist. We started to talk, and I broke down and cried like a baby. I told him what I had lost, who I was, and all the reasons that this injury had devastated me. I told him that I wasn't sure how I could go on. He just looked at me kind of blankly and basically said, "Brad, I don't know what to tell you."

That's when I knew that if I were going to get through this, I had to do it on my own.

Another time I was sitting outside and the same psychologist came jogging up; he liked to exercise during his lunch hour. A pretty girl had just walked past, and the guy stopped running for a second and made some kind of rude remark about the girl, laughed, and jogged on his way. I thought, "You son of a bitch, you don't have a clue."

Whenever I'd see anyone walk, I would get angry and resentful. The emotional struggles were like a giant roller coaster that seemed to go forever. I might be fine for a few minutes at a time, and then something would happen that reminded me of my situation, and the emotions would be released in a torrent.

Losing my career was one part of it. I had just come off my best year ever, and I felt like my career still had room to grow. Now, I felt like I had lost all my independence. I was a hands-on person who always made my own way, and at this point all that had stopped. I couldn't comprehend that it would ever get any better.

When I took my first shower a week or so after the crash, they lifted me off onto a netted gurney, and a nurse gave me a shower. I was still too much out of it to really understand. But I realized that the lady was giving me a shower, and I just lay there, literally wishing I could die.

No matter what anybody tells you, you can't see far enough ahead to think it's going to get any better, or that it's not always going to be this way.

I was enveloped in this huge fog of sadness, and I couldn't get away from it. Every few minutes, I had this jolt in my stomach, the pain of realization that my situation was permanent. People tried to cheer me up, but I just couldn't hear them. They smiled, but I had forgotten how.

18

Race fans are the greatest people in the world. From the first day following my crash, racing people lined up to help us. Today, years later, it is difficult for me to talk about without getting choked up.

During all this misery, and pain, thank God we didn't have to worry about money. We had a big motor home payment, and a house payment, so we had liabilities. But money started coming in so quickly that we could handle our short-term liabilities without all the anxiety that so often is a part of a crisis like this.

Kenny and Kim Jacobs came up with the idea of raffling off my motor home. Before I was even out of the hospital, people began buying tickets. When it was all said and done they raised enough to pay off the motor home, and we were out from under the payment.

At tracks they passed the helmets, and at Knoxville they raised money with an auction of memorabilia.

I've always made it a point not to single out the people who helped me, because there were so many race tracks and individuals that we couldn't keep a record of them all. And it would break my heart to leave someone out in my thanks. But the scope of all of this was just overwhelming.

All of this support had a profound effect on our life. We were able to focus on life issues, not money. The money situation just took care of itself, leaving us to work on dealing with all that this injury had brought.

And the incredible thing is that the money didn't stop. A month passed, then two, then six, finally a year, before it began to slow. People sold T-shirts to help us, and it kept coming. We got cards with a small check, or maybe a few dollars. But the messages in the cards and letters were so heartfelt; it was unbelievable how much people cared.

As my weeks in Columbus passed, I was allowed to return home on weekends. That was a mixed blessing. It was meant to help me ease back into life outside of the institution, so that I could make a better adjustment. And it was great to spend time with the kids, in familiar surroundings. But when each weekend ended, it was extremely painful to leave home for the two-hour trip back to Columbus. I was so upset...there I was, an adult, forced to return to a place where I didn't want to be. Really, they might as well have been taking me back to prison. In a sense, it was the same thing.

I always tried to be strong in front of the kids on those Sunday nights when I left. I still didn't like them seeing me cry. One night Kenny was there to drive me back to Columbus, and the kids and Laurie and I were saying our good-byes out by the car. I was choked up with emotion, but I was holding it all inside, not wanting to break down in front of the kids.

We got into the car and closed the door, and Kenny said, "Man, that's hard." And I just broke down, and leaned my head down and sobbed in great heaves, the emotions released in a torrent of anguish and tears. In a moment I lifted my head and looked to the right, and Brandy and Braden were standing right outside the car door. Their eyes were focused through the window on their daddy, with a look of puzzlement and sadness. We stared at each other for a moment, as the car began to slowly back away.

After my 30 days in Columbus, they sent me home. For the first few days I was so weak that I just stayed in bed. This continued for the first week or so after I came home. It was probably an emotional issue as well as physical. It was the same home that I used to run up and down the steps to the basement. Now, I could only sit in a wheelchair at the top of the stairs, and stare down into the basement. I eventually decided to use the handrails to carry myself downstairs, just to prove that I could get down in that basement. That was a big hurdle.

For nearly a year, I hardly did anything other than watch TV at home. I had a recliner that we raised four inches so I could get from the recliner to a wheelchair.

I spent a lot of time feeling sorry for myself. But I began to make tiny bits of improvement. Sometime during the late autumn of 1988 I was sitting outside in my chair looking at my Ford Bronco, which had big, oversized tires. I thought I would never sit in it again. I rolled over there and opened the door, and it looked like that seat was a mile off the ground. I began to wonder if I could get up in there. I somehow pulled myself up onto the floorboard, slipping and sliding, and I almost fell a couple of times. Finally I got up into the seat and relaxed, basking in a moment of tiny triumph. I began honking the horn, and Laurie heard me. She came outside and was shocked.

In a way, Laurie had four children to deal with, including me. I wasn't able to help her much at all. That really bothered me, and in fact maybe that motivated me. Since she was doing all the yard work, I tried to help more in the house (that was a mistake, because now that she knows I can fold clothes and do dishes, I've got no way to get out of it).

We had to put a lift in the garage, and we changed the door hinges, and widened the bathroom door, and moved the sink around some. We were very fortunate that we lived in a one-floor ranch house, with no stairs other than the basement. But it was a very small house, so moving around in the chair was tough. Try to imagine a two-bedroom house, with three kids and a wheelchair to deal with. It was tight.

Before my accident, I loved to get down on the floor and play with Brandy and Braden. I would sometimes pretend to be a bull, and put my fingers on my head and charge at them. They would howl with laughter and excitement, running to get away. During Halloween, a month or so after I had returned home from the hospital, Laurie was getting the kids dressed up for trick-or-treating. She dressed Braden up in a little devil costume, complete with little horns.

He was so excited, and his tiny hands reached up and felt the horns on his head. He suddenly got a serious look on his face. "Daddy can't be a bull anymore," he said.

It was hard to be strong during moments like that.

For a long time, we couldn't go anywhere because we didn't have a way to go. We had the Bronco and a pickup truck, and three kids in car seats.

Some dear friends provided us with a van equipped with a wheelchair lift, and that made a big, big difference. Now we had mobility. Life was starting to come back, an inch at a time.

During my rehab at Columbus they had a driving class, to teach us how to use hand controls in a car. I adapted to that really quickly, and on the very first day the teacher allowed me to get out into traffic. He said I was the first person ever to get into traffic on the first day. I was very proud of that.

I was trying to come out of my shell. I began to remember how to laugh again. Which was harder than you might think.

From the time of my crash, I went many months without a cigarette. One day at home I was having a bad day, and I thought maybe if I started smoking again, I'd feel more like I used to. So I started hacking and coughing, all over again. I smoked for a few years before I finally quit for good. Laurie and I, along with Ed and Tammy, all quit at the same time.

I never seriously considered suing anyone. Insurance covered our bills, even though our insurance company was going bankrupt. But it made it a lot easier because with the money coming in, we didn't have financial difficulties.

I was bitter at the sport for a couple of months, but that didn't last long. I could have gotten into a lot of trouble as a kid, and racing gave me a focus. So I felt like it had still given me more than it had taken.

Plus, it was my choice to race. I don't think I could have faced myself if I had sued someone. A lawsuit was never a topic of serious discussion between Laurie and me.

A lot of people have asked why I didn't sue, especially after Doug Wolfgang successfully sued for a sizable judgment after his 1992 accident. But I personally didn't feel I should sue anyone. I just didn't.

A decision like that is highly personal, and you have to follow your conscience. We chose not to sue, and that was our business. It would be wrong for me to say what somebody else should do, because that's their decision.

Sometime during the fall of 1988 I got a call from Larry Nuber about doing an interview on ESPN's *SpeedWeek* program. I told them I'd do it, but I wouldn't allow them to show the chair. I really didn't want to do the interview, but I wanted to use the chance to thank everyone for their help, and to show everyone that I was doing okay.

At that point I still hadn't seen the film of the crash. I actually saw it by accident some months later. Seeing it kind of set me back, but by then I was curious. Later I watched it frame-by-frame, to try to understand what had happened.

My first trip back to the races was the Knoxville Nationals, 1989. To be honest, I didn't want to be there, but I felt obligated because race fans had done so much to help us. It was a way to thank people for their help. It was awkward; I really didn't want anyone to see my chair. So I stayed in my van.

A year or so later I finally agreed to do an interview with *Open Wheel Magazine*, and I told them that it was okay to take a picture of me in the chair. That was part of the healing process.

I stayed away from racing for several years. I still read *National Speed Sport News* every week, and one day I saw a picture of the new Weld spoked wheel, with five studs to hold the front wheel on. I hadn't seen one personally, and it bothered me that things seemed to be passing me by.

As time went on, I began to get restless, sitting in the house watching TV. There had to be more to life than that. I began to spend a lot of time out in the garage, tinkering with an old jigsaw. I was making scroll cuts, cutting out shapes and patterns, learning how to do woodworking. I was trying to find out what I could do.

It bothered me to watch Laurie mow the yard, because that was something I had always done. I figured out how to clamp a piece of tubing onto the clutch pedal on our riding lawn mower, so I could use my hand to operate the clutch. It was kind of like a home-made hand control. I worked on the setup for an hour or two, bending it and making it fit. I didn't want Laurie to see what I was doing until I had it finished, I wanted to surprise her. The first time I hopped up onto the mower seat, I had a death-grip on the steering wheel, because I struggled to get used to my balance again. That was a real accomplishment for me.

I hadn't done much welding for a while, but within a couple of years after the crash I began doing more. At first I didn't even own a welder, but one day Gary Stanton came by to visit. He had sold everything and gotten out of racing at the time, and somehow had a welder left over. He dropped it off and told me, "You might need this thing one of these days."

Not long after that an Amish machine shop nearby began building clothing irons. My dad hauled machinery for them, and he heard they needed some welding done. He brought a batch of irons down, and I gave them to Ed to see if they could be welded properly. Ed did such a smooth job; it gave me a challenge to try to weld them as expertly as he had.

So I started welding. That, and the jigsaw work, was therapy for me. It proved that I could still be productive. It was very, very meaningful to me.

But I was still depressed. It was like being in a blue funk every day; I just didn't feel like there was any way out of this trap. I still had many capabilities; but I couldn't stop thinking about what I *couldn't* do. For a long time, each morning when I'd wake up and see that wheelchair, I'd think, "Aw, shit, not another day of *this*."

Then one day in 1990 Laurie discovered a lump on her breast. After some tests they discovered many more spots, so they referred us to the Cleveland Clinic, which is one of the finest medical facilities in the world.

That incident yanked me out of my depression. As we drove to Cleveland, Laurie and I talked about what I would do if something happened to her. How could I raise three kids on my own? That started a new thought process. I suddenly realized that my recovery wasn't optional; it was mandatory.

God was smiling on us, because it turned out that the spots were simply calcium deposits that were completely harmless. But my awakening had begun, and from that point forward I had a new attitude, a new outlook that was far more positive than before.

Life was worth living again. I felt that I had a purpose, a reason for being on earth. My children, and Laurie, are enormously important to me, and when I realized that they still needed me, it was all the motivation I needed to begin my *real* recovery.

Instead of complaining about an obstacle, I began to consider things as a test. I'd look at a hurdle and try to figure out how to overcome it.

I had my wheelchair, and I also used a Pace Saver electric cart. At Columbus they tried to drill into me that I didn't need an electric cart, because I had the use of my arms. But the cart enabled me to do things so much more quickly. Hey, it's like any other labor-saving device. We can add a long column of numbers with a pencil and paper, but how many of us use a calculator? I felt no shame in using the cart, because it really extended the things I could do.

We had a sidewalk that buckled outside our house from freezing, and everybody tripped on it all the time. It bugged me. I was going to hire someone to fix it, but I didn't know who to call. I thought about calling my friend Art Smith, a racing buddy who goes with me to the track sometimes. He and his son Lonnie have done some work for me in the past, but I knew they'd be busy, so I was hesitant to hire them for such a small job.

So one day I went out there on my scooter with my short shovel. I pulled myself out onto the ground, and began shoveling the dirt around this sidewalk. I got it cut out about a foot around the sidewalk, then went into the garage and welded two screws on the bottom of a curved rod. I used the rod to gouge the dirt from under the sidewalk, until it settled down just how I wanted it. I got a tremendous amount of satisfaction, to look out at that sidewalk and know that I did it without help. It meant a lot to me.

Fixing up my old Chevy pickup was a big accomplishment. I used a torch and a grinder and all the usual tools, all either in my chair or sitting on the ground. It's slow, but I can get it done. And I did get it done. That's the stuff that kept me going, little victories like that. I could see the progress, and it lifted my spirits.

As I continued to recover, we were getting a handle on our finances, and learning to adjust our lifestyle. We had never lived an extravagant lifestyle, which was fortunate. We had a small savings, and at the time of the crash all we owed on was our house and our motor home. So we weren't in bad shape.

But if Laurie would have had to get out and get a job, it would have crushed our lives, because during that period we needed each other almost every minute of every day. That's why I'm so sincere today when I say that the donations and generosity of race fans truly made a difference in our lives.

We invested the money in trust funds for our kids, to make sure they have an education, things like that. We never spent any of the money on anything that we didn't have to have. That wasn't our nature, anyway. We wouldn't have spent money on toys even if we had hit the lottery. Laurie and I are down-to-earth people. We just don't buy luxurious stuff. We never have.

When I buy a vehicle, I buy something that's a couple of years old. If it needs work, I do it myself. I don't like spending too much money. That's the way it's always been.

By 1991, our kids were getting bigger, and we needed more room. We were bursting at the seams in our two-bedroom house. Five people, two bedrooms, one bathroom. It was a tight squeeze.

We bought seven acres from my parents, next to our original farm. We wanted to build a wheelchair-accessible home with more space for the kids. I actually wanted to be closer to Wooster. Plus, I was hesitant to buy the property from my parents, because I didn't want people thinking that Mom and Dad were handing us something. It was important to me that we pay our way.

We wanted something wooded, and we couldn't find much. So we bought the land from my parents and had the home built. I built the shelves and hung towel racks, stuff that any new homeowner would try to do for themselves, trying to save a few bucks.

I also built a nice trundle bed. I had to learn new ways to handle material, and it got frustrating at times. The trundle bed was an angle-iron frame with wood all the way around. It was big and hard to handle, but I just had to stop and figure out ways to move the thing, and get it workable. But I did it.

Sometimes I look at Laurie and I'm amazed that she hung around. A high percentage of marriages fail in a situation like ours, something like 80%.

But she's a special person. She's always been caring and unselfish, probably to a fault. She is the most giving person I've ever met.

Right after my crash I was scared that she would take the kids and leave me. They were my reason for living, and without them my life would have been beyond empty, to the point of not wanting to live anymore.

Everything was an adjustment between us. We now saw each other every day, almost every minute. We had no space. That wasn't healthy, for either of us. And we struggled with that.

Up to that point I had taken the lead on running the family. Now, all of a sudden, everything was thrust onto Laurie. But she responded, in a big way. She amazed a lot of people, I think. They probably couldn't believe that a person could be that strong.

Any time there is a crisis like ours, the goal is to get back to normal. But for us, normal was never again possible. We had to redefine normal, in terms of what our everyday life would be like.

We had tremendous help from many people, and they saved us in many respects. But when they finished helping us they gradually went back to their own lives, which is natural, and proper. But for us, we were still stuck in our abnormal situation. It was ultimately up to us to survive, to find a new way to live with our circumstances.

Each day was getting a little better. But there were many things that made me feel a little bit empty. One thing I really missed was being involved in racing. I had no way of knowing that one day my phone would ring, and my life would be changed yet again.

19

A guy by the name of Pat Patterson put together a televised winter series in 1992 called the Slick 50 series. It featured the World of Outlaws on a Sunday night program from Manzanita Speedway in Phoenix, and was broadcast live on The Nashville Network.

I watched the series the first year, and it was cool. One of the producers called me one day and asked me several questions, and told me to watch the show that week. That was about halfway through the series, I think. They did a very nice video tribute to me, and it made me feel good that people remembered me. I hadn't been in a race car for over four years, so I naturally assumed that interest in my career was dying down.

Watching everyone on TV was hard for me. I felt like the sport was passing me by, in a hurry. I sat at home in the snow every Sunday night while they were out in Arizona racing, and that kind of drove the point home that not only was the sport surviving without me, it was flourishing. That's kind of painful to face.

Not that I expected that it wouldn't survive, of course. But it's hard to make yourself accept that life goes on. That was still during a healing period in my life, and I wasn't quite there yet.

Going in to the next winter, Jeff Swindell called me one day. He had done the color commentary that first year because he didn't have a ride. He was pretty good, too. By the second year he had a ride, so he wasn't going to be able to do the TV work. Would I be interested?

I was out in my garage when he called, and it caught me off guard. I didn't know what to think. It triggered a flood of thoughts, like a VCR on fast forward. I hadn't flown since my accident; could I physically get up into the booth; I don't know anything about TV. I stuttered and stammered, and told him that I needed some time to think about this.

He said I didn't have a lot of time, because they needed an answer. He said he'd call me in a few days.

The allure of getting involved again was very strong. But the idea intimidated me. And I was very concerned about the logistics of travel. Getting there was an issue for me, an issue I had not yet confronted.

I just knew, though, that I couldn't pass this opportunity up. I knew I would regret it if I had said no.

Part of my concern about traveling was that I was afraid I'd be embarrassed about getting on the airplane in that little aisle chair. It's a helpless, awkward feeling. But in the end, I just didn't care about that stuff. I was willing to accept those inconveniences in order to do something that seemed very exciting to me.

Laurie and I talked about it, and while she said it was my decision, she agreed that it would be something that I would probably regret if I said no.

Another benefit was getting to spend three days a week in Phoenix. Leaving the Ohio snow for the Arizona sunshine sure sounded inviting.

I called the airlines and car rental places to quiz them about things. I had lots of questions. They seemed like they knew what they were doing, and the more I talked with them, the more I was reassured that I could make the travel part of it work.

Jeff called me a few days later, and I had an answer. I said I would be willing to try it.

Pat Patterson also anchored the show *RaceDay* on TNN. He called me a few days after I talked with Jeff. I'm sure they had their reservations; maybe they were going out on a limb to try me. Pat and I talked a lot about logistics, things like that.

The first year had been at Manzanita, but the next year the series was held at Canyon Raceway in Peoria, in the middle of the desert.

My dad traveled with me for the first broadcast, just to help me get through the traveling process. But I knew I would eventually want to do it on my own. It was important to me that I regain my independence.

I had a lot of questions about the booth, and whether my chair could fit in there. Guy Forbrook is a very successful sprint car mechanic who also uses a wheelchair, and they took his chair up the stairs to see if it would fit, and it was okay. So they reassured me that getting into the booth was not an issue.

The problem was, my chair was a little wider. And we didn't find this out until just a couple of hours before air time.

At first I panicked. Then I calmed down and began to think about this. I figured out how to use some blocks of wood to narrow my folding chair up. They wanted to just take me out of the chair and carry me up, but I didn't want to do that. I didn't like how that looked. It was important to me, a principle. It's a sensitive issue for anyone in a chair.

When we approached air time, I was too ignorant to be nervous. Nobody told me what to do, so I literally had no preparation or experience. I didn't even get into the booth until a half-hour before air time. I kept looking at my watch, and I knew the time was approaching. But Mike Joy and Dick Berggren were just standing there, laughing and joking. That helped me, because it was a relaxed atmosphere.

The whole program was laid back, really. But when you put the headsets on, it's like buckling into a race car. There is an adrenaline rush, just like racing. When the producer does the countdown in your ear, you start to get excited.

It was a lot harder than I thought. More was happening than I thought, anyway. It's hard to keep track of what's going on when it's happening live. It's very easy to make a tiny mistake because things are happening very fast. You've got two or three voices in your ear, you're watching a monitor, and it's very confusing.

I didn't say much that first night. I was hesitant, because I wasn't sure what they wanted. Plus, I had never paid much attention to this job before now, so I really wasn't sure what a "color guy" did. I just tried to add things that seemed important to me; things that I figured people watching might be interested in.

After that first night, I realized that I was out of my element. I was still in awe of the travel, and the whole scene. But I knew I kind of liked it, and hey, I might even get better.

After the first few weeks I became familiar with the airline people, and the car rental people, and it got a lot more comfortable. I was traveling alone by then, and I had overcome a lot of my earlier fears. So I was getting more encouraged each week.

They also had Legends cars on the broadcast, and a couple of shows after I started there was a big pile-up in the Legends race. I noticed during the crash that one of the cars had a broken radius rod, and I mentioned that maybe that caused the crash. They showed the replay, and sure enough, you could see the radius rod dangling off the car right before the impact. So I had been right. We went to commercial, and Mike and Dick said, "Hey, that was great, that's what we want!" So I felt good that I had contributed a little bit.

I was spreading my wings, enjoying my introduction to the world again. One morning I was in my rental car on the road headed out toward the track, running about 70 mph. Jeff Swindell passed me going about 90 in a custom pickup truck he had borrowed. I grabbed the throttle and caught up to his back bumper, and we were running 90 mph on the road. Our cars were actually catching air on the rises in the road. What a blast!

Still wide open.

Maybe all of this is like a kid starting his racing career. At first, you're a little overwhelmed, but you get accustomed to things. Then you start wanting to improve, and then it becomes an issue of confidence.

Mike Joy and Dick Berggren were really good to work with. They were very patient with me, and they took the time to offer help. During commercials Mike would talk with me, giving me tips and advice, and I tried to listen and learn. I tried to respond with good feedback, and it seemed like we were getting better as a team. By the end of that year, I think the team was getting pretty good.

The racing was entertaining, and I thought the broadcasts were okay, but the series was struggling. Canyon is a long way from Phoenix, and they had trouble attracting enough fans to make the events financially viable.

By the end of the series it looked kind of bleak for next year. I know Pat Patterson had suffered through a tough series. So when things wrapped up in January, nobody knew what was going to happen the following winter.

Plus, I think the teams were worn out as well. It was an expensive deal to keep your crew out west all week for just one night of racing. The novelty had worn off a little bit.

And racing in the winter took away the off season. There was no time to regroup. When can you do the maintenance on the hauler? When do you build new cars for next season? It was tough on the teams, and after two seasons of year-round racing, a lot of people weren't very excited about racing again that winter.

But it was fun while it lasted. I was getting paid, and having a ball. We'd go to Bobby McGee's restaurant for dinner after the show, and *everybody* was there. It was very relaxed and fun.

They told me the favorite drink there was "Goat-slobber." It was actually Goldschlager, but after three drinks you couldn't say it right, so it sounded more like Goat-slobber.

Ralph Sheheen was doing the pit reporting, with aspirations of getting into the booth. That's when I got to know him better. One of his first interviews was with me in the 1980s when I was still racing. He had gone to college at Chico State University, and he interviewed me for a local television program at Silver Dollar Speedway.

After the Slick 50 series ended I later did a one-shot broadcast with Roger Hess of TCI in Tulsa. He produced a show at the Historical Big One at Eldora that was shown on Prime Sports Network. I worked in the booth with Larry Nuber, and Larry Rice was in the pits. I had worked with Larry Nuber once at Phoenix, and he was good to work with. Like most guys, he has his own style, and he was also very helpful to me.

That winter the Slick 50 series was not continued, so I saw no Arizona sunshine. I understood why it didn't happen, but I was disappointed, because I really liked the series.

TNN had been involved with the Outlaws for a few years with Diamond P Sports, but they had primarily done tape-delayed broadcasts, including the Knoxville Nationals. Dave Bowman had been working really hard to find a way to do some live shows on TNN, and by 1995 they put the package together. They did the Nationals live, with Ralph and Dick Berggren in the booth.

The show was a success, and it looked like they had some momentum. In the meantime, I continued doing some work for Roger Hess in Tulsa.

I did work on the radio broadcast of the 1995 Nationals with Bruce Ellis, and it was fun. One nice thing about radio – you don't have to worry about shaving.

During the early summer of 1996 I had a chance to work the broadcast of a World of Outlaws event from Eldora, but this time it was on CBS. We were supposed to do it live-to-tape, which means you're doing a live show but instead of broadcasting it immediately, you're going right to tape for a later broadcast. The big difference is that you can push the pause button if there are long delays, but everything else is pretty much the same as live.

I was a little bit intimidated to be working with Ken Squier of CBS. He hadn't followed the World of Outlaws much, so he wasn't that familiar with the series. At the last minute they changed the plan for the broadcast, and instead of live-to-tape the plan was to drive to Cincinnati, Ohio that night after the Eldora races, and produce the show the next morning. The next morning we went to the local CBS station. Eric Mann was a highly-visible producer for CBS at that time. He and his crew had spent all night working on the tape, and they were disappointed with what they had. The lighting hadn't worked out like they had planned, so the video wasn't as strong as they wanted.

They put it together as best they could, then I proceeded to do a terrible job as an analyst. I was still pretty new, but that was no excuse. I definitely didn't help the broadcast any. The show aired that Sunday afternoon – we barely beat the deadline. The mood wasn't good in the studio. I think everybody was really disappointed with how it turned out.

Still, TNN planned on doing some additional live shows in 1996, and I was hoping that I'd get a chance to work some of the broadcasts. I finally got the call I was hoping for, and soon enough I was working in the booth, joining Ralph Sheheen for the first time.

I've enjoyed working with Ralph. He's a high-energy guy, and we've had a lot of fun working together. Timing is everything in the analyst's role, knowing when to jump in and speak, and when to stay quiet.

I've learned to stay pretty calm. Ralph tends to be more keyed-up. The more we work together the better we get, I think. At least it seems like it flows better today than when we first started working together.

There are a lot of times when I want to comment on something, but time won't permit it. Maybe we're going to commercial break, or something has just happened that changes the flow, or the tone, of the show. You have to follow the general flow of the broadcast, focusing on what's on the monitor, without needless chatter. It has to seem natural.

I don't know how the guys in the production truck keep their sanity. There are all kinds of people barking orders, and it's chaos. It sure looks like a highly stressful environment. Just when they've got the show going in a certain direction, we might get a red flag that completely changes the complexion of the race. They have to adjust to that, on the fly, with a million people watching at home.

The anchor has it tougher than the analyst. They have to lead the broadcast and take care of a lot of details. I can sit and analyze why things are happening. That's less scripted, and a lot more flexible and fun.

I take a lot of notes before the race, with all kinds of stories and details, but most of the stuff I'm not able to use. There just isn't enough time.

I've also worked with Steve Evans in the booth. He has a different style than Ralph. I'm comfortable working with both. It has brought more out of me to do things differently, because it's forced me to learn how to adjust to different ideas, different styles.

I had obviously never thought about making television a career, but it just happened. Kind of like my racing career. But I knew it might not come along again, so I didn't want to let it pass by.

Then, in 1998, my telephone rang again. Somebody mentioned that they had a sprint car that would look familiar to me.

20

Ever since my 1988 crash, a lot of people asked me why I didn't return to driving a race car with hand controls. I didn't have any interest. I knew how long it took me to get to the World of Outlaws level, and I wasn't sure if I could ever be that competitive again with hand controls. So I really didn't have any interest in returning to competition.

Besides, after what I'd already put my family through, I don't think they would have stayed with me. I really believe that. And, honestly, I wouldn't have blamed them for feeling that way.

I was aware that Larry Wood had restored a sprint car to look like one of my old Coors Light cars. Bill Holder was going to write a story about the car for *Open Wheel Magazine*. Bill called me and told me to get out my old firesuit. He wanted to get some pictures of me in the car.

I wasn't sure I wanted to do this. But Bill is pretty persistent, and he talked me into it. I got out my old Coors Light uniform, and it still fit pretty well. My old Coors Light helmet still had specks of mud on it, as a matter of fact.

The deal was for me to meet Larry and Bill at Muskingum County Speedway in Zanesville, Ohio, to get some photos. In the spring I drove to Zanesville. They opened the track for us, and we all pulled into the infield.

When Larry and his guys opened the trailer doors and started rolling the car out, it was a very powerful moment. It was eerie, but it was a good feeling at the same time. I got in the back of my van and got my suit on.

I hadn't been in a sprint car for almost 10 years. Part of my issue was that I didn't want to be lifted in and out of the car. That was very important to me. If I was going to do this, I needed to find a way to get in and out of the car on my own. I wheeled my chair up to the left rear tire, and stopped and studied it for a moment or two. I just hopped up on the left rear, and put my feet on top of the frame rail beside the seat. I leaned forward and grabbed the top of the cage with my left hand, and pulled myself into the seat.

In one fluid motion, I was back in the saddle again.

It was so easy, and I told myself that I should have done this a long time ago. When I grabbed the steering wheel and looked out over the hood, it felt like I had driven the car the night before. The feelings were so strong; it felt very natural sitting behind the wheel again. It was awesome.

The car had a dummy motor, so they had to push me around with a four-wheeler. They snapped a bunch of pictures, and by the end of the day Larry was pushing me down the front straightaway with his four-wheeler. I wished that I could just flip the switch, and drive it down into the corner, one more time.

We got back to the trailer, and someone grabbed my chair and brought it up to the left rear tire. In one motion, I was sitting back on the left rear tire again. It wasn't nearly as tough as I thought it would be.

It all felt so good. I was kind of overwhelmed by the whole episode. We all sat around talking for a few minutes, until they finally loaded the car. I got into my van and peeled off my firesuit. I then pulled up alongside them to say goodbye.

As I pulled out of the parking lot, I glanced in my side mirror and saw their rig pulling out. For a moment, I felt like I was still driving, and we had just finished a night of racing.

I drove home kind of slowly, with a lot on my mind. I thought, "Man, it would be so nice to drive just a few laps in the car. Just once more. I don't want to race, I just want to fire it, one more time."

The more I drove home, the more I thought about that upcoming July being the 10th anniversary of my accident. I had made a promise to Laurie that I would never race again, so that was an issue. A big issue. I wondered how I was going to approach her.

That night I carefully brought up the idea. I asked her what she would think about me pacing the field at the King's Royal that July. She paused for only a moment before she said, "I think you should go for it."

I immediately got on the phone to Larry. I told him what I was thinking, and he started laughing. He said, "I told my buddy when we were pulling out of the parking lot today, 'I wouldn't be surprised if Brad calls me to see about running the car sometime.'"

Larry took care of getting a motor together. I took care of my state of mind, to make sure I was ready. I counted the days until July 18th. We went to Eldora two weeks before the Kings Royal to practice.

We installed a Honda four-wheeler throttle setup, and mounted it at about 2 o'clock on the steering wheel. We also mounted a hand brake on the left side of the cockpit. You couldn't race competitively with the brake off to the side like that, but for what we were doing it was fine.

I buckled in, and the truck pushed me away. The car fired, and the throttle was held about half-open. I was able to get the car out of gear and the truck pushed me back to the pits. Larry adjusted the idle stop, and we were ready to try again.

When we fired it up again, it was okay. I leaned the fuel mixture out to build the heat in the engine quicker. Then I made several slow laps to warm the engine.

The first time I hammered the throttle...what a thrill. Remember, the track was dry, with no preparation. When I finally did get going I could only run a couple of laps because the dust was kind of thick, so I'd slow down for a couple of laps.

I was driving harder and harder, until I felt like I was getting around the track pretty well, all things considered. I was able to get the car out from under me and let the back end slide out some, to control the throttle with my thumb, feeling the tires hooking up. It surprised me that it was that controllable.

We were ready for the Kings Royal.

I was nervous, with the big crowd on hand and national TV. It was kind of like the days when my high school class came out to

Lakeville and my wheel fell off. I didn't want the embarrassment if anything went wrong.

I was working the broadcast that night with Steve Evans. Right after the B-main, I left the booth and quickly went to my van. I put my suit on, and went to the race car, which was parked behind the main grandstand. There was already a crowd gathered there. I climbed into the car, and a push truck took me past the pond just past the main pit gate. I locked it in gear, and then we fired the motor to warm it up. I popped it out of gear, and pulled up to the pit entrance.

People started swarming around the car. That's when the significance of the moment began to sink in. Up to that point, all I wanted was to drive the car at that event, to slay the dragon, and to prove that I was still here.

I drove the car down through the pits, with the engine idling, and I could hear the crowd beginning to cheer. Other drivers and crew members approached my car, offering a handshake. I was waiting for TNN to give me the signal to push off. I was nervous, anxious, and very excited.

As the truck pushed me away, everyone along the pit lane was giving me thumbs up. As I drove around the track, people came to the fence and were waving, pressing against the fencing as if they were trying to touch me as I rolled by.

The flagman waved the green flag, and my thumb pressed the engine into a roar. Although thousands of people were waving at me, and maybe a million more were watching on television, at that moment I was all alone. It was me and the race car, alone on Eldora's steep banks.

As I went through turn two, my mind flashed back 10 years to a night that shaped the lives of many people. A night that took me several years to fully deal with.

In a way, this moment was the closure I had been looking for. As the concrete wall swept past, I felt a renewed sense of spirit, a euphoria that I thought I had forgotten.

For 10 long years the dragon had trailed me, trying to steal my hopes, my dreams, my life. But now that dragon was dead, forever silenced and put out of my heart.

If it hadn't been for Laurie, the dragon would have won. She was there with me, sharing my joy. She looked on from the infield, with Brandy, Braden, and Brittani. They fought through the tears, and their eyes followed the blue-and-silver car around the track. Really, they saved me. They gave me the reason to hold the dragon at bay, until I could slay him for good on this night.

It was a night of joy. A night of closure. A night of healing. I had beaten the dragon. Thank God, the dragon is forever dead.

21

These days, life is pretty good. Although it was a long haul, I have learned to live with my circumstances. When I get up in the morning, the chair isn't the first thing I think of. My recovery goes on, day after day. It will never be completed until I'm walking again.

At the time I got hurt, people said there would be a cure for spinal injuries in a few years. I needed that glimmer of hope at the time. At the same time, they are careful to not give you false expectations. They want you to accept things and go on with your life. I'm not waiting around for a cure, but I also haven't given up. I hope it comes someday, and not just for me. I hope it helps people in the future, to help them recover from injuries like mine.

It's taken me 11 years to get to this point. And in 11 more years, I'll be even farther along. I'm okay.

That's not to say that things are perfect. I still get depressed sometimes. I still hate what's happened, and wish things would have been different. People might say, "Oh, you're on TV, you've got a nice home, you've got the world by the ass." But I'd trade them for their legs in a heartbeat. In a heartbeat.

But I spend very little time thinking that way. That's something I've just learned to throw away, because if you're not careful that kind of thinking will steal your happiness.

If they came to me and offered surgery that would correct my spinal injury, I'd be interested. But if they also said there was a chance I'd lose the use of my arms if it wasn't successful, I'd say no. Being in the chair isn't perfect, but I've learned that you can still be happy. I wouldn't trade everything I have today just for a chance to walk again. I just wouldn't.

I've never done much counseling, or testimony to others. Maybe

I should, I don't know. During my rehab they brought in some people to talk to us, people who had gone on to live productive lives in spite of their injuries. But at the time I couldn't grasp that, so the stuff they told us just went over my head. So I'm a little skeptical about talking to others, because I'm not sure they would listen anyway.

As you progress and heal following a spinal injury, your body adjusts to the trauma in many ways, and life gets better. You reach far more toward normalcy than you can comprehend early on. You think it's always going to be horrible, but it's not.

For example, in the months that followed my crash I had to give myself shots of Heparin in the legs to prevent blood clots, but I didn't have to do that forever. So it's not nearly as hard as you think it will be at first.

At first, I couldn't feel anything from my injury on down. I couldn't even tell when I was hungry. But I've regained much of those kinds of things. Even my legs, I can feel cramping and things like that in the muscles. So your body finds a way to recover and adjust to many different things.

I have to admit that this ordeal made me a much stronger person. I am far less intimidated by situations than I used to be. If I ever walk again, face to face and eye to eye, I won't be intimidated by anyone in the world, no matter who they are. After looking at things from down here, I've learned to deal with the lack of self-esteem that a chair brings. Some people look at you as less than an equal, and that pisses me off.

It's not that I'm mad, or bitter, because I pretty much got over that a long time ago. But it frustrates me that people aren't more aware, or more sensitive. Then again, they don't know what I know, so I suppose it isn't really their fault. I'm always polite, but sometimes I do try to shatter the stereotypes.

Here's the bottom line: being in a wheelchair isn't a handicap; it's an inconvenience. I've learned to do so many things, and work around it. It doesn't stop me from doing pretty much everything I need to do.

As time went on, I wanted to reach the limit of my capabilities. Whether that was just to get strong enough to wheel my chair on my own, or to fly across the country, rent a car, do my job, and go home. I wanted to reach the limit, and nothing less.

Using my Pace Saver electric cart, I shovel snow in the winter, and every spring I shovel a dump truck load of mulch at our house. I take that kind of thing as a personal challenge. Not everything is a challenge, but many things are.

I've tried to take things on head-on. If I feel like I can't do something, I have to prove to myself that I can't before I will accept it. If it is something important to me, I have to at least try my hardest before I admit defeat.

For example, I still like to wash my own cars. I use the brush, and the hose, and it takes me forever, but I do it. I'm still proud, with a good feeling that I did it. It's not so much where I am, but whether I'm trying to make it better.

I do get aggravated when people say things like, "Oh, you can drive?" Or, "Oh, you can dress yourself?" Or, "You mean you don't have to have someone with you when you travel?" Or, "Wow! You mean you really work on your own car?"

Man, that bugs me. I'm sure before I got hurt I was just as uninformed, but now that I've seen things from this side it's hard to be patient with people.

You know which stereotype I hate the most? "Poor old Doty, it sure is sad, since all he can do is sit home and watch television."

The truth is, I wish I had *time* to watch television. Right this minute, I've got so much to do I don't think I'll ever get caught up. Out in the shop, I've got a crate full of tanks to weld that's a couple of weeks overdue. Laurie's van needs new brakes. I've got to get my old van cleaned up and ready to sell. I need to get on the phone to make some travel arrangements that are getting critically close. I need to get started getting my place ready for winter.

I'll bet that sounds a lot like your life, doesn't it?

You see, just because somebody is in a chair, life doesn't stop. I've got many of the same issues to deal with as anybody else, but

I'm in a chair. That's really the only difference. I worry about finances, health, chores, family, friends, pretty much the same stuff as anybody.

I see every day that people treat me differently because I'm in a chair. When Laurie and I go out, people talk to her, instead of talking to me. A lot of it is because in a chair, you seem like a really small person because you're way below eye level. I've learned to live with that and not be offended, but it's frustrating sometimes.

A few weeks ago I was traveling, and I was waiting on the rental car shuttle to pick me up. They wheeled up and I got into the van, and as we pulled away the shuttle driver got on the radio and said, "Hey, I picked up the handicap. I'll be there in a minute." The other passengers in the shuttle looked at me and it was kind of awkward. I just laughed and said, "Man, I hate that." But it's irritating, that people sometimes treat me like I'm not a human being. I'm amazed, really, that they aren't a little bit more understanding.

I still like to shock people with what I'm able to do. I can swim pretty well, and we have a pool in our back yard for the kids. The first time I went swimming I just rolled over to the pool and dove in. Everybody was shocked. Brittani and I like to race in the pool, and I can swim really well underwater. I can still beat her at that, but as she gets older I'm sure dad will find himself getting beat at some point.

When I drive, I try to only use the lift on the van when I have to. I feel less handicapped if I pull myself up into the van by myself. So I'll usually just wheel up beside the van and lift myself in. I do that a lot with rental cars, and it really only slows me down for a few seconds.

At the mall, I'll ride the escalators. That's something they taught me during rehab, how to use the handrails and get the chair onto the escalators. Most buildings have signs saying no wheelchairs on the escalators, because they're afraid of somebody getting hurt. But if nobody's looking I'll do it anyway. It's my way of rebelling, I suppose.

I don't hate my chair. Actually, without it, I'd be up the creek without a paddle. It is my mobility. Sometimes I think about what if something happened to my hands. That would seem huge, because now they are so important to me.

Growing older concerns me, because I haven't given up on walking again. Plus, I'm afraid that someday I might be unable to get around on my own if my condition slips. I'm so independent now that I don't want to lose it. I feel like I could lose my mobility quicker than the average guy could, so I'm worried about that.

If I keep myself in good shape, that should help. But it plays on my mind. Getting older is scary for anyone, but in a chair it becomes more of an issue, more of a challenge.

I think it's a little harder to raise kids, but again, I'm working on that. It's just another hurdle, and I'm finding ways to adjust to it. Of course, raising kids is hard for anybody.

The only ongoing fundraiser we're involved in is the Brad Doty Classic at Attica Raceway Park in Ohio. I'm proud to have my name associated with that event, because it's always an excellent race. The promoter at Attica, Gene Frankart, has been a great friend over the years. Our arrangement today is that I get half of the 50/50 drawing, which is a nice gesture on Gene's part. We don't have the severe financial needs that we had during the first few years, and we make between $600 and $1,000 each year from the event. If I need the money at the time, I use it. But if I don't, I'll donate it to the Spinal Cord Research Foundation.

Plus, I sell T-shirts, and that kind of helps us out. I'm amazed that people still remember me, since I haven't raced in over 10 years. I think that shows just how loyal, and wonderful, race fans are. When I do autograph sessions, I don't sense that people feel sorry for me, which suits me just fine. I don't want pity, or sorrow. I want them to just be friends because we love racing. That's something I have in common with any race fan.

For a long time, I felt uneasy about selling T-shirts. I felt like people might think they were obligated to buy them because of guilt, or that we needed the money. I was a little embarrassed, frankly, because I was finished racing. But then I looked around and realized that a lot of retired drivers still sell shirts and collectibles, so I guess it's okay if I do, too.

I'm often amazed at how supportive people can be. After I got back into the sprint car at Eldora in 1998, a lot of people told me they were very excited as they watched that night. I've even had great big, macho biker dudes come up and tell me that they openly cried as they watched me. Wow. That really means something, to hear someone tell me that.

After that ride, many people have asked me if I'll drive the car again, either in competition or in an exhibition. I'm sure I won't. I made a promise to Laurie, and I'm going to keep that promise. I am officially retired from driving.

I think people in racing are far more aware of paralysis issues than they used to be. Not just because of me, but also because of people like Guy Forbrook, who despite being in a chair has enjoyed great success as a sprint car mechanic and car owner.

Guy has been in a chair for a long time, and he's owned race cars for a long time as well. When I first got hurt, a lot of people urged me to buy a car, and I would constantly hear, "Forbrook has a team, you could do that!" I got tired of hearing it, to be honest. I didn't want to own a race car. It didn't interest me. But I absolutely admire what Guy has done. Who wouldn't?

He likes to needle me, and I give it right back. He'll see me and say, "Hey, Doty, you need a push? You sure you can get going all right?" I'll come back with, "Forbrook, you couldn't keep up." Then I'll give him some more, saying, "Hey, man, all you do is work on that race car! Who mows your yard? I mow my own yard." Then he'll come back with the needle for me. It's actually kind of fun.

I think sprint car racing is on the verge of some very big things. It could really explode over the next few years, in terms of growth.

And that may not be all good. One of the great appeals of the sport is that the drivers and cars are approachable as they roll into Hometown, U.S.A. We've got to make sure it stays that way.

A lot of people look at Winston Cup racing as an idea of where sprint car racing could be. I don't think it will ever be that big, for a lot of different reasons. Yes, it can and will be bigger than it is today, but I don't think it will reach the proportions of Winston Cup.

As a fan, I'm concerned about all this growth. I hope we can keep the spirit and intensity of the sport, without becoming just another show. Television raises the program to a higher level, allowing fans to see their favorite driver several times a year, instead of just once or twice.

It's hard to explain, but there is something about being seen on that little box. An aura; a magic. If it's on TV, it's bigger than reality, bigger than life. It brings a higher level of excitement, because when you see the drivers and the cars on television, there becomes a celebrity associated with them.

That's okay, and it's exciting. But we have to make sure it doesn't steal the hometown flavor of the sport, because that's what built sprint car racing.

I hope to stay involved in the sport through television, and I hope TNN stays with sprint car racing for a long time. After being involved in racing nearly all of my adult life, and getting a second chance to remain involved, it would be hard for me to be away from the sport for any length of time.

I've had opportunities with other racing-related companies, but I've never found anything that I was all that excited about, except television.

Boy, those days at Lakeville Speedway sure seem like a long time ago. Racing has been an incredible, exciting ride, and I wouldn't trade a day of it away. I've met hundreds of neat, interesting people, some of whom became very dear friends.

I'm still very close with my original racing buddies: Ed, Jac, and Kenny. Those guys mean more to me than I can say. Despite a few little scrapes along the way, we've always been there for each other. Guys, you are my friends for life. There is no doubt about it.

As my kids grow up, I can see my life changing. I'll watch them mature, and become adults, and then go off to seek their own life. Someday Laurie and I will look at our grandchildren, I suppose.

But for now, I'll take it a day at a time. I've learned not to live in the past, because I can't change it. I've also learned not to dwell on the future too much. After many years of soul-searching, I've decided to live more for today, because that's all we really have: today.

Someday I hope to get out of this chair. But if I don't, I don't. I don't have to walk again to have a happy life. I've learned to be content with what I've got.

Life goes on, whether we are ready or not. So I'll just hang on for the ride, and see where this wonderful adventure leads me.

In the meantime, I'm pretty sure of just one thing:

I'll see you at the races.